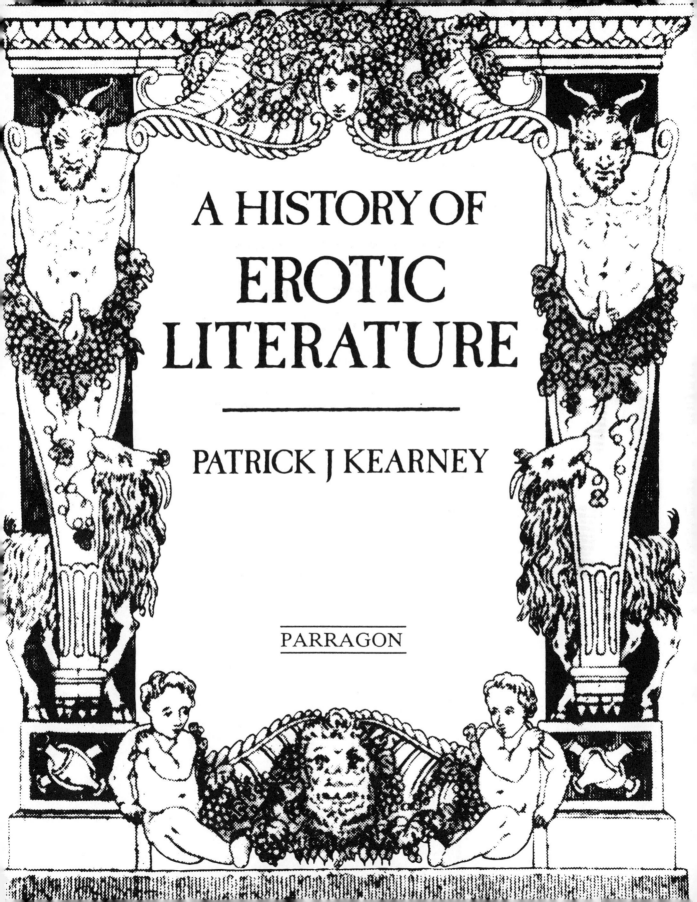

A HISTORY OF
EROTIC
LITERATURE

PATRICK J KEARNEY

PARRAGON

HALF-TITLE Lithograph from the first edition of *The Pearl*,
see colour plates opposite page 104 and following and page 111
FRONTISPIECE Frontispiece of the first edition of
La Philosophie dans le boudoir, see page 100

CONTENTS

ACKNOWLEDGMENTS

A subject like erotica admits to few authorities or 'fellow travellers' even in 1982, and it is fortunate therefore that of those who exist the majority make good friends and are generous with their time, knowledge and not infrequently their precious books as well. Among this company I am pleased and honoured to list the following without whose help the present book would probably not have materialized. Firstly, I must raise my cap to the patience of the staff of the Bodleian Library, Oxford, University Library, Cambridge, and the British Library at London; also to the staff at the Public Records Office, London. Secondly, I must acknowledge the invaluable assistance of the following individuals. In no particular order, they are: Gérard Nordmann of Geneva; Karl Ludwig Leonhardt and his wife Sieglinde of Hamburg; Denis Crutch; Peter Mendes; G. Legman of Valbonne, France; Timothy d'Arch Smith; Charles Lister: Neil Crawford; C. J. Scheiner of New York; Charles Peltz of Crouch End; J. Crowhurst; Allen Jones; Dr E. J. Dingwell. And finally a note of *special* thanks to Linda Troncelliti Perkins of California without whose encouragement I couldn't have written a word.

By special request this book is not dedicated to my parents

Y glaua' ei davod, y butrav ei din.
(The more prudish, the more unchaste.)

Old Welsh proverb

There is no such thing as a moral or an immoral book.
Books are well written, or badly written.

Oscar Wilde

INTRODUCTION

Of the several words used to describe the representation of sexuality in literature, *erotica*, which of them all possesses the greatest measure of respectability, is the most difficult to define. A combination of factors has created this situation, ranging from the debasing indignities of the gutter press, and those who should know better, compilers of dictionaries and encyclopedias, to the personal preferences or prejudices of the individual.

Homosexuals would no doubt find *Le Livre blanc*, a work ascribed to Jean Cocteau, erotic; and it is conceivable that there are in existence indviduals of a perverse sort who derive pleasure from books dealing with Nazi and Japanese war crimes. That the authors of this latter class of book are themselves perverse is questionable, but it is difficult to accept that their enormous sales can be completely explained as a symptom of a detached and academic interest in the subject. Why books such as this, and others with titles such as *The Pleasures of the Torture Chamber*, whose purpose is all too obvious, should be permitted open and unrestricted sale, while Cleland's sexually balanced *Memoirs of a Woman of Pleasure* is pilloried in the courts, is a question that is beyond the scope of the present volume. Those interested in pursuing it are referred to Mr G. Legman's pioneering book *Love and Death: A Study in Censorship* (New York, 1949; repr. New York, 1963), in which the whole subject is examined in depth.

Enough has been said to show how wide is the variety of books that may, according to taste and other considerations, be described as erotic. Providing a definition clearly presents problems, and yet for a work of this sort, which sets out to provide the reader with what will, I hope, prove to be a useful guide to erotic literature, a definition of sorts must be ventured.

Broadly speaking, the chapters that follow will concentrate on fiction, and sometimes verse and theatre, that appeared clandestinely. Erotica, for the purpose of this book, is seen as a matter of intent in that the authors and publishers had it in mind to provide the reader of their wares with sexual stimulation of one sort or another. As a definition, this has obvious drawbacks and not all the works that will be described or mentioned will fit conveniently within its perimeters. *Histoire d'O*, for example, was originally published quite openly, albeit under a pseudonym, yet there is no doubt that it is an erotic novel. The Marquis de Sade's works, on the other hand, were issued in most cases secretly; and although unquestionably obscene they were not intended, at least by their author, primarily as works of erotica, but rather as political and social polemics. Other exceptions will reveal themselves, such as the publications of the Olympia Press in Paris between the years 1953 and 1965, but the guideline of the clandestine will be the general rule.

The reason for limiting discussion to works published *sub rosa* is that it avoids what might be seen as a too generous casting of the selective net. A large volume of popular fiction could in a very general sense be described as erotic; the present author found Burton Wohl's novel *A Cold Wind in August* extraordinarily arousing in his youth, and the sales enjoyed by Harold Robbins, an author noted for the liberal use of sexual episodes in his books, indicate a high level of acceptance among readers of material of this type. But to include *A Cold Wind in August* here would be an absurdity. Similarly, previous popular histories of erotica have, it seems, included much that is irrelevant. Accounts of the writings of Rabelais, Chaucer and Boccaccio are all very well, but in their own day these authors were not regarded as being particularly erotic. The notion that Chaucer and others, such as Swift, were disgusting was born in a later age when everything was considered disgusting, chair legs included. Likewise, in more recent times, Miller, Lawrence and Joyce have frequently been recruited as examples of libertine writers, and while it is true that the frankness or realism of their language forced them to publish outside their own countries, they could hardly be thought of as pornographers, a fact only just being appreciated in some quarters. It is, however, books of precisely this character, rather than so-called hard-core pornography, that find themselves embroiled in sordid and disagreeable court cases, cases in which the prosecution – in England this not infrequently means the Crown – seldom fail to make fools of themselves. The roll call of authors honoured in this way is a long and distinguished one, and interesting accounts of many of the more celebrated prosecutions will be found in Mr Alec Craig's *The Banned Books of England* (London: Allen & Unwin, 1962) and Mr Donald Thomas's *A Long Time Burning* (London: Routledge & Kegan Paul, 1969), although this latter work deals with literary censorship generally as opposed to 'indecency' in particular.

Even given the limitations set out above, this survey or history will of necessity merely skim the surface of a very large and complex subject, an admission that should be made at the outset. The standard reference work for German erotica alone, compiled by Hugo Hayn and entitled *Bibliotheca Germanorum Erotica*, started life as a single volume printed at Leipzig in 1875. An enlarged second edition, still in one volume, appeared ten years later. The third edition, published between 1912 and 1914 with the editorial assistance of Alfred N. Gotendorf, ran to eight substantial volumes, and in 1929 it was found necessary to issue an *Ergänzungsband*, or supplementary volume, of 668 pages, compiled by Paul Englisch. Ignoring the other reference works in the field, a bibliography of which entitled *Catalogi Librorum Eroticorum* (London: Cecil & Amelia Woolf, 1964) by Terence J. Deakin may usefully be consulted, this must vividly illustrate the daunting scope of erotic literature, its bibliography and history.

All genre fiction share these difficulties. Purists will argue endlessly over such arcane matters as whether Zamyatin should be allowed into the ranks of accepted science fiction writers on the strength of his novel *We*, a sort of anti-Utopian fantasy that seems likely to have influenced both Huxley and Orwell, or whether he merely employed as a convenience the conventions of science fiction to make a political statement. Similar controversies doubtless beset the devotees of westerns and detective fiction.

However, with the possible exception of books on religious matters, condemned as unorthodox depending on which church held the reins of power at the time, erotica possesses one quality that is shared with no other type of literature so completely. Already mentioned, together with the boundaries that have governed the selection of the works to be discussed below, this quality is its secrecy, its 'underground' nature.

* * * * *

Henry Spencer Ashbee

Everything about erotica is invariably disguised behind false authors, publishers, dates and places of publication. Nothing is what it seems, and it is this more than anything else that is the fascination of the subject for its collectors and bibliographers. There is an unspoken challenge here, which transcends whatever pleasures the texts of the books might provide, to find out who these authors and publishers were. John Carter, in his witty and informative *ABC for Book Collectors* (London: Hart-Davis, MacGibbon, 1974; 5th edition), defines 'bibliomania' as 'literally, a madness for books' and a 'bibliomaniac' as 'a book collector with a slightly wild look in his eye'. Although Mr Carter did not have erotica collectors specifically in mind when formulating those definitions, they are symptoms of a condition that is all too familiar to the present writer and friends of his who are engaged in similar pursuits. Once in possession of a clue as to the author or publisher of a particular book, the hunt is on and no librarian or archivist can feel free to rest in peace until the quarry is run to earth.

To take one example, a number of years ago I noted with interest the following entry in *Catena Librorum Tacendorum* (London, 1885), the third and final volume of Henry Spencer Ashbee's bibliography of erotica written under the pseudonym 'Pisanus Fraxi':

> *The Romance of Lust* is not the produce of a single pen, but consists of several tales, 'orient pearls at random strung', woven into a connected narrative by a gentleman, perfectly well known to the present generation of literary eccentrics and collectors, as having amassed one of the most remarkable collections of erotic pictures and bric-à-brac ever brought together. He was also an ardent traveller, and *The Romance of Lust* was composed during a voyage he made to Japan. He visited India in the months of December, 1875, to April, 1876, and on his return, in 1876, had printed, for private circulation, some interesting *Letters* which he wrote during that journey. He died January 16th, 1879, in his 74th year, at Catania, whither he had repaired for the sake of his health. (*Catena*, pp. 188–9)

9

The Romance of Lust (1873–6; four vols) is not a particularly well-written book even by the low standards usually set by English pornography, yet Ashbee had thrown down a gauntlet before any enterprising literary detective who cared to pick it up. Had I been more observant I would have seen that in his usual roundabout way Ashbee identifies the author or editor quite clearly; although his name appears nowhere in the entry for the book, it is listed in the Index to the *Catena*, where the reader is referred, in connection with the destruction of his erotic bric-à-brac, his *Letters from India* and his death, to the appropriate pages in the article on *The Romance of Lust*. I missed this, however, and instead took myself off to the Records Office at Somerset House in The Strand and checked the registers there for the names of any British nationals who had died abroad on 16 January 1879. There was only one listed as dying at Catania: William Simpson Potter. Returning to Ashbee's bibliography, I checked the Index and there he was. My delight at having unearthed Potter at Somerset House was somewhat diminished at the discovery that Ashbee had identified him anyway, but it was exciting while it lasted and I consoled myself with the thought that I had been taught a valuable lesson of the importance of checking thoroughly first before embarking on any similar ventures; the answer is not infrequently staring one in the face.

Ashbee's importance to serious students of erotica is so great that it might not be out of place here to say something of his work, and that of other bibliographers of the subject. Full details of all these reference works will be found in the *Authorities Consulted* section at the conclusion of the text.

The three volumes of Ashbee's bibliography together constitute the key to much of the clandestine book production of the 19th century, and particularly to what was happening in England. Through his friend James Campbell Reddie, himself a writer of pornography, Ashbee was acquainted with many of those involved in the trade, and where he deemed it prudent he named them. In the third volume, the *Catena* already cited, he remains silent on these matters when dealing with books published after the death in 1868 of the notorious Holywell Street bookseller and publisher William Dugdale. The actors still being alive, he naturally felt it necessary to protect them, particularly in view of the strong possibility that one of them, Edward Avery, had a hand in the distribution – if not in the actual production – of his bibliographies.

When Ashbee died in 1900, his collection was willed to the British Museum Library (now the British Library). Not all his books were of an erotic nature; that portion of his library devoted to his other passion, the works of Miguel de Cervantes Saavedra, was the finest outside Spain. But those that were erotic considerably enhanced the Private Case of the Museum Library, helping to build it into one of the finest collections of erotica extant. Included in the Ashbee bequest were the first two volumes of his bibliography, his own working copies that had each been bound into two separate volumes, interleaved and annotated, and with extra illustrations and letters inserted. This additional material is of great interest and contains much curious information. Unfortunately, no similarly augmented

The Romance of Lust, vol. 1

copy of the third volume, which would certainly have unveiled the names of many of the later 19th-century publishers and authors, appears to exist. A rumour that it did, and was kept locked up in the office of the Principal Keeper of the Library, came to my ears late in 1973, and I accordingly wrote to the Keeper to enquire after it. The reply that I received, dated 4 January 1974, was disappointing:

> I have looked into the missing copy of *Catena Librorum Tacendorum*. There is a copy in the room of the Keeper of Printed Books ... with Ashbee's bookplate and the yellow British Museum accessions stamp dated 10 November 1900. It is pretty certainly the third volume which you refer to. It contains no annotations whatever and no inserted papers; nor does it bear any pressmark and is kept in the Keeper's room for occasional reference use ... You would, of course, be free to see the copy ... if you wish to do so.

This was, needless to say, a great blow, but in the near future the gap left as a result of Ashbee's timidity – if that is what it was – is to be more than adequately filled by the labours of Mr Peter Mendes, an enterprising academic, who is well on the way to completing a comprehensive bibliographical study of English clandestine erotica, 1885–1930, in which many of the puzzles left unresolved by Ashbee will be answered.

Ashbee's three volumes are in a sense unique and very much the product of his own eccentricity. He was wealthy, and could afford to have them printed to his own specifications which, in their bold mixtures of type style and colour, were as exacting as they were generous. Unlike many bibliographies, which are little else but dry listings of titles and dates, Ashbee's have a life of their own. While they lack the scientific precision of modern bibliographical practice, they are nevertheless in advance of the sort of thing usually passed off as bibliography in the 1870s and 1880s; they are reliable and – a rarity in books of this sort – an excellent read. He quotes liberally from books he considers worthy of special attention – a blessing when it is considered that many of the works he notices no longer exist at all or, if they do, only in single unique copies in libraries or private collections – and his own comments are seldom without interest, and frequently amusing. As much of Ashbee himself comes across as the people and books he describes. To illustrate this quality, the following brief paragraph, extracted from his notice of a work entitled *Lascivious Gems* (London, 1866) is not without its charms:

> Although these tales are by several hands, the chief contributor was a barrister of some standing, who died about ten years ago. The object for which the writers appear to have striven is to outdo each other in cynicism, obscenity and blasphemy; they have failed to impart to the work that literary value which it was undoubtedly in their power to have done, but have, on the other hand, produced a volume that is a disgrace even to erotic literature. (*Catena*, p. 313)

By his suggestion that they were capable of better things, Ashbee clearly implies that he knew perfectly well who the authors of *Lascivious Gems* were, and they are indeed very probably the same people responsible for the excellent

THE

INDEX EXPURGATORIUS

OF

MARTIAL,

LITERALLY TRANSLATED;

COMPRISING ALL THE EPIGRAMS HITHERTO OMITTED BY
ENGLISH TRANSLATORS.

TO WHICH IS ADDED

AN ORIGINAL METRICAL VERSION

AND

COPIOUS EXPLANATORY NOTES.

PRINTED FOR PRIVATE CIRCULATION.

LONDON:
MDCCCLXVIII.

CYTHERA'S HYMNAL;

OR,

FLAKES FROM THE FORESKIN.

A COLLECTION OF

Songs, Poems, Nursery Rhymes, Quiddities,

ETC., ETC.

NEVER BEFORE PUBLISHED.

OXFORD:
Printed at the University Press,
For the Society for Promoting Useful Knowledge.
MDCCCLXX.

[Cum Privilegio.]

---

translation into English of those epigrams by Martial usually left in the decent obscurity of the original Latin, published in 1868 under the title *The Index Expurgatorius*, and which Ashbee praises so highly in the first volume of his bibliography, *Index Librorum Prohibitorum* (1877). The 'barrister of standing' referred to was Frederick Popham Pike, whom Ashbee identifies in the annotated working copy of his *Index* preserved in the British Library as being the chief contributor to a collection of obscene verses entitled *Cythera's Hymnal* (1870).

Concerning Ashbee's life, much useful information has been gathered together by Mr Peter Fryer in his Introduction to *Forbidden Books of the Victorians* (London: Odyssey Press, 1970), an abridgment of Ashbee's bibliographies in one volume; and Ashbee's diaries are at present being edited for publication by Mr Ian Gibson, but I am reliably informed that they are incomplete, odd years being missing, and contain very little concerning his interest in erotica.

The other major bibliographical work in English concerning itself with the subject in a really big way is the *Registrum Librorum Eroticorum* (London, 1936; two vols) of 'Rolf S. Reade', the anagrammatical pseudonym of Alfred Rose. Details of Rose's life are obscure, but during the course of a short correspondence with his daughter, the novelist Christine Brooke-Rose, in connection with obtaining permission to have a photocopy made from her father's typewritten

LEFT *The Index Expurgatorius*

RIGHT *Cythera's Hymnal*

supplement to the published catalogue of *L'Enfer* (1913), the erotica collection of the Bibliothèque Nationale in Paris, I learned the following.

> I'm afraid I can't tell you very much ∴... about my father, who died when I was a child... He was born in 1876, son of a small farmer, or gentleman farmer, in Warwickshire. He was more or less self-educated as far as I can gather, at least did not go to university, and went to America in his twenties, where he did some sort of business in Mobile, Alabama, and married his first wife, whose name I do not know. In his forties he met my mother and married her after the first World War, settled in London where he was the director of a small mail addressing company for doctors (mailing publicity to doctors), called The Addressing Co., which has since been bought up, but which was quite original at the time. He died in 1934, of pneumonia.

Self-educated or not, Rose must have had some influence with the authorities at the British Library in his day, for he contrived to include in his *Registrum* the titles and pressmarks of the Private Case as it stood in the early 1930s. At the time this must have been a considerable feat, for historically the British Library has been extremely sensitive about its erotica holdings; only in the last fifteen years has it demonstrated a more liberal policy in this area and entered the collection in the General Catalogue.

Unfortunately, Rose was not able to see the fruits of his work through the press before his death, and the job was done for him by a bookseller named Stanislas who came into possession of Rose's manuscript or file cards. The result was not a happy one, and is so full of mistakes as to make its use an unreliable proposition.

As with many of those in the clandestine or semi-clandestine publishing business, little is known of Stanislas. In David Low's book *With all Faults* (1973), he is said to have started as an assistant in the bookshops of London's Charing Cross Road, and progressed to running shops of his own in Fleet Street, Tottenham Court Road and St Martin's Court. His final shop seems to have been at 52 Charing Cross Road, where he took over George Winter's premises and called himself the International Bookshop. This did not last long, and he took up freelance bookselling from an office in Holborn in about 1935, where he was presumably when publishing Rose's *Registrum*.

Two other works that have been published in England should also be mentioned. The first, entitled *Bibliotheca Arcana*, was issued in 1885 by George Redway. The authorship on its titlepage is ascribed to 'Speculator Morum', the pseudonym of William Laird Clowes. The value of this book is limited; although it is heavily cribbed from Ashbee, it is little more than a random list of titles, with no pretence at any alphabetical arrangement (although there is an index), and with occasional auction prices appended to the entries that have been culled from unidentified sale catalogues.

The British Library possesses a copy of *Bibliotheca Arcana*, at pressmark C. 134. d. 7, which is of considerable interest, however. Originally, it was in the collection of Ashbee and contains a letter to him from the publisher. At a later date there has been inserted a further letter from Redway to Alfred Rose, in which is given the history of the book and the information that Clowes was the anonymous author of a work entitled *Confessions of an English Haschish Eater*, together with the contract between Redway and Clowes.

The second book is *The Private Case*, published at London in 1981 by Jay Landesman. This is the first fully comprehensive bibliographical record of the British Library's erotica collection. Since it is the work of the present author, I shall refrain from making any remarks about it, other than to point out that it is the only such book on the subject in English not to employ a ridiculous Latin title.

The principal German reference work, the *Bibliotheca Germanorum Erotica et Curiosa* (1912–14, 1929; nine vols) compiled by Hayn, Gotendorf and Englisch, has already been mentioned. As might be suggested by the size of the work, not all the books listed are strictly of an erotic or pornographic character, but it is unlikely that many of them have been overlooked. As a bibliography, it is of immense value; yet the eccentricity of its arrangement, to which there is no effective guide, makes its use vexing in the extreme, particularly for those of us who are not versed in the German language.

There are some of the opinion that the *Bilderlexikon der Erotik* (Vienna, 1928–31; four vols), edited by Leo Schidrowitz, is of sufficient importance to rank with all the other major reference works of the genre. While not wishing to appear to be making an *ex cathedra* statement on the subject, this is not a view that I am able to share. Only volume two, and part of volume four, deal with erotic literature, and then in an arbitrary and capricious manner. It has, for example, the annoying habit of ascribing publication of almost all erotic books appearing in France after about 1910 to Georges and Robert Briffaut, two brothers who for many years published *galante* books, mostly reprints of works that appeared originally in the 18th century, from their shop on the rue de Furstenberg, Paris. While the bulk of their books were legitimately published, and carried their imprint and address, it is nevertheless true that there was also a clandestine side to their business, but not to the extent alleged by the *Bilderlexikon*. Their *sub rosa* productions were very much in line with their legitimate ones, both in appearance and the type of material that they published. One such, in 1909, was a reprint of Andréa de Nerciat's *Les Aphrodites*, first published in 1793, in three volumes, with the false imprint 'À Lampsaque' and carrying an Introduction, unsigned, but cobbled together from other sources by the poet Guillaume Apollinaire, who added a few flourishes of his own to justify his cheque. Apart from the fact that this edition of *Les Aphrodites* looks like a typical Briffaut publication, the presence of introductory matter by Apollinaire more or less clinches it, since he provided introductions to many of the legitimate Briffaut books, under his own name.

Another publisher whose name the *Bilderlexikon* makes free with, although usually correctly in this instance, is Charles Carrington, a person of Portuguese descent whose real name was Paul Ferdinando. Although born in England, he operated in Paris from about 1890 until his death in the early 1920s.

Carrington, however, was dead and buried by the time the *Bilderlexikon* was published. The Briffauts were not and as late as 1949 were still doing business from the rue de Furstenberg, in which year they published J. Rives Childs' bibliography of Restif de la Bretonne. It is interesting to speculate how the brothers reacted upon learning that their name was being bandied about literary circles as the chief producers of French pornography from 1910 onwards, much of it of a very low calibre indeed.

My personal view of the *Bilderlexikon* is that its scope and method prevent it from being of solid bibliographical value. Unlike the equally wide-ranging *Bibliotheca Germanorum Erotica et Curiosa*, which confines itself to merely describing books as objects with the occasional critical comment, the *Bilderlexikon* comprises numerous short articles by various hands, and is profusely illustrated throughout. In these circumstances, a thoroughness comparable with that of the Hayn/Gotendorf/Englisch compilation is impossible.

For French works published up until 1870 or thereabouts, the chief source of information is the third edition of the *Bibliographie des ouvrages relatifs à l'amour*, etc. (Turin, Nice, San Remo, 1871–3; six vols) of Jules Gay, who compiled the work under the pseudonym 'M. le C. d'I***' but whose real name appeared on the titlepage as publisher, along with that of London bookseller Bernard Quaritch. The arrangement of the entries in this edition was alphabetically, by title, whereas in the preceding two editions, both in one volume and published at Paris in 1861 and 1864, the arrangement was by subject.

A fourth edition, expanded by J. Lemonnyer, appeared between 1894 and 1900 in four large quarto volumes. Referred to in auction catalogues and such like as the 'Gay/Lemonnyer' for convenience, this edition is usually considered the best of the four and is the one most frequently cited as a reference and quoted from. It has, however, one very serious drawback. Many of the valuable notes that graced the earlier editions, especially the third, have been either completely abandoned or severely abridged. This was presumably done by Lemonnyer to make room for new material, notices of books published for the first time after 1870–3 – and to be fair he was not to know that Perceau's incomparable bibliography of clandestine French erotica, covering the period 1800–1929, which was to be published in 1930, would make his new material largely redundant.

As a personal preference, the third edition of Gay is the more desirable. Jules Gay was himself a prolific publisher of erotica. Like the Briffaut brothers who came after him, he looked to earlier ages for many of the books he printed, taking a scholarly interest in the subject and adding to his publications erudite introductions, frequently anonymous or pseudonymous, by such authorities as Gustave Brunet and Paul Lacroix. As may be expected from this, the notes appended to his *Bibliographie* are scholarly and reliable, except in the cases of works noticed other than French ones, where caution must be exercised. As Ashbee points out (*Catena*, p. xlviii): 'Probably all the English books which are to be found *correctly* noticed in M. Gay's *Bibliographie* ... were communicated by J. Campbell [Reddie], whose name figures in the preface to the third ... edition.' (The emphasis on 'correctly' is Ashbee's.)

With the publication of his *Bibliographie du roman érotique au XIXe siècle* (Paris, 1930; two vols), Louis Perceau became the first to bring to erotica the application of something seriously approaching scientific bibliography. Unlike his predecessors, and in particular Hayn/Gotendorf and Gay who fairly uncritically attempted 'national histories' of erotica, Perceau narrowed his sights and concentrated on a specific period and a well-defined area of study: clandestine French erotic and pornographic prose works published between 1800 and 1929. The arrangement he adopted was by year, with the first editions of each work appearing under their appropriate dates and their reprints being noticed immediately afterwards in chronological sequence. There are two appendices, one for works that have been announced as forthcoming but which have not appeared and one for unpublished manuscripts, and no less than ten indices. It is an extraordinary achievement by any standards, and there is little likelihood that anything of importance was omitted.

Perceau's life – he was born in 1883 and died in 1942 – seems to have been an interesting one, for apart from his literary pursuits he was also involved in extreme left-wing political activity, something rare if not unique among workers in the field of erotica for some reason, and he was imprisoned in 1906 for being one of the signatories to a 'seditious' poster. As Jean Cabanel rather neatly puts it in a biographical article on Perceau in *Triptyque* (June–July, 1932): '*Il partage dès lors son temps entre l'agitation dans la rue et le silence des bibliothèques.*'

Together with Pascal Pia (1901–80) and Fernand Fleuret (1883–1945), Perceau is generally considered to have been one of the pillars of French clandestine book production between the two world wars. As far as it goes, this is true, but as Mr G. Legman has shown in his Introduction to *The Private Case* (1981, pp. 25–26) Perceau actually published his first under-the-counter book in 1909, a collection of erotique spoonerisms or *contrepéteries* ('cross-fartings') entitled *Le Trésor des équivoques*, under the pseudonym 'Jacques Oncial'. Continuing with his interest in erotic folk humour, he published anonymously in 1913 *Histoires d'hommes et de dames*, which included riddles, charades and more spoonerisms. A copy of this very rare little volume is preserved in the Private Case of the British Library.

In 1913 also, in collaboration with Fleuret and Guillaume Apollinaire, he published his first bibliographical venture, the catalogue of *L'Enfer*, the erotica collection of the Bibliothèque Nationale, Paris.

After the First World War, Perceau produced a series of scholarly editions of reprints of 17th- and 18th-century anthologies of libertine verse, either alone or in collaboration with Fleuret, and provided learned Introductions under the pseudonym 'Helpey, Bibliographe poitevin' for critical editions of many of the major erotic works of the 18th and 19th centuries, editions that were invariably published *sous le manteau* in fine, limited printings by Maurice Duflou and others. Using the pseudonym 'Alexandre de Vérineau' he issued several collections of his own verses, including *Priapées* (1920) and *Au bord du lit* (1927), and it is thought that before he died he prepared bibliographies of Ronsard, erotic novels of the 17th and 18th centuries and clandestine erotic poetry, all as yet unpublished.

OPPOSITE Titlepage of the first edition of *Histoire d'O*. The vignette is by Hans Bellmer, and is rumoured to have appeared on as few as 60 of the 600 copies of the book that were issued

HISTOIRE D'O

PAR

PAULINE RÉAGE

AVEC UNE PRÉFACE
DE

JEAN PAULHAN

A SCEAUX
CHEZ JEAN-JACQUES PAUVERT
39, *Rue des Coudrais*
MCMLIV

OPPOSITE ABOVE The lithograph frontispiece to *The Exhibition of Female Flagellants* (London, *c.* 1860), typical of the illustrations adorning William Dugdale's publications

OPPOSITE BELOW A Victorian view of the Earl of Rochester. One of the lithographs from a spurious autobiography of the Earl of Rochester published at London, *c.* 1860, by William Dugdale

The last of the great French bibliophiles and *amateurs* of erotica was Pascal Pia, already mentioned, who died in 1980 at the age of 79 after delivering himself of *Les Livres de l'Enfer* (Paris, 1978; two vols). This is essentially an updating of the catalogue of the erotica collection of the Bibliothèque Nationale, published in 1913 by Mercure de France and compiled by Perceau, Apollinaire and Fleuret, but with a considerable amount of additional material gathered together from Pia's own collection and those of his friends.

The announcement that Pia's work was about to be published created not a little excitement among those who interest themselves in these matters, for he is known to have been acquainted with the publishers of *sub rosa* literature between the wars, and to have himself been involved in many of the more important productions, including the first edition of Pierre Louÿs's novel *Trois filles de leur mère* (1926), which he designed and which was published by René Bonnel.

Hope that he might 'reveal all' was not entirely fulfilled, however, for while he was forthcoming in many areas he remained infuriatingly guarded if not actually obstructive in others. Pia is reputed to have been something of a practical joker in his younger days, and one area in which he displayed noticeable pre-varication concerns a number of small poetical works, allegedly by Apollinaire, Baudelaire and others, which are rumoured to have been written by himself and passed off, at least to their purchasers, as the genuine article.

RIGHT Titlepage and frontispiece of *Histoires d'hommes et de dames*, edited by Louis Perceau and possibly published by J. Chevral at Paris. The frontispiece has been ascribed to Lobel-Riche

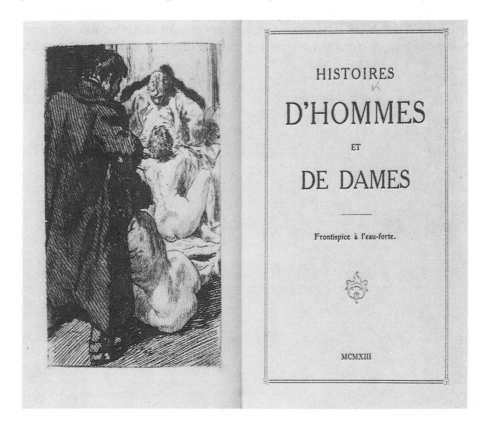

HISTOIRES

D'HOMMES

ET

DE DAMES

Frontispice à l'eau-forte.

MCMXIII

With Pia's death, the truth behind many of these mystifications may never be known. It is to be hoped that he prepared a *memoire*, for publication in the near future, as did the late Eric Losfeld, the original publisher of *Emmanuelle* and much else besides, with his entertaining volume *Endetté comme une mule ou la Passion d'éditer* (Paris: Belfond, 1979). If not, certain important aspects of the underground literature of pre-war France will be as lost to us as that of the late 18th century has been.

*   *   *   *   *

By starting with the 17th century, it is possible to avoid much of the sort of irrelevant material that has been spoken of earlier in this Introduction; it was also the century in which for their own sake erotic and pornographic books began to find themselves in trouble with the authorities. Previously, prosecutions had been made against books and their publishers chiefly on the grounds of political or religious unorthodoxy. Some of these works were of an erotic character as well, but that aspect of them was not seen as being particularly dangerous, an interesting reversal of the situation that currently prevails – at least in the West, where it might be assumed that sex is seen as a more subversive force than political ideas, a notion that has not escaped some of our more radical artists, like the anarchist film director Luis Bunuel and the equally libertarian French novelist Octave Mirbeau. They might be right. I hope that they are, for love is an infinitely finer and more enjoyable method of rebelling than the barricade and the machine gun.

PATRICK KEARNEY
Camden Town, London
June 1981

CHAPTER ONE

THE 17ᵀᴴ CENTURY

SODOM'S PALACE OF PLEASURE

> Thus in the zenith of my lust I reign,
> I eat to swive and swive to eat again.
> Let other monarchs, who their sceptres bear
> To keep their subjects less in love than fear;
> Be slaves to crowns, my nation shall be free;
> My pintle only shall my sceptre be.
> My laws shall act more pleasure than command,
> And with my prick I'll govern all the land.

King Bolloxinion's opening speech in the obscene tragi-comedy *Sodom, or the Quintessence of Debauchery* is also the opening blast of libertine writing in England. Although single poems and miscellany collections of erotic verse had been circulating in manuscript since at least the time of Thomas Nash's *Choise of Valentines, or the Merie Ballad of Nash his Dildo* in the late 16th century, *Sodom* marked the first appearance of an extended home-grown product, and is probably the earliest attempt in any language at a full-length play on an openly sexual theme.

The history of *Sodom* is a classic example of the sort of obscurity, rumour and speculation that plagues so much of erotica. The authorship has been ascribed to John Wilmot, the second Earl of Rochester (1647–80), a 'Cavalier poet' during the reign of Charles II whose verse satires were to get him into trouble more than once, and whose love lyrics are among the finest in the English language. He was also given to composing poems of gross obscenity and cynicism, a fact that has led to almost everything of a similar nature by his peers and contemporaries being laid to his credit as well.

Rochester's first collected book of verse, *Poems on Several Occasions* ('Antwerp' or 'Antwerpen' [London], 1680), is of considerable interest. It appears to have been put together with little regard for the establishment of an authentic selection of Rochester's muse, and may indeed be merely a printed version of one of the peregrine manuscript miscellanies already spoken of. The indecency of many of the poems, coupled with Rochester's unfortunate reputation and recent death, probably prompted the publishers to add his name – or, rather, his initials – to the titlepage as a selling point. Several of these printed editions of '1680' survive, but they are not identical in either content or physical appearance, which indicates that variant editions appeared over a number of years. One of them, preserved in the Henry E. Huntington Library at San Marino, California, was reprinted in

OPPOSITE John Wilmot, 2nd Earl of Rochester, after J. Huysmans

BELOW LEFT One of the Earl of Rochester's more vigorous compositions in *Poems on Several Occasions* (c. 1680)

BELOW RIGHT Titlepage from the spurious autobiography of the Earl of Rochester, published at London, *c.* 1860, by William Dugdale. See colour plate *opposite below*, p. 17

facsimile in 1950 by Princeton University Press, with notes by James Thorpe, while an undated 'Antwerpen' edition in the British Library was similarly reprinted, but without scholarly annotation, in London in 1971 by the Scolar Press.

The printed editions of the poems, and the manuscript miscellanies on which they were based, were the subject of an admirable study in depth by Professor David M. Vieth in his *Attribution in Restoration Poetry* (New Haven & London: Yale University Press, 1963). In this, Professor Vieth discusses all the various poems ascribed to Rochester and shows that many of them are by other writers entirely. Of those that are unquestionably by Rochester, a number are equal to the obscenity of *Sodom*. Professor Vieth's study of 1963 led, in 1968, to his fine *Complete Poems of John Wilmot, Earl of Rochester* – also from Yale University Press – in which there appears for the first time what may be considered a definitive gathering of the poet's work. Apart from those fortunate enough to possess copies of the now scarce Thorpe facsimile of 1950, this was probably the first

(14)

A Ramble in St. James's Park.

MUch Wine had paſt, with grave Diſcourſe,
Of who Fucks who, and who do's worſe ;
Such as you uſually do hear
From them that Diet at the *Bear* ;
When I, who ſtill take care to ſee
Drunk'nneſs Reliev'd by Letchery,
Went out into St. *James's* Park,
To cool my Head, and fire my Heart ;
But though St. *James* has the Honour ont !
'Tis Conſecrate to *Prick* and *Cunt.*
There, by a moſt Inceſtuous Birth,
Strange Woods Spring from the teeming Earth :
For they relate how heretoſore,
When Ancient *Pict* began to Whore,
Deluded of his Aſſignation,
(Jilting it ſeems was then in faſhion.)
Poor penſive Lover in this place,
Wou'd Frig upon his Mothers Face ;
Whence Rows of Mandrakes tall did riſe,
Whoſe Lewd tops Fuck'd the very Skies.
Each imitated Branch do's twine
In ſome Love Fold of *Aretine* :
And nightly now beneath their Shade
Are Bugg'ries, Rapes and Inceſts made,
Unto this All-ſin-ſheltring Grove,
Whores of the Bulk and the Alcove,
Great Ladies, Chambermaids and Drudges,
The Rag-picker and Heireſs trudges ;

Car-

NEW EDITION—WITH RICH ENGRAVINGS.

THE
SINGULAR LIFE,
AMATORY ADVENTURES,
AND
EXTRAORDINARY INTRIGUES OF
JOHN WILMOT.
THE RENOWNED
EARL OF ROCHESTER:
The constant Companion of that Merry Monarch,
KING CHARLES THE SECOND,
In most of his famous Freaks and Intrigues,
INTERSPERSED WITH
CURIOUS ANECDOTES
OF NELL GWYNNE—JANE STANLEY—LADY CASTLEMAINE—SOPHIA WALLER
—COUNTESS OF SHREWSBURY—DUCHESS OF PORTSMOUTH, &c. &c.,
AND OTHER CELEBRATED BEAUTIES OF THAT LICENTIOUS COURT.
In which is now given for the first time,
THE AMATORY ADVENTURES OF LORD ROCHESTER IN HOLLAND, FRANCE,
AND GERMANY,—THE WHOLE FORMING A PICTURE OF
GALLANTRY AND GAIETY
UNRIVALLED IN ANY AGE OR COUNTRY :
TO WHICH ARE ADDED, THE
POEMS OF LORD ROCHESTER,
Carefully Collected and Revised, including all his Scarce and Curious Verses.
Now first printed from the Manuscript in his Lordship's Hand-writing by a Living Descendant of the Family.

ILLUSTRATED WITH RICHLY COLOURED PLATES.

Printed and Published by Henry Smith, 37, Holywell Street.—Where may be had a choice Catalogue of French and English Facetiæ.

opportunity for the general public to sample such poems as 'A Ramble in St. James's Park,' which commences:

> Much wine had passed with grave discourse
> Of who fucks who, and who does worse
> (Such as you usually do hear
> From those that diet at the Bear),
> When I, who still take care to see
> Drunkenness relieved by lechery,
> Went out into St. James's Park
> To cool my head and fire my heart.
> But though St. James has th' honour on't,
> 'Tis consecrate to prick and cunt ...

and proceeds in a similar vein for 166 lines in all. The earliest 'standard' edition of Rochester, edited by Professor Vivian de Sola Pinto and published at London in 1953, omits this satire with the rather prim note 'This poem has been excluded from the present edition at the request of the publisher.'

Although Rochester has been shown as the author of obscene verses, there is considerable doubt that he wrote *Sodom*. Professor Vieth, who is certainly the foremost scholar on the subject of Rochester, considers the ascription to be 'spurious'. In a letter written in October 1970 to the present writer, Professor Vieth reiterated this view, but apropos the obvious importance of dating the play, irrespective of its authorship, he made the interesting point that the opening line – 'Thus in the zenith of my lust I reign' – is a clear parody of the opening line of Dryden's play *The Conquest of Granada*, Part I, 'Thus in the triumphs of soft peace I reign'. The first production of *The Conquest of Granada* was in December 1670, and for the *Sodom* parody to have any point it is unlikely to have been written much later than the early months of 1671, when the first manuscript copies would have begun to circulate.

Another opponent of Rochester's authorship is Rodney M. Baine who in an article printed in *Review of English Studies, 22* (1946), argues that it was written by one Christopher Fishbourne, an otherwise obscure versifier known chiefly for an 'Ode to St Cecilia's Day' (1683) which had the distinction of being set to music by Purcell. Many other writers have, however, championed Rochester as being responsible for *Sodom*, but on seemingly emotional rather than bibliographical or textual reasoning.

A third and somewhat novel possibility was proposed by Mr A. S. G. Edwards in a most interesting analysis of the extant manuscript copies of *Sodom* that appeared in the Autumn 1976 issue of *The Book Collector*. In his article, Mr Edwards suggests that on textual evidence the play may have been a sort of round robin. Although the question of authorship was not Mr Edwards' prime concern, and he made no commitments on the subject, Rochester may well have had a hand in the play's composition if his theory is correct.

No early printed edition of *Sodom* has come down to us, although there is ample evidence that there were at least two printed within twenty-seven years of the supposed author's death. Two of the surviving contemporary manuscripts seem to derive from a printed version by having 'Antwerp. Printed in the Year 1684' on their titlepages, but there were no prosecutions for publishing such a printed edition until 1689, when Benjamin Crayle and Joseph Streater were indicted for the offence and it is possible that this was the '1684' version on which the manuscripts were based, actually printed about 1689 but predated. This has always been a favourite trick of erotica publishers. Another prosecution took place in 1707, when John Marshall was indicted for the same offence. An article by Mr D. S. Thomas on early prosecutions for both *Sodom* and *Poems on Several Occasions* will be found in *The Library*, fifth series, XXIV, 1969.

Ashbee, in his notice of *Sodom*, states that an early printed edition of the play existed in the collection of Richard Heber, an eccentric bibliophile who died in 1833. Heber was a likely candidate for possessing a copy, too. He was a compulsive collector, who would systematically fill one house with books, lock it up, buy another and start all over again. 'No gentleman', he is reported to have once said, 'can afford to be without three copies of a book, one for show, one for use and one for borrowers.' He meant it, for at his death his library filled four houses in England, one each at Ghent and Paris, and there were smaller collections at other Continental locations. It took four years to auction off his collection, at sixteen separate sales. Unfortunately, according to Ashbee, the volume of *Sodom* was destroyed 'together with one or two other obscene works ... by the executors.' (See *Ashbee*, 2, p. 327.)

It is possible, however, that another of the early editions survived until as late as about 1865 for in *The Playhouse of Pepys*, Montague Summers asserts that Edmund Gosse had seen a copy, and Gosse was not born until 1849.

The earliest printed edition extant appeared in 1904. It was published at Paris by H. Welter, and edited from the manuscript in the Hamburg Staats- und Universitätsbibliothek (Cod. 115, pp. 7–39) by L. S. A. M. von Römer who, in adding his own blunders to those of an already far from perfect manuscript, did a pretty poor job of it. The following year, this same text was printed again in volume nine of *Kryptadia*, a series in twelve volumes published between 1883 and 1911 that was devoted to the serious study of erotic folklore under the editorship of Friedrich Krauss and Isidore Kopernicky. The first four volumes of this remarkable series were published at Heilbronn by Henninger Frères, and the others by H. Welter at Paris.

In his unpublished *Study of Erotic Literature in England*, the manuscript of which is preserved in the British Library, Charles Reginald Dawes states that two other editions – presumably in English – were published in 1911 and 1930, but I have been unable to locate details of these. Most recently, a version edited possibly by Robert Nurenberg with some gesture toward variant readings was published in 1957 by The Olympia Press, as volume 48 of its Traveller's Companion Series. With the collapse of censorship in the United States in the late 1960s, several presumably pirated reprints of this appeared.

German translations of *Sodom* were published in 1909 and 1924. Both were clandestine printings. The earlier of the two, according to the titlepage, was issued at Leipzig and it was illustrated by Julius Klinger in a grotesque manner reminiscent of Aubrey Beardsley. The edition of 1924 formed volume fourteen of a '*Sammlung Bibliotheca Erotica et Curiosa*', and was actually published at Vienna by Klement von Treldewehr although the titlepage gives 'Volosca ... Verlag Dr. Alexander Trianta'. It was illustrated with drawings by an artist calling himself 'Dietz', apparently a pseudonym.

OPPOSITE Pietro Aretino. A woodcut portrait from the third edition of the third part of the *Ragionamenti*, published at Venice in 1539 by Marcolini

*　　*　　*　　*　　*

In terms of book-length erotica, *Sodom* may have been an isolated example of native English enterprise, but connoisseurs were not starved of reading matter. Continental works, in both their original versions and in translation, had been circulating in England since at least 1584 or 1585 when John Wolfe published the first collected edition of Pietro Aretino's *Ragionamenti* at London. These were two sets of three dialogues between an older woman and a younger, more inexperienced one in which the lives of women in various occupations or roles are explained in a realistic and satirical, but not obscene, manner. The two parts were first published separately at Venice in 1534 and 1536.

The earliest trace of Aretino's work in English was *The Crafty Whore, or, the Mistery and Iniquity of Bawdy Houses laid open* ... (London: Henry Marsh, 1658). This is a rather free rendering of the third dialogue of the first part of the *Ragionamenti*. As this particular dialogue dealt with the life of whores, it enjoyed enormous popularity as a separate entity from the rest of the book and went through numerous editions and translations, including *Pornodidascalus, seu colloquum muliebre* (1623) which was a Latin translation done by Caspar Barthius from the Spanish version of F. Xuarez entitled *Coloquio de las damas*, first published in 1547.

The only complete English edition of the *Ragionamenti* appeared in 1889, when it was published, and translated, by Isidore Liseux at Paris, in six volumes.[1]

Pietro Aretino (1492–1556), called *Flagello de' principi* (the Scourge of Princes) because of his biting, satirical wit, was the *ne plus ultra* of pornography, especially in England, but not for the *Ragionamenti*, rather for something that he actually played only a peripheral part in. These were the so-called 'Postures of Aretino'.

In 1524, Giulio Romano had Marcantonio Raimondi engrave sixteen plates from drawings that the former had executed of erotic postures, scenes in which various positions for love-making were graphically portrayed. The appearance of these illustrations did not find favour with the Pope, Clement VII, who took steps to have them suppressed. Romano fled Rome for Mantua, or was safely there when the trouble started, but Raimondi was not so fortunate and was thrown into prison.

What happened next is not altogether clear. According to the art historian Giorgio Vasari (1511–74), Cardinal Hippolyte de' Medici and Baccio Bandinelli interceded with the Pope on behalf of Raimondi and secured his release (*Vasari*,

RAGIONAMENTO

NEL QVALE M. PIETRO ARETI NO FIGVRA QVATTRO

Suoi Amici, Che fauellano de le
Corti del Mondo, e di
quella del Cielo.

IL DIVINO PIETRO
ARETINO

M. D. XXXIX.

Florence, 1906; vol. V, p. 418). Aretino, on the other hand, claims in a letter that he wrote to Battista Zatti that it was he who persuaded the Pope to release Raimondi (Aretino, *Lettere*: Venice, 1538).

Whichever it was, once Raimondi was free Aretino made it his business to see the engravings that had so offended the Pope, upon which he felt moved to compose a series of sonnets, one for each engraving, which became known as the *Sonneti lussuriosi*. By November 1527 a book incorporating both the sonnets and engravings was in print, for in that month Cesare Fregoso received a copy sent to him by Aretino. Copies of this book have not survived, but a solitary specimen of a related work, published at Venice about 1550, has. It contains a number of poetical pieces, in addition to Aretino's sonnets, and fifteen of sixteen woodcut copies of the engravings. The book was discovered by Max Sander in Italy, from whom it passed to Walter Toscanini, a collector who spent many years researching every aspect of it and who came to the conclusion that it is an exemplar of the edition of 1527 rather than the later, unauthorized reprint that Mr David Foxon believes it to be. In 1978 it was sold at auction to Mr Hans Kraus and is presently in the possession of an eminent Swiss collector. There is a microfilm copy in the British Library.[2]

Despite Aretino's marginal connection with these illustrations, his name was nevertheless associated with them, and they are referred to a number of times in

ABOVE LEFT Nine fragments of Giulio Romano's *Sedici Modi*, illustrations that inspired Aretino's *Sonetti lussuriosi*. Formerly belonging to Pierre Mariette in the 18th century, they are now in the Department of Prints and Drawings of the British Museum

ABOVE A late edition of Aretino's *Sonetti*

the English drama of the Restoration and earlier. Ben Jonson makes Sir Epicure Mammon speak favourably of them in *The Alchemist* (1612), and they are mentioned also in Wycherley's *The Country Wife* (1675) and John Leanard's *The Rambling Justice* (1678). In *Sodom*, the first act takes place in 'an Antechamber hung round with *Aretin's Postures*'.

The *Rettorica delle puttane* (1642) of Ferrante Pallavicino recommends 'Le figure dell'Aretino', but the English adaptation of this work, first published at London by George Shell [i.e. John Wickens?] in 1683 as *The Whore's Rhetorick*, completely reverses this advice and has the bawd Mother Creswel say: '*Aretin's* Figures have no place in my Rhetorick, and I hope will find no room in my Pupils apartment. They are calculated for a hot Region a little on this side of *Sodom*, and are not necessary to be seen in any Northern Clime.'

After these xenophobic strictures, Mother Creswel describes the 'postures' and refers to them endearingly as numbering 'Six and Thirty Geometrical Schemes' which is considerably more than the original sixteen. A hundred years later, in a letter in the *Correspondence de madame Gourdan* (1784), this number is increased again:

> *From* Monsieur de B***, student
> at the School of Painting.
> Paris, May 1st, 1776.

I have, madame, a collection of Aretin's Postures in forty oval-shaped illustrations. As I am to leave shortly for Rome, I am anxious to dispose of them; it occurs to me that they would prove ideal for decorating your *boudoirs*. The price is one thousand

RIGHT Frontispiece and titlepage of the 2nd edition of *Le Porte-feuille de Madame Gourdan* under its new title. This copy was used by the Brussels erotica publisher Auguste Poulet-Malassis as the basis of his 1866 reprint

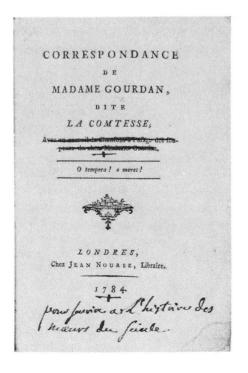

écus; last year I refused an offer of one hundred *louis* for them from the Duke of ***.
Should you wish to examine them, I will be at home this evening after dinner and
all tomorrow morning.[2]

Someone had clearly been adding to them, or else different sets of illustrations
entirely were being circulated under the same name. A full account of the history
of the 'postures', with excellently argued solutions to the many bibliographical
difficulties that they offer, will be found in the second of Mr David Foxon's series
of four articles that were published in *The Book Collector* during 1963, under the
general title *Libertine Literature in England 1660–1745*.

Aretino's *Sonneti lussuriosi* by themselves, which may have been originally
entitled *La Corona di Cazzi*, under which name they appeared at least once in the
16th century and subsequently, have never been satisfactorily translated into
English, although French editions appeared at Brussels in 1871 and Paris in 1882,
and a number of German versions – variously as *Die wollüstigen Sonnette* (Berlin,
1907) and *Die tausend Künste der Liebe* (Privatdruck [?Berlin: Johndorff], 1918) –
have also been published.

Mr Wayland Young in his *Eros Denied* (1965) mentions an English version of
the sonnets fancifully ascribed to Oscar Wilde but without further identification,
and another by Samuel Putnam which appeared in the second volume of *The
Works of Aretino* (New York, 1926), but he is unable to recommend them. In the
case of the Putnam translation this is surprising, for Putnam's translation of *La
Cazzaria* (1531) of Antonio Vignale, which circulated for many years in manuscript among *amateurs* of erotica, before finally being published in a disgracefully
shoddy paperback from a firm of sordid pornographers in California in 1968, is
quite good in its slangy way and deserves a more edifying exposure.

The following sonnet may give an idea of Aretino's style:

> As I can now feel such an impressive tool
> That's opening up the edges of my quim
> I wish I was nothing but quim
> And that you were all tool.
>
> If I was quim and you were tool
> For a while I'd sate my quim
> While you would strip my quim
> Of all pleasures wanted by a tool
> So take the good wishes of this quim.
>
> You too. Take from this modest tool
> The same good wishes. Lower the quim
> And I will raise the tool.
>
> Then on my tool
> Go made with your quim.
> I will be all tool. You – all quim.[3]

L'ESCOLE
Des
FILLES,
Où
LA PHILOSOPHIE
Des
DAMES.
Divisée en
DEUX DIALOGUES,
Agere & Pati.

Corrigé & augmenté, d'un combat du
. . . & du . . . d'une Dialogue entre le . . . & Perrette ; & une
instruction des Curiositéz, dont la
methode de trouver, est marqué par
leur nombres suivant les tables.

Imprimé a Fribourg,
Chez ROGER BON TEMPS,
l'An. 1668.

Frontispiece and titlepage
of an early edition of
L'Escole des filles, a work
usually ascribed to Michel
Millot. The imprint is false;
probably printed in Holland

If the edition of Aretino's works in which Putnam's translations of the *Sonneti* appeared was openly published, then on reflection it is probably not altogether surprising that Mr Young found them '. . . so coy, guilty, timid and periphrastic that the eye involuntarily erases them from the page and leaves a sonnet-shaped blank there and in the memory.'

*   *   *   *   *

The mark left on the erotic literature of the 17th century by Aretino, and in particular his *Ragionamenti*, was considerable, for the dialogue form that he used was followed by almost all the important works in the genre up until the latter part of the century when *Le Zombi du grand Pérou ou la Comtesse de Cocagne* (1697) was published, a work allegedly by Pierre Corneille Blessebois, in which for what was probably the first time in erotica the form of the novel was employed.

One of the best known of the earlier works in dialogue form is *L'École des filles*.

29

It is the book that Samuel Pepys writes about in his diary in January and February 1668, when he recounts amusingly how he paid two visits to his bookseller John Martin, trying to make up his mind whether or not to buy a copy of 'L'escholle des filles', which he found to be the 'most bawdy, lewd book that ever I saw...'. Eventually Pepys bought one, but after reading it through he justified his choice of the cheaper 'plain binding' by burning it, 'that it might not be among my books to my shame'. This was unfortunate, since it is now impossible to know which edition it was that he acquired.

Unlike many other erotic books of the period, however, *L'École des filles* is possessed of a good deal of reliable documentation, at least so far as the first edition is concerned, although the question of authorship remains uncertain. *Gay* (3rd ed. vol. 3, p. 141) records the titlepage of the first edition thus: '*École (L') des filles, ou la Philosophie des dames* (ou, dans les édit. suiv., *des femmes*), *leur indiquant le secret pour se faire aimer des hommes, quand même elles ne seraient pas belles, et le plus sûr moyen d'avoir du plaisir tout le temps de leur vie ... par A. D. P.*' He adds that it was printed at Paris in 1655 and that the edition is '*introuvable*' which is correct, although one might reasonably surmise that he had seen a copy at some time in order to have been able to quote the title so exactly.

The story of the original edition was first told by Frédéric Lachèvre, who discovered the dossier of the interrogation and trial of the main characters involved in the Archives Nationales and published them with a commentary in a splendid article in his *Mélanges* (Paris, 1920; pp. [82]–126), a collection of short pieces comprising volume seven of his series *Le Libertinage au XVIIe Siècle*. More recently, the documents were reprinted in the edition of *L'École des filles* '*présentée par Pascal Pia*' for Claude Tchou's *Cercle du Livre Précieux* at Paris in 1959.

Early in 1655, Jean L'Ange, or de Lange, and Michel Millot had a printer named Louis Piot run off three hundred copies of the book, fifty of which were on fine paper. It had an engraved '*figure*' [i.e. a frontispiece] by François Chauveau, an artist from Poitiers, and the titlepage bore the false imprint '*À Leyde*'. A binder, Louis Framery, was employed who, under the watchful eye of L'Ange, bound up twenty-two copies in parchment, eight or nine of which were delivered to the poet Paul Scarron (1610–60).

At this point in the proceedings, Piot and Framery got cold feet; printing unlicensed books was a serious offence. Despite the fact that they had been paid for their work, they informed on L'Ange and Millot. The former was arrested while keeping an appointment with a bookseller named Nicolas de la Vigne, who was to buy fifty copies of the book, and his rooms on the rue des Roziers searched. Copies of the book and of a manuscript of it in L'Ange's handwriting containing passages not included in the printed version were taken away. Millot was more slippery. Although the arresting officer found him at home in his rooms on the *quai* of the '*isle Nostre Dame*' he was intimidated by the presence of some of Millot's heavier associates – '*plusiers particuliers*' as the documents put it – and had to make do with taking away more copies of the book.

On 12 June, L'Ange, Framery, Piot and Chauveau were all interrogated by Claude Hourlier concerning their respective roles in the publication of *L'École des filles*, which was stated to be '*contre l'honneur de Dieu, de l'Église et fort contraire aux bonnes moeurs et dissipline chrestienne.*'

Piot and Framery merely repeated what they had presumably said when informing on Millot and L'Ange, and Chauveau, although admitting that he had engraved the frontispiece, claimed he had no idea what sort of book it was supposed to be for. L'Ange, who seems to have been questioned first, put up some stiff resistance, saying that the book had actually been printed at Leyden and that the entire print run had been given him by somebody called Dumas in payment of a debt. He claimed at one point that the author was the Comte de Cramail, who had died thirteen years previously, and then said it was by the Comte d'Etelan, the author of a satire against Cardinal Richelieu entitled *La Milliade*.

The following day, 13 June, at his second interrogation, L'Ange was told of the testimony given by Piot and Framery and he confessed. He accused Millot of being the author of *L'École des filles*, but stated that for his own part all he had done was some editing, proof reading and the cutting out of a few of the more obscene bits.

When the trial took place, L'Ange was found guilty, fined 200 *livres* and exiled from Paris for three years, and ordered to make formal penance. Millot fared rather worse. He was sentenced to be hanged and have his property confiscated. Fortunately, he had had the presence of mind to abscond to a safe distance and the authorities were obliged to carry out the sentence in his absence by hanging him in effigy, and burning the books. Two days afterwards, on 11 August, Millot appealed on the curious, not to say flimsy, grounds that he had been in the service of the King in Lombardy at the time the offences he was supposed to have committed had taken place. Surprisingly, this was accepted, and it seems likely that the proceedings taken against him and L'Ange were not altogether serious in the first place, or else pressure had been brought to bear shortly after the arrests to hush things up. Pierre Louÿs, a friend of Lachèvre, suggested to the latter that since a number of copies had been delivered to Scarron, he might be the author of it. Scarron had edited the *Gazette Burlesque* since the beginning of 1655 and it may be significant that the issue for July, the month after the arrests took place, failed to appear. Lachèvre, in his *Mélanges*, reprints some verses by Scarron's editorial successor on the *Gazette* which ask what had become of the poet. If Scarron were the author of *L'École des filles* and was being protected, a likely candidate for protector was Nicolas Fouquet, the Superintendent of Finances, to whom Scarron had dedicated *Le Gardien de soi-même*. Fouquet fell from favour in 1661, and in a house that he had furnished for a mistress was found a copy of the 1655 edition of *L'École des filles*.

Whether it was Millot who wrote the book, as was claimed by L'Ange, or Scarron is clearly doubtful, but what is certain is that copies escaped the destruction order, for reprints, mostly published in Holland, soon started to appear. Gay and Lachèvre record editions of 1659 and 1667, both with false 'Paris' imprints, and the British Library has one dated 1668 ('*Imprimé à Fribourg, chez Roger Bon*

Temps') which reproduces the frontispiece by Chauveau from the first edition. Copies of a French edition reached England possibly as early as 1667 for, as has been shown, Pepys was reading one in January of the following year, but the first appearance of an English translation was about twelve years later in 1680 when John Coxe, alias John Tarter, was prosecuted for publishing and selling one, as is shown in J. C. Jeaffreson's calendar of *Middlesex County Records* (vol. iv, 1892, 146).

Eight years afterwards, in 1688, Crayle and Streater, the two reprobates who were prosecuted in 1689 for their edition of *Sodom*, were in trouble for *L'École des filles* as well. Two other editions were circulating about 1744. One was the subject of legal proceedings in 1745 when Daniel Lynch and John Stevens were prosecuted and convicted of selling copies; the other was falsely imprinted 'Rotterdam, printed for J. Johnson 1,000,000' and may have actually been printed in Ireland.

Legal records show that in 1788, John Morgan and Lewis McDonald were fined £200 and sentenced to a year in prison and a session in the pillory for publishing four books, one of which was a reprint of the 1745 edition of *L'École des filles*. Although it is unwise to make claims of this sort, it is nevertheless possible that the 1788 edition is the same one listed by J. Campbell Reddie in his *Bibliographical Notes*, an unpublished three-volume manuscript forming part of the Ashbee bequest to the British Museum and preserved in Department of Manuscripts. The title, as quoted by Reddie, is *The School of Venus, or amorous fancies and the postures of love described in two instructive and confidential dialogues between a woman and a virgin*, a work of seventy pages. (BM Add. MS 38829 ff. 381, 382.) The authorship is absurdly ascribed to Aretino, which indicates the extent to which his influence on erotic literature continued to be exerted.

None of these early editions has survived – a point that is well worth emphasizing for similar claims by David Foxon in his 1963 articles in *The Book Collector* resulted in the sudden appearance, as will be seen below, of a unique copy of an English translation of *Vénus dans le cloître* (1725) – but the indictments against Lynch and Stevens in the Public Records Office in London (KB 28/176/19, 20) conveniently include extremely lengthy quotations from the edition of *L'École des filles* they were convicted of selling, and extracts from these appear in the Introduction to Mr Donald Thomas's new translation of the book that was published at London in 1972 by Panther Books. Another modern translation, perpetrated by one 'Rudolf Schleifer', was put out by Brandon House [Milton Luros] of North Hollywood, California, in 1967 under the title *Lessons in Seduction*.

The subtitle of the edition cited above by Reddie provides an adequate idea of the content of *L'École des filles*; it maintains the Aretinesque dialogue form of the *Ragionamenti*, in which an experienced older woman explains the facts of life in realistic terms to a young virgin. Although the method of explanation is direct and to the point, and couched in language not normally found in even modern 'marriage manuals' and the like, it lacks the gloating crudity of commercial pornography, emphasizing instead sexual happiness and a warmth of feeling. The following extract from the first dialogue, taken from Mr Donald Thomas's translation, illustrates the style and tone of the book. Susanne, named Fanny in the 18th-century translation, has just explained to Fanchon, originally Katy, the mechanics and purpose of an erection.

FANCHON   And when it grows, as you describe it, that's when he inserts it into the girl?

SUSANNE   Of course. He couldn't do it any other way, though there's still more enjoyment in watching the trouble he goes to in order to get it in. It doesn't go in all at once, as you might think, but bit by bit. Sometimes the boy is absolutely sweltering before he's got it all in, because the girl isn't big enough – though there's more pleasure in that if the girl feels his tool open her boldly and rub hard against the rim of her fanny, exciting her gently and exquisitely.

FANCHON   Not for me! I should be afraid it would do me some damage.

SUSANNE   Out of the question, my dear. It does the girl a great deal of good. Certainly the first thrust of the yard, to get it in, gives her a slight twinge of discomfort because she isn't used to having it there, but after that it does nothing except arouse and excite the greatest pleasure in the world.

FANCHON   And what do you call the girl's organ?

SUSANNE   I call it the *cunny*. Sometimes it's called the *sheath* or the *thingummy*, the *little hole*, the *mossy hole*, and so on. And when a boy does what I've described to a girl, it's known as *putting his yard in her cunny*, or rather one says that he *mounts* her or *rides* her. Boys teach us to use language like this when they hold us in their arms. But do be careful not to talk like this in front of everyone because they are supposed to be vulgar words which make girls blush when they're used.

FANCHON   I promise to be careful, love. But what does the boy do so that he can insert his stiff instrument into the cunny?

SUSANNE   As soon as he'd lodged it in the girl's opening, he pushes forward with his rump. Then he draws back a little and pushes forward again still harder. The girl, for her part, pushes towards him to thread it in further until it's completely engulfed in her. All this time she feels the rhythm of the boy's hips as he straddles her.

FANCHON   He has to keep moving, then, without stopping at all?

SUSANNE   Certainly.

FANCHON   How does he manage to push it in bit by bit with these precise movements?

SUSANNE   Watch me. This is how he does it. Now watch how I move. And while the girl sees him moving like this she embraces him, kisses him on the mouth, strokes his stomach, backside, thighs, calling him her dear heart and soul. All this time she feels his yard entering her cunny as gently as you could dream of.

FANCHON   You know, love, I think I should rather like to try this thing, in the way you've just described. I'm quite sure I should get the greatest possible enjoyment out of it. Girls certainly ought to be grateful to boys for doing such things to them. But isn't there anything in it for boys, who devote themselves so completely to giving pleasure to others?

SUSANNE   Well, what do you think? Of course there is! You can tell that from the way they carry on! When they almost swoon with delight in doing this to a girl, you hear nothing from them except 'Ah! My Heart! Ah! My love!

I'm dying! Faster! I can't go any further! Faster!' And of course, the girl's enjoyment is even greater when she sees that the boy who is doing it to her is getting such pleasure from it. She enjoys it much more than if he received no pleasure at all. If the boy delights the girl, there's no doubt that she delights him. (*The School of Venus*, trans. by Donald Thomas. London, 1972, pp. 84–86.)

*   *   *   *   *

About five years after the first publication of *L'École des filles*, there appeared the most outspoken erotic work of the 17th century, and certainly the one nearest to true pornography. These were the Dialogues of Nicolas Chorier, published originally in Latin and purporting to be a translation by the Dutch philologist and historian Joannes Meursius (Jan de Meurs: 1579–1639) of a work in Spanish by an erudite woman named Luisa Sigea (*c.* 1530–60), who was born at Toledo and styled by her contemporaries as the Minerva of her day.

Chorier, the real author of the book, was born at Vienne, Dauphiné, in 1609 or 1612. Educated by the Jesuits, he eventually took a degree in law in 1639 and until about 1658 conducted a successful legal practice in his home town at the *Cour des aides*, a law court which tried suits arising from the collection of taxes. While he studied law, he also developed a flair for literature and from 1640 he published a number of historical and literary works that bought him a measure of fame and the acquaintanceship of many of the leading scholars of the time.

Shortly after 1658, the *Cour des aides* was suppressed and Chorier was obliged to leave Vienne and move with his family to Grenoble, where he again became successful and published in 1661 the first volume of a work entitled *Histoire générale du Dauphiné*, which resulted in his being voted an endowment of 500 *louis* by the Provincial States. It was about this time too that his celebrated Dialogues were first published.

In articles appearing in series II-IV of *La Curiosité littéraire et bibliographique* (Paris, 1880–83), Isidore Liseux and Alcide Bonneau explore the history of the work and its author. According to them, the first edition appeared in 1659 or 1660 as *Aloisiae Sigeae Toletanae Satyra Sotadica de arcanis Amoris et Veneris, Aloisia Hispanice Scripsit, Latinitate donavit Joannes Meursius, V.C.* It is in two parts of 245 and 111 pages, and the presence at the conclusion of the first part of six pages of *errata* tends to confirm its priority. Liseux and Bonneau argue that from the absence of catchwords it was printed in France,[4] and by comparing it typographically with *Recherches du sieur Chorier sur les antiquités de la ville de Vienne* (1658) further localize it to Lyons, where Chorier's other books were published. Other authorities have disagreed with these conclusions. J.-Ch. Brunet, in his *Manuel du Libraire* (5th ed., 1862, vol. 3), gives the first edition as having 156 and 78 pages, and being of Dutch origin. *Hayn/Gotendorf* (vol. 6, p. 521) have nothing to say on the subject of pagination, but favour Grenoble as the place of publication, probably on the authority of Edmund Maignien's

L'imprimerie ... à Grenoble (Grenoble, 1884), which proposes that the work was printed there by Jean Nicolas.

The balance of evidence would seem to favour the findings of Liseux and Bonneau, but the truth of the matter is unlikely to be settled. The depressingly recurrent fact that the first edition has been lost to us applies to Chorier's dialogues as it does to so many works of erotica. Assuming that the edition described so fully by Liseux and his colleague was the first, as appears likely, then it has dropped from sight during the past hundred years or so, although it was undoubtedly before them about 1880. Aside from internal bibliographical evidence, it is a totally anonymous performance, lacking both date and impress. Like one or two reprints done from it shortly after its appearance, it contains six dialogues and an Introduction, styled 'Advice to the Reader', which provides the fictitious history of the work and confusingly states that while Luisa Sigea composed seven dialogues in all only five are to be included. Since the sixth dialogue, entitled *Veneres*, occupies the second part of the book by itself and is separately paginated it is possible that Chorier added it as an afterthought or was working on a tight schedule with his printer. The seventh dialogue, *Fescennini*, emerged about eighteen years later, at which time it was added to a dated edition printed in 1678,

LEFT Titlepage of an early dated edition of Chorier's *Satyra Sotadica de arcanis amoris et veneris*. This is the first edition to contain the seventh dialogue

RIGHT Titlepage of the only known copy of the first French translation of Chorier's *Satyra Sotadica*

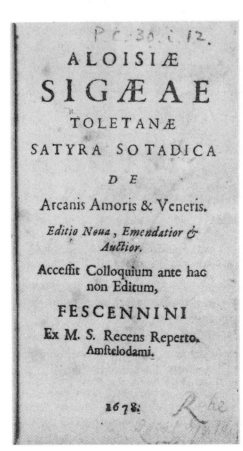

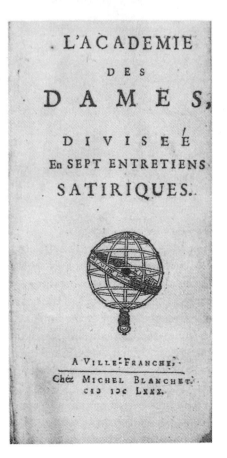

supposedly at Amsterdam. Brunet argues that this was actually published at Geneva, but it seems unlikely. *Fescennini* is something of a curiosity; it transfers the action of the first six dialogues, which were set in Italy, to Spain and likewise changes the nationalities of the characters. Whether this was done by Chorier to reinforce the fiction of the book's Spanish origin is uncertain.

About 1680, an edition appeared as *Joannis Meursii Elegantiae latini sermonis*, a change of title that was adopted for all subsequent editions until the one published at Paris in 1885 by Isidore Liseux and Théophile Belin, which reverted to the original title.

The first French edition also appeared in 1680. Entitled *L'Académie des dames, divisée en sept entretiens satiriques* ('À Ville-Franche, chez Michel Blanchet'), it was believed to have been translated by Jean Nicolas, the son of the bookseller

36

credited by Hayn/Gotendorf with publishing the first Latin edition, and to have been published at Grenoble. The only known copy is in the British Library. Pascal Pia, however, among others, believes that an undated edition of the same translation, entitled more briefly *L'Académie des dames* ('Á Venise, chez Pierre Arretin [*sic*]') and containing a frontispiece and thirty-five obscene plates, is the first French edition. (See Pia, *Les Livres de l'Enfer*, vol. 1, cols 325, 6.) This is certainly an error. A copy of what appears to be this edition is in the British Library, but clearly dates from about 1775 rather than 1680 as is stated by Pia.

A second French translation, ascribed to Jean Terrasson, appeared as *Nouvelle traduction de Meursius, connu sous le nom d'Aloisia au l'Académie des dames. Revue, corrigée et augmentée* ('Cythère' [Paris?], 1749) and as *Le Meursius françois* ('Cythère' [Paris], 1782) from the celebrated printer and publisher Hubert-Martin Cazin,

LEFT and OPPOSITE Two
engravings by Elluin after
designs by Borel for the 1782
Cazin edition of Chorier's
Le Meursius françois

who illustrated his edition with a frontispiece and twelve plates that were unsigned but were designed by Antoine Borel and engraved by Elluin.

The book was known in England soon after its first publication. A manuscript commonplace book of the 17th century preserved at Princeton University (MS AM 14401) contains a spirited English rendering of Book IV: 'The Duell, Being a translation of one of ye dialogues in Satyra Sotadica De Arcanis amoris et Veneris A^o Dom^ni 1676'. Whether the date 1676 refers to when the manuscript was written, or was transcribed from the printed version from which the translation was taken – or even, as is possible, from a printed English version – are questions that cannot be answered. But its position as the earliest surviving specimen of English pornography makes it *nonpareil* in any study of the subject.

The earliest evidence of a printed English edition is to be found in the legal records relating to the prosecution of William Cademan in 1684 for 'exposing, selling, uttering and publishing the pernicious, wicked, scandalous, vicious and illicit book entitled A Dialogue between A Married Lady, and a Maid Tullia Octavia'. The brief passage quoted in the indictment – 'He took his pricke out finding it all wet with my spending, and having wiped it and me, he immediately put it in again and began to thrust with great vigour' – closely follows the relevant passage in the French version of 1680, and is probably translated from that. Further translations – or reprints of the same one with different or slightly changed titles – followed, and may be traced through the legal proceedings against them.

In 1688, Joseph Streater was prosecuted for *A Dialogue between a Married Lady and a Maid*. In 1707, it was John Marshall's turn for *The School of Love* and in 1745–6 there were two prosecutions against *Aretinus Redivivus*. A unique copy of *A Dialogue between a Married Lady and a Maid* printed in 1740 survives in the Bayerische Staatsbibliothek, Munich, and a microfilm of this has been presented to the British Library.

Without copies of all these various editions it is impossible to be able to determine whether they were translations or adaptations, or even if they represent English versions of Chorier's entire work. The 1740 edition has only forty-eight pages and is therefore greatly abridged, but from the evidence of the legal records *Aretinus Redivivus* seems to have been considerably longer, perhaps the whole of the original work since it was said to have been 'Adorn'd with twenty-four curious copper-plates', and was selling for the sum of five shillings which, at 1745 prices, implies a fairly substantial volume.

In 1709, a rather strange variation in the English history of Chorier's dialogues took place. During that year was published *The Cabinet of Love*, a repertoire of more or less obscene poems that was afterwards appended to various of the editions of *The Works of the Earls of Rochester, Roscommon, and Dorset* appearing in the first fifty years or so of the eighteenth century. Included in this, and by far the longest piece, was *The Delights of Venus*, which is a section of Chorier's work done into verse. While of equal indecency with its frequently prosecuted prose original, and certainly not alone in its outrageousness with the accompanying

OPPOSITE Frontispiece to the first edition of the second French translation of Chorier's *Satyra Sotadica*, see illustrations on pages 36 and 37

OVERLEAF LEFT AND RIGHT Two of the ten original watercolour drawings inserted into an 1868 reprint of *Venus dans le cloître*. The artist is unknown, but may have been Jules Adolphe Chauvet

L'Volupté Enchaine L'Amour, Et Presen. La Chai. A L'Hym.

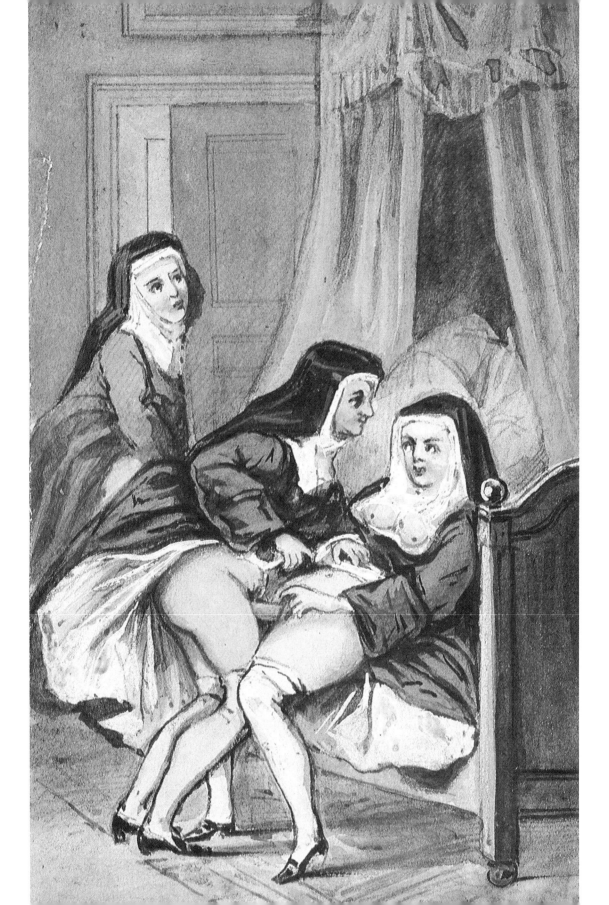

OPPOSITE Frontispiece of an early edition (*c.* 1748) of *Thérèse Philosophe*, see page 54

poems which included *Dildoïdes*, an amusing and neglected burlesque usually ascribed to Samuel Butler (1612–80) the author of *Hudibras*, the volume contrived to escape legal entanglements. In 1798 and 1809, however, John Cole and Edmund Rich respectively were indicted for the publication of what would appear to have been editions of *The Delights of Venus* printed on its own, presumably as a broadsheet or a *plaquette*.

The later history of the work is dominated by the editions published by the erudite ex-priest Isidore Liseux at Paris; a reprint of the original Latin text in 1885, and new French and English translations in 1881 and 1890. All subsequent editions stem from these, and in the instance of the English version usually in the form of smudgy photo-offset reprints on paper with a built-in self-destruct ingredient that causes them to go brown, turn brittle and eventually fall to bits unless kept in optimum library conditions.

The Dialogues of Luisa Sigea represents a significant advance – some might say retreat – on what had gone before in erotica. The proceedings display a grim seriousness, an unhealthy emphasis on defloration and an all-too-ready acceptance of male domination. In these respects, the book is not dissimilar to many of the pornographic effusions of the mid-Victorian period, written by Edward Sellon and others. The Liseux translation, despite its idiosyncratic use of English, nevertheless reveals a vigorous and interesting style which to some extent recommend it as worthy of consideration. And as David Foxon points out: 'The plot continually provides new shocks as apparently stable background figures like mothers and husbands are disclosed as having highly irregular relationships; it is as though a series of gauzes were lifted showing each time more complex groupings. As a demonstration of the falsity of appearances and the hypocrisy of society it is brilliantly anarchistic.' (*The Book Collector*, Autumn, 1963.)

The first dialogue, *The Skirmish*, opens with Tullia and Ottavia discussing the forthcoming marriage of the latter to Caviceo who has already been 'making free' with his intended, much to her distress.

OTTAVIA   I shall ever hate those roguish hands, from the very fact that they with their fire impregnated me, tortured and wearied!

TULLIA   A nice affair!

OTTAVIA   Why? Having stuck his hand in my breast, he seized one of my paps, then the other; and, while he was handling each of them rather hard, lo he tossed me hover [*sic*] on my back in spite of me.

TULLIA   Thou art blushing; the deed was accomplished.

OTTAVIA   His left hand was laid on my bosom (I am stating how this thing was done), he easily overcame all my efforts: he next slipped his right hand under my petticoat. I blush, I blush to tell it.

TULLIA   Lay aside that ridiculous modesty; fancy thou art relating to thyself what thou art telling me.

OTTAVIA   Having speedily lifted my petticoat above my knees, he handled my things. Oh! hadst thou beheld his sparkling eyes!

TULLIA   So thou wast happy then!

41

OTTAVIA   Having carried his hand higher, he invaded that place which, they say, distinguishes us from the other sex; ay, it is now a year ago, and ever since a lot of blood runs from me every month during several days.

TULLIA   Bravo, Caviceo! ah! ah! ah!

OTTAVIA   O the rascal! 'This part', he says, 'will soon rejoice me exceedingly. Do consent, my Ottavia.' A little more and I had fainted at these words.

Unfortunately for Caviceo, he suffers a premature ejaculation.

TULLIA   Withal Caviceo did not even pierce thee with his lance? it did not enter thy trench?

OTTAVIA   I seized it and held it aside; but unlucky event! I felt myself completely drenched with a regular shower like fire, and, naked as I was, wet up to the navel. I put my hand to it again; but, when falling on that sort of slimy fluid with which the mad fellow had flooded me, my hand recoiled with fright and horror.

In the further discussion, Ovid is quoted by Tullia who is evidently supposed to represent Luisa Sigea herself, the alleged authoress of the dialogues, and Ottavia reveals her secret attraction to Caviceo. Tullia, in her concluding speech in this section, tells Ottavia: 'Thy mother begged me in person to disclose to thee all these hidden secrets of the bridal bed, and to teach thee what thou oughtest to be with thy husband, what thy husband will be also, concerning the things of this nature, for which men are inflamed. So, to teach thee everything in plainer language, we shall lie together tonight in my bed, which, would to God! I might properly style the sweetest list of Venus. After me, thou wilt taste a more agreeable bed fellow than I have been.' Which leads to the second dialogue entitled, appropriately, *Tribadicon*:

TULLIA   As thou lovest Caviceo, so I love thee.

OTTAVIA   Speak clearly: what enigmatical discourse is this?

With the assistance of botanical metaphors, and Greek and Latin euphemisms (printed in the original language), Ottavia is given a quick lesson in female anatomy, and in between some energetic love-making the historical aspects of female inversion are touched upon. Ovid is again quoted, there is a reference to Sappho and an interesting, though brief, digression on the dildo: 'The Milesian women were wont to make themselves leather mentules eight inches long and broad in proportion. Aristophanes informs us that the women of his time were wont to use them. Even nowadays among Italian, especially Spanish as also Asiatic women, this tool plays a considerable role in the female boudoir, as being their most precious piece of furniture; it is held in the highest esteem.'

Fabric, the third dialogue, treats of the female sex organs in much greater detail, with Tullia adopting some uncomfortable-sounding postures in order that Ottavia may examine the real thing, after which the male sexual apparatus is the subject of similar attentions, a discourse that begins with a piece of news for Ottavia that causes her some understandable agitation: 'Thy mother told me that he [Caviceo] was admirably well furnished, so she is exceedingly glad of it; she thinks there is not a single man in our town better set off than he. I answered her, while thus bragging, that my husband, Callias's dagger, was eight finger breadths in length. She replied that he is a man of nothing at all, compared to Caviceo. She pities and at the same time envies thee thy lot; she congratulates thee exceedingly on it. She says that Caviceo's tool is eleven inches long and as thick as thy arm, at the place it is joined to the hand.'

Ottavia is comforted by Tullia, who then proceeds with the biology lesson. Further Greek and Latin euphemisms are introduced, and some sweeping generalizations: 'Now, those women who love and have had experience, brag in different tones of that virile part which is so intractable and hasty; none has tasted it without loving it.'

The fourth and fifth dialogues, *The Duel* and *Pleasures*, deal respectively with the wedding nights of Tullia and, after a lapse of time, Ottavia. Both are described in graphic and painful terms that make far from pleasant reading. Callias, Tullia's husband, is particularly brutal and when he finds the initial love-making more difficult than he expects gives voice to views and demands of an exceedingly reactionary character: 'Tullia ... if thou didst love me, thou wouldst not refuse, as thou dost, wretched me, who am burning with love for thee, the true fruit of thy love ... Knowest thou not ... that this part of thy person is no longer thine, but mine by full and lawful right? why dost thou prevent me from freely enjoying my own goods? Does it become one versed in the *belles-lettres*, as thou art, my spouse, my delight, to be so careless about thy duty? For it is thy duty not to quarrel with me about these gifts of Venus.'

Until about a third of the way through *Pleasures*, everything has progressed in a relatively straightforward manner, but after Ottavia's account of her wedding night the 'shocks' mentioned by David Foxon begin to emerge. Tullia announces that her earliest sexual experiences were with Ottavia's mother, Sempronia, when they were both young girls. Two other girls, Lucrezia and Vittoria, were also involved in these experiments, and later a boy of fourteen named Giocondo. Tullia then proceeds to argue forcibly against the popular notion of virtue and in favour of discreet libertinage, and one or two things that she says recall to Ottavia's mind an incident in her girlhood that involved her mother and the same Giocondo which at the time she ignored, not having actually seen anything, but now realizes was a bit of Tullia's discreet libertinage in practice.

Ottavia is greatly vexed by these revelations, having been under the impression that her mother was a bastion of virtue.

OTTAVIA One thing I clearly understood: my mother spared no pains to give me a high opinion of herself, and to persuade me that she was the most exemplary woman in our town.

TULLIA I know it; she earnestly entreated me on several occasions to recommend her to thee as a very chaste and holy woman. Well, what I am now disclosing to thee about her secrets shall, nevertheless, lie buried, for everybody else, in dark oblivion.

OTTAVIA   I would be a parricide if I did not spare the reputation of my mother, who always cherished me so tenderly, that reputation which outweighs even life itself. But see what a cunning trick she wanted to play on me. About three days before I was to be given to Caviceo, she addressed me as follows: 'Daughter, the day after tomorrow, thou wilt be wedded to Caviceo; only this short space separates thee from contaminations and filth; until now thou wast holy and pure, being a virgin. When thou wilt have lost thy maiden-head, many virtues will flee thee, so stained with corruption; nor canst thou by any means, whether violent or dexterous, conserve those which a severe gravity suits. Nothing is more heavenly than a virginal maid, and nothing is more despicable than a polluted girl.' – 'Mother, what shall I do?' I answered, 'let me then conserve my virginity intact the remainder of my life. Cloister me among the Vestals.' – 'God forbid!' she replied; 'neither our fortune, nor the love I bear thee would ever suffer me to bury thee alive. Make a vow to hate and abhor every idea and desire of lust. Remove thy mind, as I have always removed mine, from those contaminations, and, on venerating with a sacrifice the chastity thou art just going to lose, weep over it when lost with another sacrifice.' – 'I will,' said I, 'but to what sacrifice are you exhorting me, mother?' – 'I wish and beseech thee, Ottavia,' said she on kissing me, 'I wish thee to decide by thyself on this sacrifice, and each of us to have a hand in its consummation. But thou must have an unflinching and resolute courage.' – 'I shall not be wanting in courage,' I answered. Then she made me take an oath and promise her that I would endure whatever she would counsel. – 'Tomorrow morning,' she added, 'since thou art as pure, good and chaste, daughter, as thou art pretty, witty and handsome, when in the temple thou shalt have promised the Gods what thou has promised me, and we shall execute a glorious, righteous and exceedingly useful thing for thee.'

The 'useful thing' turns out to be a confession to a priest named Teodoro, 'a man of that sect whose adherents, thanks to their faces and squalid beards and straggling gray locks, seem to the vulgar to make a great display of holiness,' followed by a flogging that would not appear out of place in the pages of the Marquis de Sade. True to her promise, Ottavia's mother undergoes the scourge as well and gives every indication of having enjoyed it: 'It is now thy turn, daughter. Dost thou think thou has courage enough for that sport?... For it is sport and not suffering.' Ottavia is less enthusiastic. After being flogged by the priest, she declines the opportunity to continue doing it herself and her mother has a go, after which the priest takes over again and finishes the job.

The ordeal over, Sempronia puts Ottavia to bed. 'In troth,' she tells her daughter breezily, 'I am well used to this sort of thing; I never experience the least inconvenience from it.'

Tullia at this juncture reveals herself as being even more knowledgeable about Sempronia, informing Ottavia that her mother has entered into a highly eccentric relationship with her childhood lover Giocondo that involves his marriage to a convent girl named Giulia – '... the fruit of my grandfather's intercourse with a concubine of his' as Ottavia describes her – who is to be kept confined to a chastity belt except for certain specified purposes. The arrangement is succinctly described by Sempronia, as quoted by Tullia: 'Thou shalt have intercourse with Giulia only for the sake of begetting children, whilst thou must satisfy all thy desires with me.'

Tullia then describes an arrangement she herself has entered into with one Lampridio, an ex-Anchorite of great wealth whose 'utensils are nicely adapted to the work of which we go to form the victory and triumph,' after which everything gets completely out of hand with more chastity belts, duplicate keys, a *ménage à trois* and a further episode with the priest Teodoro and his scourge.

In the sixth dialogue, *Frolics and Sports*, two male actors are introduced into the action and group sexual activity takes place interspersed with reminiscences and some discussion on sodomy that provokes Tullia into a long lecture on male homosexuality, a subject of which she takes a dim view.

OTTAVIA Thou hast forgotten to say whether thou approvest of or abhorrest this kind of Venus, as, by Hercules! I abominate it.

TULLIA If I do approve of it, I am not in my wits. The fulminating voice from heaven, though the earth be silent, condemns this guilt. Lucian discourses very shrewdly on both Venuses without blaming either. So we cannot tell which one he preferred. Achilles Tatius, in 'The loves of Clitophon and Leucippe', likewise couches his opinion in ambiguous terms, the peevish fellow. Both were Greeks. Not one of the Latin writers reproves or commends this unnatural lust. What is still more surprising, none of the legislators forbids it: doubtless they made no crime of pleasures which did not incur capital punishment. Be that as it may, I shall freely give my opinion on them without recourse to any Socratic quibbling. The posterior Venus deserves every species of torture and reprobation. The thoughts of one sex turn naturally to the other. He who seeks Venus in a boy offers violence to his own natural propensity. Cupid inspires love: who has ever committed unnatural crimes with Cupid? He would not commit them himself, or tolerate another to commit them with him. Youths, be they ever so inexperienced, preconceive in spite of them, from the moment the amorous flame begins to work in their veins, that the remedy for calming the fiery tempest is to be really had in women's embraces. A young girl sets a stripling on fire, a stripling sets a young girl on fire. They are possessed by mutual longings; one desires the other. Such is the course of love ...

The dialogue concludes with Tullia expressing herself on coital postures:

There are as many ways of doing Venus as the body has windings and alterations. It is impossible to compute or indicate those that are best qualified for pleasure. Each one regulates the shape he wishes to take after his humour, place and leisure. Love however is not the same for all. Elephantis, a young Greek lady, represented in paintings the postures which she knew to be fashionable among libertines, that they might be henceforth pleased to 'execute the business after the pictures.' Another devised twelve different ways of copulating, ways calculated to afford the tilter the greatest possible amount of voluptuousness. On this account they called her *Dodecamechanos*. In our own time, a man of divine genius, Pietro Aretino, has described very many of them in his witty satirical Dialogues; after him, the unrivalled painters, Tiziano and Caracchio, have represented them in painting. Yet several of them are impracticable, although the limbs and loins of those coupling together in generation be flexible, beyond the power of imagination. Of course, by force of meditating and reflecting, more ideas present themselves to the mind than can be realized. As nothing resists the desires of an impetuous mind, so nothing is difficult for an enthusiastic, disorderly imagination. It insinuates itself into whatever it pleases, and that by whichever way it adventures; it finds, for instance, a level road where there are precipices. Everything that right or wrong minded people counsel is not so easily performed by the body.

Liseux didn't bother to include the seventh Dialogue in his English edition, explaining himself in a *Note of the Editor*:

Here ends Nicolas Chorier's work, such as it came out for the first time, about the year 1660. There was a reprint, issued in 1678, containing a seventh Dialogue, entitled Fescennini, which the Author had announced in the Preface to the first edition ... But unfortunately this latter Dialogue, which is full of gaps, seems to have been printed after an incomplete manuscript. There is, moreover, hardly any connection between it and the other Dialogues. The scenes lie no longer in Italy; they are laid in Spain. The interlocutors: Tullia and Ottavia, being made Spaniards, look as it [*sic*] they were moving in a new world. This series of fragments is a sort of outline or sketch which spoils the harmony of the book, instead of heightening the interest. So we think it is better to leave it out.

*   *   *   *   *

The speed with which English publishers were able to import foreign erotica, or produce translations of it, is most easily demonstrated with *Vénus dans le cloître, ou la Religieuse en chemise*, a work that appeared first in France in 1683 and was offered for sale in an English translation about April the same year from a publisher named Henry Rhodes. Such an almost parallel event seems extraordinary, suggesting some sort of connection between Rhodes and the French publisher of the original, and brings to mind the simultaneous publication of the first English and French editions of *Histoire d'O* by Maurice Girodias's Olympia Press and Jean-Jacques Pauvert in June 1954. At the time, the two men were sharing office accommodation in a building on the rue de Nesle at Paris, and an arrangement was made whereby M. Girodias's translators, Baird Bryant and his wife Denny, produced their English version from the original manuscript in the possession of M. Pauvert. The furore that resulted on the publication of the novel, which appeared quite openly in both editions, involved Girodias and Pauvert being subjected to prolonged and bitter verbal third degrees by the French vice squad, known with deceptive charm as *La Brigade mondaine*, concerning who 'Pauline Réage', the pseudonymous author of the work, really was. To their credit both men remained silent. An amusing account of this episode will be found on pp. 289–92 of *The Olympia Reader* (New York: Grove Press, 1965).

The authorship of *Vénus dans le cloître* is given on the titlepages of the first and some subsequent editions as being the work of the Abbé du Prat, although in other editions this name is confined as the signatory to a prefatory note or dedication addressed to a 'Madame D. L. R., très-digne abbesse de Beaulieu'. According to Antoine Laporte in his *Bibliographie clérico-galante* (Paris, 1879), a work devoted exclusively to erotica written by members of the clergy of which there is rather more than one might imagine, du Prat was the pseudonym of François de Chavigny de la Bretonnière, an unfrocked Benedictine monk living in Holland as a refugee. Other authorities, however, believe that the book was written by Jean Barrin, the vicar-general of the diocese of Nantes. Neither ascription has been

Frontispiece and titlepage to an early edition of *Vénus dans le cloître*, a work ascribed to Jean Barrin

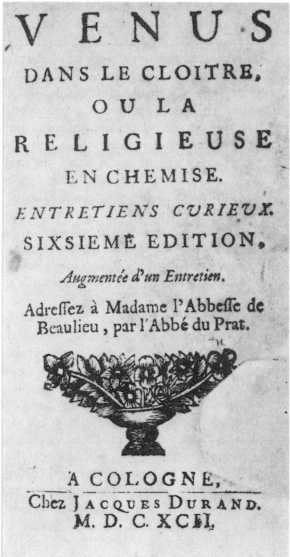

supported by anything resembling hard evidence and it is, therefore, impossible to determine which, if either, is correct. Barrin's established literary output appears rather negligible, consisting of a translation of Ovid's elegies and epistles published in 1676 as *Œuvres galantes et amoureuses d'Ovide*. Chavigny on the other hand – who assumed the name 'de la Bretonnière' for effect, it seems – wrote a number of slightly free pieces, including one divertingly entitled *La Galante hermaphrodite* (1683), a fact which on circumstantial grounds makes him the more likely candidate of the two.[5] Laporte's opinion however, unlike that of Gay's which is neutral, is quite dogmatic but suspect by his strangely vitriolic view of the book, which he considers to be 'shamelessly obscene', a judgment that hardly stands up even under a cursory examination of it, as will be seen, and posits the suspicion that he had never actually read the book or considered the question of its authorship objectively.

In the first edition of *Vénus dans le cloître*, there are three dialogues. They take place in a convent between two nuns, the Sisters Angélique and Agnès, who are aged nineteen and sixteen respectively. David Foxon mentions an edition of 1685 with a fourth dialogue, while the British Library has one of 1692, which although advertising the additional dialogue on the titlepage actually omits it on the grounds that it was not by the same author as the rest of the book. The publishers of an 'eighth edition' dated 1702, a copy of which the British Library also possesses, were less scrupulous and include not only the possibly spurious fourth dialogue, but a fifth one for good measure. Seventeen years later in 1719, an edition was published containing a short sixth dialogue between two entirely new characters – Virginie and Séraphique – and a reprint of a somewhat eccentric religious pamphlet, *L'Adamiste, ou le Jésuite insensible*, as an added attraction.[6] It was this edition that was used for the two important reprints of 1866 and 1868, which although they have 'Genève' as their place of publication on the titlepages, were actually published at Brussels, the earlier of the two certainly by Jules Gay and the latter by either Gay again or by Auguste Poulet-Malassis. A 'Londres' edition of 1737 returns to the three dialogues of the original, but in general the 19th- and 20th-century reprints follow the six dialogue version of 1719.

The history of the book is clouded by the appearance early in the 18th century of a pamphlet containing two dialogues, the first between Julie and Dorothée and the second between Julie and Brother Cosme, which came out variously as *Les Délices du cloître, ou la Religieuse éclairée* and *La Nonne éclairée, ou les Délices du cloître*. Since these titles were sometimes applied to reprints of *Vénus dans le cloître* as well, it is difficult to know exactly when the pamphlet was first printed. Gay lists one in 1709, but fails to provide the number of pages which would have been one way, although an imprecise one, of knowing whether he was citing the original work or the pamphlet, the latter being the briefer work of the two. The earliest edition I know of that is described reliably is dated 1737 (*Galitzin* 467), while the British Library has three others, dated 1757, 1761 and 1763. This shorter work is actually an '*imitation adoucie*', as the compilers of the catalogue of *L'Enfer de la Bibliothèque Nationale* put it, of *Vénus dans le cloître* and in fact the two works appeared together several times. Whether they are both by the same author, as is frequently asserted, is uncertain; David Foxon's only comment is that '[the pamphlet] is a different work on the same subject', which leaves the question open to speculation.

The English version of the book that appeared during the same year as the first French edition has already been mentioned. Entitled *Venus in the Cloyster, or the Nun in her Smock*, it was advertised openly in the *Term Catalogue* for Easter 1683 by its publisher, Henry Rhodes. The usual reason for books of this sort not surviving is that they were suppressed, but not in this instance, for its freedom from interference was one of the mitigating defences put forward by Edmund Curll in 1725 when he was prosecuted for publishing the work. Curll's case was complicated, and although it is not strictly appropriate for it to be dealt with in a chapter devoted to the 17th century, it nevertheless requires attention in order to understand the notoriety surrounding a book that would otherwise have been relegated to an unremarkable place among the many other merely *galante* works of the time.

Curll was charged with two books initially: two editions of *Venus in the Cloyster* in 1724 and 1725, and a rather boring pseudo-medical work called *A Treatise of the Use of Flogging in Venereal Affairs* (1718), which was a translation by George Sewell of the *Tractus de usu flagrorum in re medica et venerea* of Johann Heinrich Meybaum, or Meibomius as he was better known, first published in 1629. The *Treatise* was published together with another work, the *Treatise on Hermaphrodites* of Giles Jacob, but although this was listed in the indictment no passages from it are quoted and it does not seem to have been proceeded against as a separate work in its own right.

The defence offered by Curll in the case of *Venus in the Cloyster*, that it had been issued unmolested almost fifty years earlier, seems hardly relevant since his edition was not a reprint of the earlier one, but a new translation entirely, done, it is generally believed, by Robert Samber who in 1729 did posterity a good turn by offering the first English translation of Charles Perrault's *Contes du temps passé*, now known as *Mother Goose's Tales*. For Curll to be able to make this defence stick, it would have been necessary for him to have shown that his edition, and hat of 1683, were to all intents and purposes the same. He was not able to, but in actuality the conduct of the trial was more concerned with theoretical legal concepts than unprovable, not to say dubious, claims relating to events of fifty years earlier. A particular stumbling block for the prosecution, and one that Curll hoped to take advantage of, was a ruling in 1708 by Lord Chief Justice Holt in which it was stated that the ecclesiastical courts were the correct venues for cases involving obscene publications. One of the judges in 1725, with this earlier ruling in mind, admitted that Curll had committed a grave offence but failed to see how he could be punished for it, and later confessed to having not thought *Venus in the Cloyster* obscene anyway, but a piece of anti-clerical propaganda which, in the 1720s, would not have been unwelcome.

Arguments and considerations of this sort created something of a problem, involving as they did such weighty matters as precedents, and although Curll was fairly quickly found guilty of publishing the books themselves – which he had never denied in the first place – the question of whether they were obscene or not occupied the court for more than two years, an account of which will be found admirably explained in Donald Thomas's *A Long Time Burning* (London: Routledge & Kegan Paul, 1969, pp. 78–84).

During the time of the trial, Curll was free to carry on his business and he published the memoirs of a man named John Ker who had been a government spy during the reign of Queen Anne. It was this kind of publication, which was hardly calculated to win him friends in quarters that mattered, that is the key to his un-popularity, his brushes with the law and a particularly unsavoury incident in which Alexander Pope, driven to distraction by Curll's attacks on him, slipped the publisher an emetic. More than anything else, Curll was a pamphleteer and a satirist in the true tradition of Grub Street hackery and involved himself in endless lampoons and scurrilous burlesques on famous and well-placed people of the day.[7] He was not, like Auguste Brancart or Henri Kistemaeckers in the late 19th century, a professional pornographer, but the fact that he sometimes issued works of a mildly erotic nature may have given his enemies the opportunity to try and silence him. Already in bad odour for *Venus in the Cloyster* and the *Treatise*, he found himself charged with publishing the *Memoirs of John Ker* as well and in 1728 was convicted on all charges, being fined £43. 13s. 4d. and sentenced to the pillory at Charing Cross for the *Memoirs*.

The importance of the Curll case in determining how similar prosecutions would be conducted in the future by establishing in English law the concept of obscene libel is outlined in the relevant pages of *A Long Time Burning*, already cited, but for the purpose of the present book it will be seen that such a spectacular trial created in the public much interest, and the view that *Venus in the Cloyster* is a pornographic book stems from this, at least in England.

No further editions of *Venus in the Cloyster* were to appear, although Curll with a characteristic flair for bellicosity continued to advertise it as late as 1735 and ten years later, in 1745, an attempt to reprint it by John Leake was frustrated by the authorities.

Until about 1964, no copies of the edition of 1683 or either of the two published by Curll were known to exist, a state of affairs reported in good faith by David Foxon in the third of his articles on libertine literature published in the *Book Collector*. No doubt prompted by Foxon's reference, however, a collector living in Bournemouth came forward with what is probably a unique copy of the 1725 edition, and a photocopy of this was prepared by the British Library for its Private Case in the autumn of 1964.[8]

The rarity of this volume, coupled with the importance that its prosecution played in shaping the English law on obscene publications, renders necessary a closer examination of it than its literary value might otherwise warrant. It is a small octavo of twelve preliminary pages numbered in roman and 184 pages of text, with what would seem to be a woodcut frontispiece (the Xerox reproduction is far from clear). Working from a Xerographic copy it isn't possible to provide a full bibliographical collation, but a transcription of the titlepage is as follows:

VENUS | IN THE | CLOISTER: | OR, THE | NUN in her SMOCK. |
[*rule*] | [*epig.*:] *Vows of* virginity *should well be weigh'd* |
Too oft they're cancelled, tho' in Convents made. | GARTH. |
[*rule*] | Translated from the *French* | By a Person of Honour. |
[*rule*] | [*device of bird with spread wings*] | [*rule*] | *LONDON*: |
Printed in the YEAR M.DCC.XXV. | Price [*obliterated*] Stitcht,
[*obliterated*] Bound.

The 'Garth' referred to who provided the two-line epigram is almost certainly Sir Samuel Garth (1661–1719), a member of the Kit-Kat Club and chiefly remembered as the author of a burlesque poem entitled *The Dispensary* (1699).

The text is in five dialogues, between Agnes and Angelica, and a comparison of the English translation and the French original shows that in general Samber executed a good, workmanlike translation, although in places Curll has contrived to insert some free advertising for himself in compensation for the absence of his name on the titlepage. On page 118, for example, there is a footnote reference to an English translation of a work by Pietro Bembo 'printed for Mr Curll, over against Catherine-Street in the Strand,' that is prompted by the inclusion in the text of brief extracts of the work in question that are not to be found in the French original.

But even with these little embellishments, it is difficult to see how *Venus in the Cloister*, though advocating a faintly libertine attitude toward sexual matters within certain conditional rules of conduct, could have been seen as indecent. There is no obscene detail and such sexual activity as is touched upon is brief in the extreme, and it is highly unlikely that the critical view of the Roman Church expressed in the book would have caused any problems with the law. The fact that Daniel Bécourt in his *Livres condamnés, livres interdits* (Paris, 1961) fails to mention any action against *Vénus dans le cloître* in France, where indecency coupled with attacks on religion might be seen as eminently actionable, is not without significance and leads one to suspect that Curll's prosecution might have resulted more from the agitation of those he had antagonised than to a genuine sense of outraged morality on the part of the authorities.

That the book is far from obscene or even, strictly speaking, erotic may be judged from the following passage extracted from the third dialogue, in which the two interlocutrix discuss in terms of stern disapproval two of the works described above.

ANGELICA   Lord! I believe thou ravest to talk after this manner, and thou oughtest to agree with me, that there are Books which have not one good Line in them, and which contain Instructions essentially opposite to good Morality, and the Practice of Virtue. What canst thou say of the *Young Women's School*

[*L'École des filles*], and that infamous Philosophy which has nothing in it but what is dull and insipid; and where the Arguments are so sottish, that they are persuasive only to low and vulgar Souls, and touch such only who are half corrupted, or who easily suffer themselves to be drawn away by all sorts of Weakness.

AGNES It must be owned, that the Book should be put into the Catalogue of those that are unprofitable, and indeed, of such as are prohibited. I wish I could redeem the Time I employed in reading it, there was nothing in it pleased me, and which I did not condemn. The *Abbé* who shewed it me, gave me another, which treats much on the same Subject; but the Author has handled it with a great deal more Wit and Address.

ANGELICA I know what it is thou speakest of, as for forming of Peoples Manners, it is not one Jot better than the former; and though the Purity of the Style, and its easy Eloquence have something agreeable in them, it does not hinder their being infinitely dangerous, inasmuch as the Fire and the *Brilliant* [i.e. glossiness or polish] which blazes out in a great many Passages, serve only to make the Poison which it is full of, spread with greater Sweetness, and insinuate itself into such Hearts as are but a little susceptible of it. It has for its Title, *The Ladies Academy; or the seven dialogues of Aloisia*. I had it Eight Days in my hands, and he who brought it me, explained the most difficult places, and gave me perfectly to understand all that was mysterious in it, especially these words in the seventh dialogue, *Amori vera lux*; and discovered to me the Anagramatical Sense they covered, under the simple Appearance of an inscription of a medal.[9] I imagine this is the Book thou hadst a Design to speak to me about.

AGNES Certainly. Ah! Lord! how ingenious is that Author to invent new Pleasures to a Soul all sullied & disgusted! what Provocatives and Incentives does he make Use of to awaken and rouze up the most sleepy and languishing Concupiscence, and even that which is impotent! What extravagant Appetites! What strange Objects! And what unknown Dishes does he cook up to debauch us!...[10]

CHAPTER TWO

THE 18TH CENTURY
THE FLOWERING OF LIBERTINISM

Now I am young; blind Cupid me bewitches.
I scratch my belly for it always itches,
And what it itches for I've told before:
Tis either to be wife or be a whore.
Nay, any thing indeed, would poor I
E'er maidenhead upon my hands should lie
Which till I lose, I'm sure my wat'ry eye
Will pay to love so great a sacrifice
That my carcass soon will weep out all its juice
Till grown so dry as fit for no man's use.

The opening years of the 18th century were marked by a noticeable absence of new erotic writing, a situation that was to remain for almost half a century until the publication in England of John Cleland's *Memoirs of a Woman of Pleasure* (1748/49) and in France a few years earlier of *Thérèse Philosophe* and *Histoire de Dom B. . . , Portier des Chartreux.* Why there was this hiatus is not altogether clear, but it appears to have been a phenomenon effective throughout Europe. It seems almost as though the world of erotica, or 'pornotopia' as Professor Steven Marcus refers to it in his book *The Other Victorians* (London, 1966), were somehow adjusting itself to a new era in which the traditional dialogue form that had effectively reigned supreme since the beginning of the 16th century was replaced by the novel, an event dated with great precision – in England anyway – by the appearance of Samuel Richardson's *Pamela, or, Virtue Rewarded* in 1740–1.

This hiatus was not absolute of course. As was shown in the preceding chapter, some of the earlier classics were dusted off and reprinted for the benefit of a new generation or two, and there were the occasional poetical bagatelles such as *The Fifteen Plagues of a Maidenhead* (1707), the 'Eighth Plague' of which heads this chapter. There was also a whole series of strange publications consisting of descriptions of the female anatomy in terms of elaborate topographical metaphor, complete with shrubs, hillocks, vales and grottoes. One of the earliest of these, Ερωτόπολις: *the present state of Bettyland* (1684), has been attributed to the Staffordshire poet Charles Cotton (1630–87) who is otherwise known for a dialogue continuation of Walton's *Compleat Angler* that first appeared in the fifth edition of that work published in 1676. Ερωτόπολις was later included in an abbreviated form in *The Potent Ally: or Succours from Merryland* ('Paris' [London], 1741).

MEMOIRS

OF A

WOMAN

OF

PLEASURE.

VOL. I.

LONDON:
Printed for G. Fenton in the *Strand*
M.DCC.XLIX.

THERESE

PHILOSOPHE,

OU

MÉMOIRES

Pour servir à l'Histoire de D. Dirrag, &
de Mademoiselle Éradice.

PREMIERE PARTIE.

A LA HAYE.

Frontispice

L'AUTEUR
Rempli de
son Sujet.

HISTOIRE

DE

GOUBERDOM,

PORTIER DES CHARTREUX.

NOUVELLE ÉDITION, revue, corrigée &
augmentée sous les yeux du St. Pere.

PREMIERE PARTIE.

A ROME.

M. DCC. LXXXVI.

FAR LEFT the first edition of the most famous erotic book ever written, familiarly known as *Fanny Hill*

LEFT Titlepage of an early edition (*c.* 1748) of *Thérèse Philosophe*, sometimes ascribed to Jean–Baptiste, Marquis d'Argens, see colour plate opposite page 41

LEFT Frontispiece and titlepage of a late 18th century edition of *Histoire de Gouberdom*, also known as *Histoire de Dom B. . .*, *Portier des Chartreux*. 'Gouberdom' is an anagram of 'Dom B[ougre]' i.e. 'Master Bugger'. The book is ascribed to Jacques Charles Gervaise de Latouche

A similar work, by Thomas Stretser or Stretzer using the pseudonym 'Roger Pheuquewell', was entitled *A New Description of Merryland* (1740), and the Private Case of the British Library contains no fewer than eight different editions of it, three of them in French. The earliest English edition in the Private Case is the fourth, dated 1741, and like the other English ones it allegedly hailed from Bath. As with *The Potent Ally* it was published in London by our old friend Edmund Curll. Also in 1741, the same author and publisher issued *Merryland Displayed*, an anonymous and mischievous criticism of the earlier book and which is churlishly credited on the titlepage to a perfectly respectable publisher and bookseller named J[ames] Leake, of Bath.

The full imprint of *Merryland Displayed*, of which the British Library possesses two copies of the second edition, is: 'Bath: Printed for the Author, and sold by J. Leake; and the Booksellers of London and Westminster, 1741.' The simultaneous existence of a James Leake in Bath, one of a whole family of booksellers and publishers operating in that city for most of the 18th century, and a John Leake in London is confusing. According to H. R. Plomer's *Dictionary of the Printers and Booksellers ... in England* (The Bibliographical Society/Oxford

BELOW Titlepage and one of the illustrations from an English translation of *Histoire de Dom B....* See colour plate opposite page 64

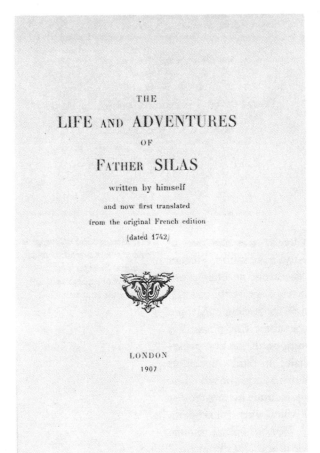

THE
LIFE and ADVENTURES
OF
FATHER SILAS
written by himself
and now first translated
from the original French edition
(dated 1742)

LONDON
1907

Thus pushed and pushing, the strokes of the uncle re-echoed...

Frontispiece and titlepage to one of the many editions of Thomas Stretser's anonymous geography of the female anatomy

University Press, 1932; repr. 1968, pp. 152–3), James Leake was the 'Son of John Leake, of London. . .'. Whether this was the same John Leake whom Plomer and others reveal was arrested for publishing obscene literature in 1745 is not clear, but it seems unlikely. James Leake died in 1764 at the ripe age of 79; in 1748, when he would have been 63, his 'father' had apparently become a reformed character, for he was printing orders for the Middlesex Sessions. The possibility of there being two John Leakes in London is therefore suggested, the one prosecuted in 1745 being, perhaps, the brother of James Leake in Bath. A further complication arises with John Leake's first deposition after his arrest in which he states that 'the first books that he ever printed on his own account he printed for Daniel Lynch living in New Street near Shoe Lane, & they were Merryland, Bettyland, Frutex Vivaria & the Flowering Shrub [sic]' (Foxon, op. cit. p. 17). Most authorities agree that these books were all published if not actually printed by Curll, including Ralph Straus, who was Curll's bio-bibliographer. Mystifications of this sort are typical of clandestine publishing, and not just of the 18th century; they serve as a ''orrible warning' to aspiring bibliographers of erotica.

Not content with a written description of the delights of 'Merryland', Charles Mosley, an engraver, and Thomas Harper, a printer, ran off a hundred copies of a suite of plates entitled *A Compleat Set of Charts of the Coasts of Merryland* (1745) for Thomas Read, himself a printer, of Dogwell Court, Whitefriars, Fleet Street. Unfortunately the law stepped in following a tip-off, and although Read and the others appear to have escaped prosecution, forty-seven sets of the plates were handed over to the authorities and presumably destroyed. The fate of the remaining fifty-three is unknown; certainly none has come down to us.

Philip Miller's *Catalogus plantarum* (1730) inspired at least two parodies, *The Natural History of the Frutex Vulvaria* and *Arbor Vitae, or, The Natural History of the Tree of Life*, both first published in 1732 and reprinted nine years later in 1741. The latter, like *Teague-Root Display'd* (1746) by 'Paddy Strong-Cock', treats of the penis; the former, I trust, is self-explanatory.

Public demand for books of this sort was enormous, as may be judged from the fact that Stretser's *A New Description of Merryland* went through ten editions between 1740 and 1742, and most of the others of a similar description were reprinted several times. By the end of the century, however, such naïve and rather charming examples of primitive sexology had lost much of their attraction. The French Revolution of 1789 and its attendant excesses created a taste for more boisterous fare, even in England. The last of these horticultural and geographical tours of the human anatomy seems to have been *La Souricière. The Mousetrap. A Facetious and Sentimental Excursion through part of Austrian Flanders and France* (London: J. Parsons, 1794. 2 vols) by 'Timothy Touchit', an obvious imitation or parody of Laurence Sterne's *A Sentimental Journey* (1768) and possibly a last defiant gesture of innocence against the horrors across the Channel.

For some reason these extended sexual metaphors did not find a great deal of favour elsewhere in Europe; some translations appeared in France, but in general they appear to have been a peculiarly English fancy. It is interesting to note, though, that the remarkable and exhaustive bibliography of Akira Ishihara and Howard S. Levy's *The Tao of Sex* (New York: Harper & Row, 1970) includes a reference to a story entitled *Wen-jo-hsiang chi* by Kuo cheng Liang in volume nine of *Hsiang-yen ts'ung-shu* (Shanghai, 1908–10) which is 'an ingenious description of a woman in terms of the geographical features in and around "Warm-Soft Village", a metaphor for a woman's sexual charms.' Unfortunately, *Hsiang-yen ts'ung-shu* ('A Collection of Feminine Fragrance') is an anthology of essays and stories spanning the fourteenth to the nineteenth centuries and it is not clear when Liang's 'Warm-Soft Village' story was originally written, or whether it owed anything to the obviously similar English stories of the 18th century, or even if this was an isolated example of the genre in China.

If Europe failed to share the enthusiasm of the English for the *double entendre* it was not because they were more prudish. France in particular had her own national literary eccentricity, so to speak, with scatological prose and verse and, in at least one instance, a full-length play. These coarse little tales which centre on farting contests and similar elevating recreations – and which actually date back at least as far as Rabelais – were so numerous that a *Bibliotheca Scatologica* was devoted to them.[1]

Titles such as *Merdiana, ou Manuel des chieurs* ('Turderie, or The Crappers' Handbook'), which first appeared about 1803 and was reprinted many times, hardly require amplification. Similarly, *L'Art de péter* ('The Art of Farting'). This curious work appeared first in French 'En Westphalie' [i.e. Paris] in 1751, but its complicated origins have their roots almost two hundred and fifty years earlier. The French text is a translation of *De peditu ejusque speciebus*, a Latin dissertation included in a prodigious two-volume anthology of scatological titbits entitled *Amphitheatrum sapientiae socraticae* (1619) that was compiled by the doctor and poet Gaspard Dornavius. This was in fact the first appearance of the work, but its existence was inspired by the *Ars honeste petande in societate*, an imaginary book cited by Rabelais in his inventory of the Library of Saint Victor (see *The Histories of Gargantua and Pantagruel*, London, Penguin Books, 1979, p. 187). Including as it does such wonderful titles as *The Codpiece of the Law, The Bald Arse of Widows* and *Tartaretus, de modo cacandi* ('Tartaret, on Methods of Shitting'), it is surprising that this remarkable inventory has not been the inspiration of more such eponymous derivatives.

Other books of this type displayed marked literary pretensions. *Caquire*, for example, which is also one of the filthiest books of the genre yet quite funny if you like that sort of thing, is not only a full-blown verse drama in five acts but also an inventive and spirited parody of one of Voltaire's finest plays, the tragedy *Zaïre* which was first produced in 1732.

'*Zaïre, vous pleurez?*' ('So, you're weeping, Zaïre?') Voltaire makes the sultan Orosmane ask. In the parody, this is rendered as: '*Caquire, vous foirez?*' Since *foirer* is a slang word for diarrhoea, the limitations of the English language unfortunately preclude a satisfactory translation although 'So, you've got the runs, Caquire?' conveys something of the idea. But the question is a rhetorical one anyway, for it is accompanied by a typically ingenious stage direction showing how Caquire's distressing condition may be simulated by the up-ending of a mug of chocolate.

The earliest appearance of *Caquire* is generally dated at about 1780. It carries the burlesque imprint '*A Chio de l'imprimerie d' Avalons, en chez le Foireux*' and a jokey '*Dernière édition, considérablement emmerdée*' ('The last and much more shitty edition'). Earlier editions are said to exist, but have not been reliably recorded. A 'second' and expanded edition appeared at Paris about 1810, and in 1866 a critical edition was printed at Brussels by Mertens for the publisher Jules Gay.

The authorship of *Caquire* is given on the titlepage as 'M. de Vessaire', but Gay in his edition proposes that it is actually by a certain de Bécombes or De Combes. This man, a native of Lyons where the edition of *Caquire* dated *c.* 1780 was supposed to have been published, was also the author of a rare little poem engagingly entitled *l'Art de mystifier dans les jardins* (1784), which might be translated as 'The Art of Practical Joking in Gardens'.

But to suggest that the French have possessed a monopoly on scatological humour would be quite wrong. While it is true that it appears to have been enormously popular there, it is not exactly unknown elsewhere. From Italy came *La Merdeide* (1629), ascribed to the poet Thomas Stigliani, and in 1806 another poem of the same title said to have been written by an abbot named Penoncelli. Spain produced the suggestively titled *Los Perfumes de Barcelona* (1843) and Germany offered *Scheissereien und Arschwische* (1834), believed to have been from the pen of a well-known comic actor of the day in Berlin named Beckmann.

England, however, lagged behind in all this and her offerings, such as they have been, are not a patch on the foreign commodity in either quantity or vulgarity. There have been a few trifles such as Sir John Harington's *Metamorphosis of Ajax* ('a jakes', 1596) which, along with some other satires, got him banished from court, and in 1722 there appeared a twelve-page pamphlet entitled *The Benefit of Farting Explained*. This was reprinted ten years later and augmented by *Meditation on a Turd*, a poem 'Wrote in a Place of Ease'. Jonathan Swift's works and the *Scarronides* (1664–5) of Charles Cotton contain scatological elements but they are not wholly taken up with the topic, and in any case the latter is translated or adapted from Paul Scarron's *Virgile travesti* (1648–52; 7 vols), a French work, so it does not really count.

It is interesting, however, that it was left up to the English in about 1978 to make a short film biography of Joseph Pujol, the celebrated Frenchman who in the 1880s kept the Paris music halls packed to the gunwales by his ability to fart at will assorted national anthems and extremely personal interpretations of the Battle of Austerlitz and similar historical events. Concerning this extraordinary individual, and prompted by the limerick

> There was a young Royal Marine,
> Who tried to fart 'God Save the Queen'.
> When he reached the soprano
> Out came the guano,
> And his breeches weren't fit to be seen

Norman Douglas wrote: 'The talent of this young Marine, though rare, is not unique. Visitors to the Paris exhibition of 1889, if they frequented certain low haunts, will remember a performer called 'l'homme pétard', who achieved wonderful effects on the same organ. His vocal range was amazing, and the soprano notes worthy of Tetrazzini. It has since occurred to me that he may have concealed about his person the musical instrument called 'pétophone', a specimen of which I bought in Naples many years ago. It is carried in a trousers' pocket and, when squeezed, imitates that particular *vox humana* so beautifully that, after a hush of general consternation, it becomes a great success at dinner parties, diplomatic receptions, Royal levées, etc.' (*Some Limericks*, [Florence: G. Orioli] Privately Printed, 1928; repr. New York, 1968, p. 38). Whether Norman

Douglas actually had the privilege of seeing M. Pujol in action is not known, but his words reflect perfectly the virtuoso performance of Leonard Rossiter in the challenging title role in the film *Le Pétomane*.

Popular as well in France were the numerous *galante* tales that frequently had exotic Oriental or Middle Eastern settings. Inspired by the first French version of the *Arabian Nights*, which had been translated by Antoine Galland as *Les Mille et une nuits* (1704–17), the plots of these tales were usually slight, mildly erotic but occasionally possessed of some amusing satirical observation. Many centred on the magical transformation of the central character into some bizarre object. One of the earliest of these, and very typical, is *Le Canapé couleur de feu* (1714), an anonymous work that has been ascribed incorrectly to Fougeret de Monbron (1704–61). The story opens with an ageing pimp named M. de La Chicane and his new wife attempting to consummate their marriage on a large red settee. Unfortunately, La Chicane's virility fails him, at which point both he and his bride are deposited on the floor by a sudden metamorphosis of the settee which becomes a young man. Announcing he has been for so long in this magically transformed condition that his real name has slipped his mind, he christens himself the Chevalier Commode, makes the necessary introductions and favours the two astonished newly-weds with the story of his life.

It seems that many years before, Commode was unable to gratify the lusts of an extremely ugly fairy princess who, by way of revenge, turned him into a settee and laid a curse on him whereby he is to maintain this guise until such time as another couple experience a faulty sexual performance while upon him. He is then transported to Paris by four *jinn* and dumped without ceremony on the Saint-Michel bridge. Here he is auctioned off to the highest bidder who happens to be the proprietor of a well-known brothel.

An account of some of his experiences in this establishment follows and since the majority of them involve an assortment of monks, priests and abbots, the author takes the opportunity to make some comments on the immorality and hypocrisy of the clergy.

Hypocrisy is the theme of chapter ten as well, in which a miserly woman of great piety takes possession of the settee which suffers at her hands, and those of her crooked business manager M. Ventru, a number of unsavoury experiences. None of these, however, are of an exactly sexual nature until Ventru loses control of himself one day while administering a flogging to the maid who has botched up an enema she was giving to her mistress.

Finally, in a most parlous state of repair, the settee reaches its ultimate destination in the home of the pimp where the story began.

A novel with a similar theme is *Le Sopha* by Crébillon *fils* (Claude-Prosper Jolyot de Crébillon, 1707–77). Written in 1737, it circulated first in manuscript form until in 1742 the first printed edition appeared clandestinely. *Le Sopha* was much admired by Horace Walpole, a fact that enraged Macaulay for some reason. 'Even of Montesquieu,' the great historian wrote in an essay on the master of Strawberry Hill, 'Walpole speaks with less enthusiasm than of that abject thing,

Crébillon the younger, a scribbler as licentious as Louvet,[2] and as dull as Rapin.[3] This trash, Walpole extols in language sufficiently high for Don Quixote.'[4]

Published in Paris about 1748 in imitation of *Le Sopha* was *B****, *histoire bavarde*, said to have been written by either François Antoine de Chevrier (1705–62) or Antoine Bret (1717–92). In this most grotesque effusion, the fairy Grossopède, insanely jealous of the success of Cyparide in wooing the lovely Urgande, takes '*une certaine partie*' of his rival and turns it into a sponge, while the remainder he transforms into a bidet.

Even more outlandish if possible, is *Le Joujou mystérieux* (Partout et nulle part ['Everywhere and nowhere'; i.e. Paris? *c.* 1780]). In this story, set in an imaginary country located between China and Japan, a Brahmin converts a young man into a dildo.

Important in this literature of erotic fantasy and metamorphosis is *Nocrion, conte Allobroge* ([Paris: Robustel] 1747), a small pamphlet of thirty-eight pages with an engraved frontispiece-cum-titlepage that has been ascribed to either Fessard or Charles Eisen. *Nocrion* – the word is an anagram of *con noir* (i.e. 'black cunt') – is a free little tale, written in old French and in imitation of the traditional *fabliau*, in particular Garin's *Le Chevalier qui faisoit parler les cons et les culs* ('The Knight who Commanded the Cunts and the Arses to Speak') of the 13th century which Gay and Doucé thoughtfully included in a reprint of *Nocrion* which they published at Brussels in 1881 together with notes by François Louis Jamet and a glossary by the probably pseudonymous Albert de la Fizelière. The authorship of *Nocrion* is not known for certain; it has been attributed to a number of different authors, most notably Anne Claude Philippe de Tubières, Comte de Caylus (1692–1765), who was certainly responsible for several other obscene pieces, and François Joachim de Pierres de Bernis (1715–94), an abbot – later a cardinal – who was a close friend of Madame de Pompadour. Interestingly, the good abbot was the author of a short comic play in one act called *L'Amour et les fées* ('Love and the Fairies'), the title of which suggests that he was no stranger to this type of exotic romance. The play was apparently never printed, but the manuscript was included in the *Bibliothèque dramatique* (1843), the sale catalogue of the great Soleinne collection of books on the theatre, at item no. 1870.

The idea that portions of the anatomy other than the mouth are able to converse – the *raison d'être* of *Nocrion* – is clearly not new, nor has time dimmed its piquancy for William Burroughs uses it to devastating effect in his novel *The Naked Lunch* (Paris, 1959), in which the device is taken to its logical and chilling conclusion whereby the 'talking asshole' actually takes over: 'Finally it talked all the time day and night, you could hear him for blocks screaming at it to shut up, and beating at it with his fist, and sticking candles up it, but nothing did any good and the asshole said to him: "It's you who will shut up in the end. Not me. Because we don't need you around here anymore. I can talk and eat *and* shit."' (*The Naked Lunch*, p. 127.) But Mr Burroughs's fantasy horrors, effective though they are, owe more to 20th-century despair and paranoia – notice that at one point in the above quotation the garrulous anus speaks in a collective sense, hinting perhaps at some rectal conspiracy – than to 13th-century chivalry or 18th-century libertinism.

Garin's *fabliau*, a text of which will also be found in volume three of Méon's edition of Barbaza's *Fabliaux et contes du poëtes des XIᵉ-XVᵉ siècle* (Paris, 1808; 4 vols), and the derivative *Nocrion* as well, were both certainly an influence on the theme of *Les Bijoux indiscrets* (1748) by the philosopher and encyclopedist Denis Diderot (1713–84), first published at Paris but with the false imprint 'Pékin' to emphasize the novel's Oriental setting.[5]

Les Bijoux indiscrets was the only work of fiction by Diderot long enough to be described as a novel that was published during his lifetime. It was written at a time when he was under considerable financial pressure from his mistress, Madame de Puisieux; stung by her challenge that he was unable to write stories in the manner of Crébillon *fils*, stories that were all the rage just then and which Diderot had dismissed as being easy to emulate, he dashed off *Les Bijoux indiscrets* in a little over two weeks at the end of 1747. It was published in January the following year, and he presented his demanding mistress with the proceeds which amounted to fifty *louis*. It has been said that in later life, Diderot regretted having written the book. This is a claim that has been made by – or on behalf of – many otherwise celebrated authors who have written erotic works, including Diderot's contemporary, and arch foe of Voltaire, the poet Alexis Piron (1689–1773) whose election to the *Académie* in 1753 was blocked by Louis XV on account of his obscene *Ode à Priape*. Even if it is true, however, these misgivings seem to be unjustified, for *Les Bijoux indiscrets* is a much underrated work in which is gathered together satire, literary criticism and eroticism in a pleasing and stylish combination.

Many characters in the book are transparently not what they seem. Louis XV and Madame de Pompadour are satirized as the sultan Mangogul and his favourite Mirzoza; the Duc de Richelieu becomes Sélim while Marie Leczinska is Mani-monbanda. Mangogul's father, Erguebzed (a parody of Louis XIV), has an interesting approach to his offspring's education which early on reveals Diderot's satirical intent.

> *Erguebzed*, who was a man of sense, and was resolved that his son's education should not be so much neglected as his own had been, sent betimes for all the great men in *Congo* [i.e. France]; as, painters, philosophers, poets, musicians, architects, masters of dancing, mathematicks, history, fencing, &c. Thanks to the happy dispositions of *Mangogul*, and to the constant lessons of his masters, he was ignorant in nothing of what a young prince is wont to learn the first fifteen years of his life; and at the age of twenty he could eat, drink, and sleep, as completely as any potentate of his age.[6]

Les Bijoux indiscrets makes some interesting criticisms of both literature and the theatre; the view held in the 18th century that French traditional drama was of a very high order is ridiculed, and in some passages it is possible to detect the conscious parodying of other authors, most notably Crébillon *fils*. But one of the most powerful episodes in the book occurs in chapter thirty-two – *Rêve de Man-*

gogul – in which the sultan, while dreaming, is taken on the back of a chimera to the land of Hypotheses and in the Temple there is entertained by Plato. During the discourse between the two, a most singular incident takes place:

> ... I saw at a distance a child walking towards us in a slow but sure pace. He had a little head, slender body, weak arms and short legs: but all these parts increased in all dimensions, according as he came forward. In the progress of his successive growth, he appear'd to me under a hundred different forms; I saw him directing a long telescope towards the heavens, estimating the fall of bodies by means of a pendulum, determining the weight of the air by a tube fill'd with quicksilver, and discomposing light with a prism. He was now become an enormous *Colossus*: his head touch'd the heavens, his feet were lost in the abyss, and his arms reach'd from one to the other pole. With his right hand he brandished a torch, whose light spread a vast way in the sky, enlightened even the bottom of the waters and penetrated into the entrails of the earth. I ask'd *Plato*, what that gigantic figure was, that was coming towards us. It is experience, said he. Scarcely had he made me this short answer, when I saw experience draw near, and the columns of the portico of Hypotheses to shake, its arches to sink in, and its pavement to crack under our feet. 'Let us fly, said *Plato*, let us fly: this edifice has but a moment to stand.' At these words he departs, and I follow him. The *Colossus* arrives, strikes the portico, it tumbles down with a frightful noise, and I awake.[7]

This vision of the conflict between the empiric and the theoretic – with perhaps a hint of a prophecy of the Revolution? – worried Mangogul not at all, except for the headache it caused him.

But the central theme of the book, the peg on which the satire and criticism hangs, is the element that has earned it the most serious censure, and derives from an ennui of satiety afflicting the sultan. He complains to his favourite, Mirzoza, of his boredom and expresses a desire to know the most intimate secrets of the ladies of the court, by way of a diversion.

Mirzoza recommends a visit to the *jinn* Cucufa, an 'old hypochondriac' who lives in conditions of abject poverty in a cave. Mangogul explains his plight and what he's after to help him, and after some initial dithering Cucufa produces from his pocket a magic ring.

> 'You see this ring,' said he to the Sultan, 'put it on your finger, my child: every woman, at whom you shall level the stone, will relate her intrigues in a plain, audible voice. Do not imagine however, that 'tis by the mouth that they are to speak?' By what then will they speak, says *Mangogul*? 'By the frankest part about them, and the best instructed in those things which you desire to know, says *Cucufa*; by their Toys [i.e. vaginas].'[8]

Armed with this worrying ornament, Mangogul embarks on a tour of the ladies of the court. The question quickly arises as to when he is going to get around to trying the ring out on Mirzoza, and sure enough his suspicions and curiosity eventually get the better of him – but not until the last chapter.

The twenty-sixth experiment with the ring, which takes place in chapter forty-seven, is probably the most extraordinary episode in the book. Headed *Le Bijou voyageur* ('The Rambling Toy'), this chapter concerns Cypria, a raddled old courtesan who has also been identified, along with Mirzoza, as Madame de Pompadour. Cypria's 'toy', displaying a penchant for formality and higher education, delivers its story like an oration complete with a title of its own – *Histoire de mes voyages* ('A Chronicle of my Travels') – and is recounted in no fewer than four different languages, not counting the French bits: English, Latin, Italian and an odd amalgam of French and Spanish, which G. Legman in his discussion of this chapter has called 'Franco-Spanish pidgin'. (See *Rationale of the Dirty Joke*, 1st series; New York, 1971, p. 751.)

The reasons for these polyglot ramblings are to demonstrate the cosmopolitan nature of Cypria and her 'toy', and to allow Diderot to express himself rather more freely than he obviously felt able to in French. As the chapter concludes: 'The *African* author [i.e. Diderot] closes this chapter with an advertisement to the ladies, who might be tempted to order a translation of those parts of the narrative, where *Cypria's* Toy expressed itself in foreign languages. "I should be wanting, says he, to the duty of an historian, by suppressing them; and to the respect which I bear the sex, by preserving them in my work; without acquainting virtuous ladies, that *Cypria's* Toy had excessively spoil'd its speech in travelling, and that its narratives are infinitely more free than any of the clandestine lectures which it ever made." '[9] The English section is worth quoting:

A wealthy lord, travelling through France, dragg'd me to London. Ay, that was a man indeed! He water'd me six times a day, and as often o'nights. His prick like a comet's tail shot flaming darts: I never felt such quick and thrilling thrusts. It was not possible for mortal prowess to hold out long, at this rate; so he drooped by degrees, and I received his soul distilled through his Tarse. He gave me fifty thousand guineas. This noble lord was succeeded by a couple of privateer-commanders lately return'd from cruising: being intimate friends, they fuck'd me, as they had sail'd, in company, endeavouring who should show most vigour and serve the readiest fire. Whilst the one was riding at anchor, I towed the other by his Tarse and prepared him for a fresh tire. Upon a modest computation, I reckon'd in about eight days time I received a hundred and eighty shot. But I soon grew tired with keeping so strict an account, for there was no end of their broadsides. I got twelve thousand pounds from them for my share of the prizes they had taken. The winter quarter being over, they were forced to put to sea again, and would fain have engaged me as a tender, but I had made a prior contract with a German count.[10]

In addition to the English translation of *Les Bijoux indiscrets* of 1749 quoted from above, another was published in 1968 by Collectors Publications [i.e. Marvin Miller], an exceedingly dubious concern operating from a post office box number in City of Industry, California. Entitled *The Talking Pussy*, and the translation credited to one 'Dr. W. H. Kayy', it would seem to be a reprint of an earlier American edition, possibly published in the 1930s. The translation is appalling; it is marred throughout by modern colloquialisms and wholesale insertions of obscenities where none appear in the original, and is rendered almost unreadable

OPPOSITE Frontispiece from an English translation of *Histoire de Dom B. . . .* The publisher was Charles Hirsch and the artist Paul Avril. See illustrations page 55

LE
PORTIER
DES
CHARTREUX

"Vigour is the gift of Heaven"

FRONTISPIECE

NOCRION

Conte Allobroge.

1747.

OPPOSITE *Nocrion*. The frontispiece of the first edition. Paris, 1747

by a rearrangement of the chapters with little or no concern for logic. Chapter forty-seven, for example, in which Cypria's 'jewel' is quizzed, becomes for no apparent reason chapter forty-one and even the passage that in the original is written in English, quoted above, is spiced up with gratuitous indecencies. It is in the worst possible taste, and the sort of thing that gives erotica – to say nothing of Diderot – a bad name.[11]

*   *   *   *   *

The word *libertin* at first meant 'free-thinker' and as an epithet was used to describe the 17th- and 18th-century intellectual heirs of Rabelais, Montaigne and others who had advocated free inquiry in the pursuit of knowledge and who had rejected the harsh doctrines and moral codes of the Church as hindrances to that objective. *Libertins* were not, therefore, primarily concerned with sexuality and excess although one of them, Théophile de Viau (1590-1626), found himself in extreme difficulties for his part in a compilation of verses entitled *Le Parnasse des poëtes satyriques* – shortened in later editions to *Le Parnasse satyrique* – first published in 1622, for which he was burned in effigy and banished from France. It has been argued that it was Théophile's irreligion that was the real cause of his troubles rather than the immorality of the poems, a suggestion that is supported by the more-or-less parallel, and unmolested, existence of such similarly free anthologies of verses as *Les Muses gaillardes* (1609) and *Le Cabinet satyrique* (1618), the latter being splendidly reprinted in 1924 by Jean Fort under the careful editorship of Fernand Fleuret and Louis Perceau.

It was the enemies of free thought, like the Jesuit François Garesse (1585–1631) whose reactionary work *Doctrine curieuse des beaux esprits du temps* (1623) went for the throat of the *libertins* in general and Théophile in particular, who really created the modern sense of the word 'libertine'. Fearful of the effects of this disaffection, bastions of the Church and the establishment like Garesse dishonestly imputed to their enemies as a whole charges of debauchery and atheism which, while very possibly applying to individual free-thinkers, could hardly be said to be elements central to *libertin* thought in general. It is highly unlikely that the *libertins* took these accusations and accepted them as a *fait accompli*, deciding quite consciously that since everyone thought them to be beasts anyway they might as well play the part and enjoy themselves. In effect, however, this is more or less what happened and by the middle of the 18th century – possibly earlier – 'libertine' as a noun had come to mean in actuality an individual of habitual licentiousness, unfettered by moral laws. As an adjective used to describe literature a definition is less easy to draw up.

There had been a libertine phase in England following the Restoration of the monarchy in 1660. As a counter-blow to the austerity of Puritan rule this is not altogether surprising, and since the King and many of his closest friends and supporters spent their exile during this period in France it is not surprising either that their outlook and subsequent behaviour when they returned should have been influenced by their hosts. But as a libertine phase it was short-lived, surviving Rochester, Etheridge, Radcliffe and the others only as occasional sparks like John Cleland's *Memoirs of a Woman of Pleasure* (1748, 1749) and *An Essay on Woman* (1763), said to be by either John Wilkes or Thomas Potter.

Cleland's novel, more familiarly called *Fanny Hill* after the edition of 1750 which the author abridged himself, is probably the most famous erotic novel ever written. For this reason, and also because texts and critical accounts are readily available, it is perhaps superfluous to go into its history in too great a depth. The most reliable account of the publication of the first edition will be found in the Appendix to David Foxon's book *Libertine Literature*; and in William H. Epstein's *John Cleland: Images of a Life* (New York & London: Columbia University Press, 1976) there is a well-researched biography of a man who would have been merely another minor 18th-century literary figure had it not been that the shortage of a bob or two had forced him to write a sensational novel.

Briefly, Cleland composed his novel while serving a sentence for debt in the Fleet Prison. According to his own testimony, it was written largely from boredom and, the early chapters anyway, was based on an idea '... originally given me by a young gentleman of the greatest hopes that ever I knew, (Brother to a nobleman now Ambassadour at a Foreign Court,) above eighteen years ago, on an occasion immaterial to mention here.'[12] Volume one appeared about November 1748, and volume two was published in early February of the following year. Both were printed by Thomas Parker for Ralph Griffiths and advertised in the press at three shillings each volume.

In November 1749, a warrant was issued for the persons responsible for the book and by the end of the month Cleland, Griffiths and Parker – together with three other men whose connection with the case is not clear – were all on bail and awaiting trial. Despite his recent experiences in the Fleet, Cleland did not seem unduly bothered at the prospect of another jail sentence for at Griffiths's suggestion he reworked *Memoirs of a Woman of Pleasure* so that most of the erotic content was eliminated, and the result was published in March 1750 in one volume as *Memoirs of Fanny Hill*. Rare as is the first edition – four are known to exist in national or major research libraries – the one-volume abridgment is rarer, and so far as it is possible to determine only one copy, that in the British Library (C. 133. a. 9), survives. The British Library also has a reprint of this done in 1841 at London by 'H. Smith' [i.e. William Dugdale].

The expurgated version seems not to have found any more favour than the complete first edition for it was suppressed very quickly – accounting for its rarity in comparison with the edition of 1748/9 that had to wait almost a year before any notice was taken of it – and the three found themselves in trouble again. Yet despite the heated exchanges of letters between the offices of the Secretary of State, the Attorney-General and the Bishop of London, to say nothing of grovelling epistles from Cleland and attempts by Ralph Griffiths to blame everything on a brother of his called Fenton who never materialized, all the evidence seems to point to the case not being pursued.[13]

BELOW Titlepage of the first French edition of Cleland's *Memoirs of a Woman of Pleasure*

NOUVELLE TRADUCTION
de
WOMAN of PLEASUR
ou
FILLE de JOYE
PAR M^R. CLELAND
Contenant
Les Memoires de Melle Fanny
écrits par Elle-même
Avec des Planches en taille douce
Seconde Partie.

A LONDRES M.DCC.LXXVII.

RIGHT Engraved titlepage from
a later French translation of
Cleland's celebrated novel.
The date of this edition is 1786,
and not 1777

67

OPPOSITE A plate from a later translation of Cleland's *Memoires of a Woman of Pleasure*, 1786. See page 67

The later history of the book has been exhaustively covered by most of the bibliographies of erotica and hardly requires amplification here. There is, however, an interesting departure on the subject concerning the celebrated incident at Hampton Court in which Fanny witnesses an encounter between two homosexuals. So far as I am aware, the idea that this was inserted by a bookseller named Drybutter, as was suggested by Henry Bohn in a note that he added to his edition of Lowndes's *Bibliographer's Manual* (1864), or was otherwise not by Cleland, is not supported by any real evidence and need not detain us. The fact remains that the first edition of the novel contains in volume two (pp. 177–9) two paragraphs which are absent from almost all subsequent editions. Since these are not commonly encountered, it may not be altogether superfluous to include them here. The passage follows a paragraph that ends with the words: '. . . they now proceeded to such lengths as soon satisfied me what they were.'

For presently the eldest unbutton'd the other's breeches, and removing the linen barrier, brought out to view a white shaft, middle sized, and scarce fledg'd, when after handling and playing with it a little, with other dalliance, all receiv'd by the boy without other opposition than certain wayward couneesses, ten times more alluring than repulsive, he got him to turn round, with his face from him, to a chair that stood hard by; when knowing, I suppose, his office, the Ganymede now obsequiously lean'd his head against the back of it, and projecting his body, made a fair mark, still covered with his shirt, as he thus stood in a side view to me, but fronting his companion, who presently unmasking his battery, produc'd an engine that certainly deserved to be put to a better use, and very fit to confirm me in my disbelief of the possibility of things being push'd to odious extremities, which I had built on the disproportion of parts; but this disbelief I was now to be cured of, as by my consent all young men should likewise be, that their innocence may not be betray'd into such snares, for want of knowing the extent of their danger: for nothing is more certain than that ignorance of a vice is by no means a guard against it.

Slipping, then, aside the young lad's shirt, and tucking it up under his cloaths behind, he shewed to the open air those globular fleshy eminences that compose the Mount Pleasants of *Rome*, and which now, with all the narrow vale that intersects them, stood displayed and exposed to his attack; nor could I without a shudder behold the dispositions he made for it. First, then, moistening well with spittle his instrument, obviously to make it glib, he pointed, he introduced it, as I could plainly discern, not only from its direction and my losing sight of it, but by the writhing, twisting and soft murmur'd complaints of the young sufferer; but at length, the first straights of entrance being pretty well got through, every thing seem'd to move and go pretty currently on, as on a carpet road, without much rub or resistance; and now, passing one hand round his minion's hips, he got hold of his red-topt ivory toy, that stood perfectly stiff, and shewed, that if he was like his mother behind, he was like his father before; this he diverted himself with, whilst, with the other he wanton'd with his hair, and leaning forward over his back, drew his face, from which the boy shook the loose curls that fell over it, in the posture he stood him in, and brought him towards his, so as to receive a long-breathed kiss; after which, renewing his driving, and thus continuing to harass his rear, the height of the fit came on with its usual symtons [*sic*], ad dismissed the action.

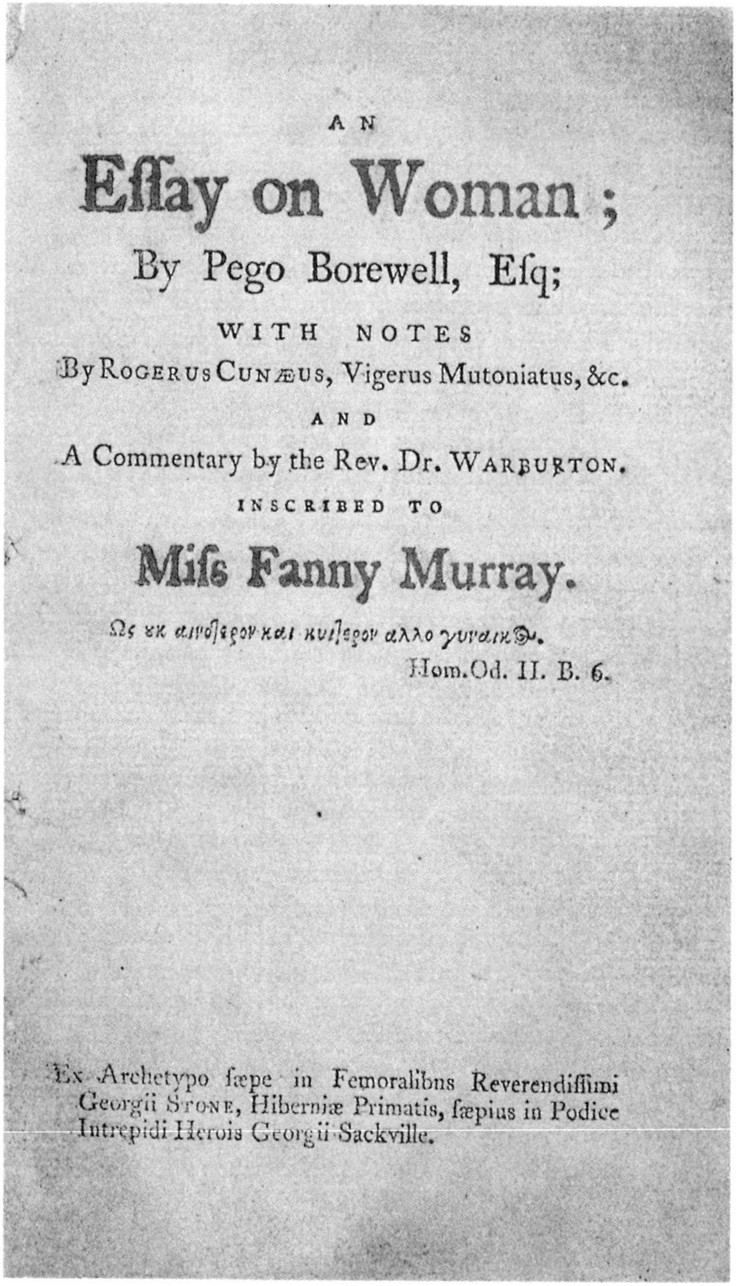

AN

Essay on Woman;

By Pego Borewell, Esq;

WITH NOTES

By Rogerus Cunæus, Vigerus Mutoniatus, &c.

AND

A Commentary by the Rev. Dr. Warburton.

INSCRIBED TO

Miss Fanny Murray.

Ὡς ꭒκ αιɴοʃεϱον και κꭒιʃεϱον αλλο γꭒναικϕ.

Hom. Od. II. B. 6.

Ex Archetypo sæpe in Femoralibns Reverendissimi Georgii Stone, Hiberniæ Primatis, sæpius in Podice Intrepidi Herois Georgii Sackville.

The edition of the *Memoirs* published at Paris in 1888 by Isidore Liseux prints these paragraphs as a footnote to the appropriate pages, but the only modern edition to my knowledge that incorporates them in their correct place in the text is the one published by M. Maurice Girodias at Paris in 1950. Entitled *Memoirs of Fanny Hill*, it was one of the last books that he published under the imprint of the Obelisk Press which his father, Jack Kahane, had started twenty years before. In 1954, M. Girodias issued the same text – as *Memoirs of a Woman*

ABOVE The earliest known edition of *An Essay on Woman*, contemporary with the first edition which appeared in 1763

of Pleasure – which appeared as the fifth volume of The Atlantic Library, the first series that he edited under the aegis of the Olympia Press and the source of the quotation above (pp. 209–10). Reverting to the 1950 title, he reprinted it again in 1956 as no. 17 in the Traveller's Companion Series, and in 1960 and 1962 in the same series simply as *Fanny*, a ruse that effectively misled *la Brigade mondaine* who, having no English and working from an alphabetical list of titles, failed to connect a book called *Fanny* with one called *Memoirs of Fanny Hill*.

All subsequent editions containing these two paragraphs, including those published in the United States by feeble imitators of Girodias, after the effective collapse of censorship there in the mid-1960s, would appear to be piracies of, or at least to originate from, the 1950 edition and its immediate progeny. The editions published in 1963 in England and America by Mayflower Books and G. P. Putnam's Sons respectively – both giving rise to court cases – are expurgated and do not contain this incident.

An Essay on Woman, although less well-known perhaps with the public than Cleland's novel, is nevertheless an important work and not just as a piece of erotica. As literary parody it is not without interest, and since it was employed as an excuse to discredit a radical politician, assuming charitably that such beings may be said to exist, it enjoys a certain historical significance as well. The first edition of 1763, of which only twelve copies are known to have been struck off, is lost to us, but a contemporary reprint is described by Ashbee (vol. 1, pp. 198–201) and a copy of this is preserved in the Dyce Collection at the Victoria and Albert Museum, London. Further reprints followed, many of them catch-penny frauds, either innocuous doggerel with no relationship to the original except the title or else crude expurgations, and the British Library has a representative selection of these.

The true work contains four poems in all, three of which are direct parodies of verses by Alexander Pope (1688–1744). The title poem is obviously a burlesque of Pope's *Essay on Man* (1732–4), and consists of ninety-four lines commencing:

> Awake my Fanny! leave all meaner things;
> This morn shall prove what rapture swiving brings!
> Let us (since life can little more supply
> Than just a few good fucks, and then we die)
> Expiate freer o'er that loved scene of man,
> A mighty maze, for mighty pricks to scan;
> A wild, where Paphian thorns promiscuous shoot,
> Where flowers the monthly rose, but yields no fruit.
> Together let us beat this ample field,
> Try what the open, what the overt yield,
> The latent tracts, the pleasing depths explore,
> And my prick clapp'd where thousands were before.

Veni Creator; or, The Maid's Prayer (twenty-seven lines in five stanzas) is an original work with no obvious influence. The *Universal Prayer* stems from Pope's poem of the same title and has thirteen stanzas of four lines apiece, while Pope's versification of the Emperor Adrian's death-bed address – *A Dying Christian to his Soul* – is rendered with delightful cynicism as *The Dying Lover to his Prick* and is short enough to be quoted in its entirety:

> Happy spark of heavenly flame!
> Pride and wonder of man's frame!
> Why is pleasure so soon flying?
> Why so short this bliss of dying?
> Cease, fond pego, cease the strife,
> And yet indulge a moment's life.
>
> Hark! cunt whispers. Don't she say,
> Brother pego come away?
> What is this absorbs me quite,
> Seals my senses, shuts my sight,
> Drowns my spirits, draws my breath?
> Tell me, my prick, can this be death?
>
> Now you recede, now disappear!
> My eye looks round in vain; my ear,
> Fanny your Murmur rings:
> Lend, lend your hand! I mount! I die!
> O Prick, how great thy Victory?
> O Pleasure, sweet thy stings.

Accompanying these poems are notes relative to the texts, which are signed 'Warburton', 'Vigerus Mutoniatus', 'Burman', and 'Rogerus Cunaeus'. Although far more indecent and possessing a high degree of profanity, these are not completely dissimilar in feel or style to the notes written by Norman Douglas to attend his privately printed *Some Limericks* (1928), already mentioned in connection with *La Pétomane*. Both own a light, irreverent humour beneath a pseudo-serious surface and Ashbee, during the course of his very full and detailed history of *An Essay on Woman*, states that the notes are probably of greater interest than the verses to which they allude.

The question of who wrote *An Essay on Woman* has never been fully resolved, but how it came to be printed and used against Wilkes, the Member of Parliament for Aylesbury, is known well enough. With Wilkes's knowledge, twelve copies of the work were run off on the private press at his home in Great George Street, Westminster. They were intended for circulation among his fellow members of Sir Francis Dashwood's Hell-Fire Club, a sort of convivial drinking and debauching society for well-placed persons which held its meetings at the ruined Cistercian abbey of Medmenham near Marlow on the banks of the Thames.

During the course of the printing, some proof sheets were discarded and subsequently fell into the hands of Wilkes's enemies. How this happened is not clear, but C. R. Dawes, in his unpublished *Study of Erotic Literature in England* (Cheltenham, 1943; ms. in British Library), tells a good story about an employee of Wilkes named Samuel Jennings who picked up the sheets and used them to wrap his lunch in, later giving them to a pal named Farmer who took them away to show some of his cronies. It seems unlikely, if this account is true, that Jennings or even, possibly, Farmer were deliberately acting against the interests of Wilkes, but nevertheless it was not long before the proofs found their way into the hands of a clergyman named John Kidgell, a completely unprincipled wretch who was chaplain to the Earl of March, afterwards Duke of Queensberry or 'Old Q' as he became known, and the author of a boring novel called *The Card* (1755).

John Wilkes (1727–97) was already an unpopular figure with the government of the day for his attacks on them in his periodical *The North Briton*, which he had founded in 1762 and ran in collaboration with Charles Churchill. No. 45 of this contained a particularly swingeing assault on Lord Bute and his Tory administration, for which Wilkes was accused of seditious libel and the offending issue of his paper was ordered to be burned by the hangman at the Royal Exchange. The burning was frustrated by Wilkes's supporters who incited the mob to riot.

It was at this time, toward the end of 1763, that Kidgell had come into possession of the proof sheets of *An Essay on Woman*. Egged on by his patron March, who had himself been urged to action by Lords Bute and Sandwich, he conspired with Wilkes's printer Michael Curry to obtain a complete copy of the work, which Sandwich then read to the House of Lords – amid shouts of 'Go on, go on!' when Lord Lyttleton attempted to halt the proceedings – and afterwards moved that Wilkes should be declared the author of it. At first this was not allowed since Wilkes, who had been injured in a duel, was laid up in Paris and unable to travel back to London to defend himself. Legal, or moral, niceties of the sort that expect an accused person to be able to defend himself did not seem to worry Wilkes's enemies, for in January 1764 he was expelled from the House of Commons, and although still in France was found guilty in February in the court of King's Bench of publishing issue no. 45 of *The North Briton*. Still absent from the country the following November, he was outlawed by order of Lord Chief Justice Mansfield.

The Government's chief witness against Wilkes in the case of *An Essay on Woman* was his printer, Michael Curry, a man who bore a personal grudge against his employer and who was by all accounts unpopular with his fellow workers in the print shop. He paid for his treachery by effectively being declared 'black' – refused work throughout London – his offence being regarded as a violation of the freedom of the press. He died in Norwich in 1778, aged 56.

While there is little doubt that Wilkes had *An Essay on Woman* printed on the Great George Street press, the allegation that he wrote it as well, as was imputed by Sandwich, Bute and the rest, seems early to have been disputed. In his *Memoirs of the Reign of King George III*, which was not published until 1845, although the author died in 1797, Walpole gives an interesting eye-witness account of the affair – he was present in the House of Commons when Sandwich gave his recitation to the Lords in the Upper House – and proposed that Wilkes might have written the poems in collaboration: 'Wilkes and *Potter*, son of the late Archbishop of Canterbury, had formerly composed this indecent patchwork in some of their bacchanalian hours...' This was an opinion mooted by the Earl of Stanhope among other historical and literary writers. If Thomas Potter were the author, either in partnership or alone, then the business assumes an even more lively aspect since it was well known that he was cuckolding Bishop Warburton – the 'Warburton' who was supposedly the author of some of the notes to *An Essay on Woman*. 'Although of a "large and athletic person," ' writes *Ashbee* drolly (vol. 1, p. 213), 'doubts seem to have been entertained as to his capability of performing certain conjugal duties, which will go far to excuse the conduct of his wife with Potter.' It is hardly surprising that Warburton 'foamed with the violence of a Saint Dominic' when he heard of the book and his inclusion in it, especially if he heard also that his wife's lover was thought to have had a hand in its writing.

Of more than passing curiosity, despite its brevity, is *The Letter Paraphras'd* by the tragic Thomas Chatterton who, in a fit of despair at his reduced circumstances, poisoned himself with arsenic at the age of 17 in 1770. As is well known, Chatterton forged a number of historical documents, many concerning his home town of Bristol, and composed some fine poems which he passed off as the work of an imaginary 15th-century poet-monk named Thomas Rowley.

The Letter Paraphras'd was written by Chatterton in reply to a note rejecting his advances that he had received from a semi-literate Bristol girl. Both originals are preserved in the British Library's Department of Manuscripts (pressmark: Ms. 5766 B. f. 92). The only printed version that I am aware of appeared in March 1933, when it was secretly published by a bookseller named Charles Heartman at Metuchen, New Jersey. The edition was limited to fifty copies and has an Introduction signed 'M. O. Hunter' [i.e. Professor Thomas O. Mabbott]. The poem, which is brief, is worth quoting in full:

> My loving Dear I send thee this
> To tell he that I want to piss.
> Pray let me speak the matter blunt
> I want to stretch my narrow cunt.
> But if you frown and turn away
> Go, with the devil dance the Hay
> Pray send me back a swelling prick
> To touch my matters to the quick
> But if your Roger cannot fill
> The water brook that turns my Mill
> Go fuck green sickness girls and wenches
> On Bulks, in Lanes, on Tombs or Benches.
>
> By God I want a strapping Man
> My Cunt is more than twice a Span
> And Faith I speak it without joking
> Last night I put a Cartwheel Spoke in
> Then if your matters cannot do
> By God I never will have you
> Unless I dangle with thy prick
> Piss in thy face and let thee lick.

* * * * *

In France, the libertine tradition in literature became more established. Books so categorized ranged from ill-written rubbish to masterpieces like *Les Liaisons dangereuses* (1782) of Pierre Choderlos de Laclos which, while not overtly erotic, nevertheless examines the world and the cynical philosophy of the libertine with such brutal reality that even today the book retains its sinister reputation. There is no sexual activity – in the sense that there is in, say, *Memoirs of a Woman of Pleasure* – and neither does Laclos moralize. His characters come to sticky ends – Valmont is killed in a duel and his female accomplice is hideously disfigured by smallpox – but there is no suggestion that this is some sort of poetic justice meted out to them for their corruption. It is as much this detached perspective of *Les Liaisons dangereuses* as the callous cynicism of its characters that roots it firmly in the libertine tradition. Had Valmont become reconciled to the Church, married somebody and sunk into respectable old age it would have been a different sort of book altogether. Laclos's novel, however, is rather a special case. As Wayland Young has pointed out, 'Boucher painted the book of libertinism, and Nerciat described the feel of it. Laclos wrote down its rules in vitriol and thereby destroyed it.' (*Eros Denied*, p. 209.) Most libertine novels appear to possess intellect and wit, and indeed it is these very qualities that make them agreeable to read, unlike the sort of erotic novels that would today be described as 'hard-core pornography'. But these qualities are not of any real depth and do not stand up too well under close inspection; the intellect is generally sophistry, while the wit is often little more than a pleasant froth. *Les Liaisons dangereuses* on the other hand has a ferocious intellect. The values of libertinism are there, but they are carried through to their logical conclusion – almost; it is but one step from the calculating evil of the Marquis de Merteuil and the Vicomte de Valmonte to the graphic horrors played out by Sade's two schemers, Juliette and Noirceuil.

The true libertine novel combines a disregard for popular concepts of morality and an emphasis on sensual pleasure. There is a frequent element of anti-clericalism as well, although this is not obligatory, to remind one of the free-thinking origins of the genre. The characters that populate these works are frequently aristocratic, wealthy, amusing, urbane. They plot and scheme, but they are not vicious and nobody is ever really incommoded. In the sense that they have personalities they are 'real' people, and yet for all their apparent sophistication and world-weariness, they are naïve, almost child-like.

There is a scene in *Le Libertin de qualité* (1784) which illustrates the humour and light qualities of such works. The book concerns a young man who decides on the life of a gigolo. 'I am prepared to fuck only for money,' he declares bluntly at the very beginning of the book. 'I shall put myself out to stud to women who are past their prime, and in return for showing them what's what I'll charge by the month.'[14] After a particularly villainous piece of sexual profiteering, the 'reader' delivers a reproof to the libertine: '... but this is outrageous; love is a pure and noble thing. You are nothing but a rotter.' In answer to this, the libertine exclaims peevishly: 'Fuck! You jest of course, and undermine the profession. She is thirty-six, and still pretty good; but I'm twenty-four and a good deal better. She lays out her love and her cash, while I lay out my virility and discretion. Aren't I entitled to any reward?'[15]

One of his earliest clients is Madame Fonteniable – '… an American, and rich as Crœsus' – to whom he is introduced by Madame Saint-Just, 'a celebrated bawd'. Madame Fonteniable looks the young libertine up and down.

'Fuck, she says to Saint-Just, where did you get hold of this pretty boy? He's rather young, and a bit on the small side. But no matter – little man, big prick … And to get better acquainted she gave me a hug than nearly suffocated me. – Good God, he's timid. – Oh, he's new to the business – We'll soon fix that … But has the cat got your tongue? – Madame, with all respect! (I was flabbergasted). – Bah! You drive me crazy with your respect … *Adieu* Saint-Just. There, there my little fucker. You stay here and we'll eat and bed together.'

Once we are alone, my lovely throws herself on a sopha; not bothering with trifles like preliminaries, I hurl myself on her; in an instant she is ready for pillage. I find a tanned cleavage, but breasts as hard as marble; a fine body, a domed *mons veneris*, a most entrancing wig … During the inspection, my dearest bellows like a bull, whinnies like a mare in heat; her arse beats a tattoo, her cunt sounds the bugle call … Jesus wept! Overcome with a Holy fury I grab one of her arms, hold her tight for a moment and plunge in … Wonder of wonders … My buggeress is tight … With two mighty thrusts I'm in up to my balls … I bite her … She scratches me … The blood flows … Sometimes I'm on top, sometimes underneath; the couch creaks, breaks, falls to pieces … The beast is down, but I'm still in the saddle; my strokes re-double … 'Keep it up my friend … Keep … fuck … Ah! Ah! … Harder … Ah! … Bugger … Ah! It's so good. Ah! Ah! Ah! … Sweet Jesus, don't take it out … Ho, ho, ho … More … more … I'm coming … Help … help … ah, youth, youth …' Stupid cow! She shakes her good-for-nothing arse so much that I am all but uncunted … I press on … My prick's on fire. … I grab her by the *chignon* (not the one on her pussy); I am back in harness … 'Ah! She cries … I'm dying …' Horrible old bag! … (I grind my teeth) … 'I'll throttle you if you don't let me come …' Finally, breathless, her eyes soften; she begs for mercy … Never, dammit … no quarter! … I dig the spurs in … Full speed ahead … My balls are in a perfect rage; She faints dead away … But I don't give a cuss, and only unsheath when we discharge together …

It is high time, I think, for her to put her underclothes back on. When we have composed ourselves, she offers me compliments and congratulations and repairs to the *bidet*. While she's out of the room, I set to work trying to fix the sopha.

'What are you up to? She asks on her return. My friend, the servants are accustomed to this sort of thing and one of them, a *valet de chambre*, is an upholsterer too and comes in each morning to mend that.'[16]

The history of *Le Libertin de qualité* is confused. It actually appeared first in 1783 as *Ma Conversion*, and was probably printed by Jean-Zacharie Malassis at Alençon, although the titlepage reads 'À Londres'. The following year it was reprinted at either Paris or Neuchâtel as *Le Libertin de qualité*, with the false imprint 'À Stamboul: de l'imprimerie des Odalisques, 1784', under which title it has usually

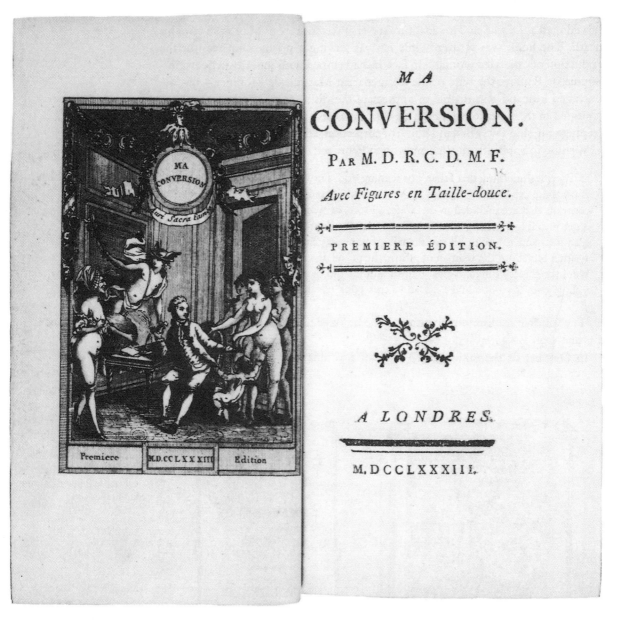

MA
CONVERSION.

PAR M. D. R. C. D. M. F.

Avec Figures en Taille-douce.

PREMIERE ÉDITION.

A LONDRES.

M, DCCLXXXIII.

Frontispiece and titlepage
of the first edition of
Mirabeau's *Ma Conversion*

appeared since.[17] The reason for this title change seems to have had something
to do with an erotic work composed in epistolary form, and called in its original
edition *Lettres de Julie à Eulalie* (1784). No doubt with an eye to the market, this
was reprinted in the same year – with sixteen additional letters and new names for
the two central characters – as *Ma Conversion* ('À Stamboul: de l'imprimerie des
Odalisques, 1783'), a piece of deception that has caused trouble ever since.

The author of *Le Libertin de qualité* was Honoré-Gabriel Riquetti, Comte de
Mirabeau (1749–91), a man noted as much for his immorality and excess as for
his enthusiastic, though moderate, participation in the Revolution which he

served well as *Député du Tiers État* for Aix-en-Provence from May 1789 until his
death. The book was written while he was serving a prison sentence 'for the
abduction of a married woman'. In fact, he had eloped with the lady in question –
Sophie de Ruffay, the wife of the sexagenarian Marquis de Monnier – but the
outraged husband was unable to appreciate the distinction, and had Mirabeau
confined in the notorious Donjon de Vincennes and his wife, who happened to
be pregnant, shut away first in a house of correction, and later in a convent.

Writing to Sophie from Vincennes on 21 February 1780, Mirabeau said:

> ... there is something that I shan't be sending you, a novel that I am writing, a totally
> crazy thing called *Ma conversion* ... You wouldn't credit the characters and amusing
> contrasts that are included in the draft; all sorts of women in all sorts of conditions
> enter into it in turn; the idea is mad, but the details are rather jolly and one day I'll
> read it to you although I'll run the risk of you scratching my eyes out. I've already
> written bits about the woman of means, the prude, the religious type, the president's
> wife, the tradeswoman, ladies at court and the old dear. Now I'm working on the
> young girls. It's a good take off, and a true book of ethics.[18]

The following month he mentioned the book again, saying that it was 'much
funnier than *Parapilla*'.[19]

In October of the same year, Mirabeau was able to write to Sophie about

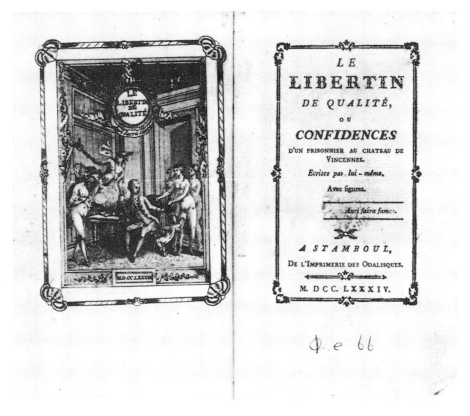

LEFT The second edition of *Ma Conversion*, with the title that it appeared under most often in subsequent editions

RIGHT Portrait of Honoré-Gabriel de Riquetti, Comte de Mirabeau

another book he was working on. 'Do you think', he asked her, 'that research could be done in the Bible and in other ancient literature on onanism, tribadism, etc., etc., in fact, on the most indelicate subjects that have been dealt with by the casuists, and the whole lot made readable to the most straight-laced class of person?'[20]

OPPOSITE Elaborate binding and titlepage of the 'lost' fifth copy of the first edition of Restif de la of la Bretonne's L'Anti-Justine

The book that he was referring to was the *Errotika* [sic] *biblion*, first published in 1783 at either Paris or Neuchâtel with the false imprint 'À Rome, de l'imprimerie du Vatican'. The answer to Mirabeau's question to Sophie as to whether the book could be made socially acceptable appears to have been 'no' since it was pursued with such vigour by the authorities that only fourteen copies of the first edition are supposed to have survived. An edition of 1792 was followed by the inclusion of the work in the Papal *Index* of prohibited books, where its original Greek title appeared with a Latin translation, as *Amatoria Bibliorum*, presumably to make sure that there was no confusion among the faithful. This entry onto the *Index* took place in July 1794 according to the *notice bibliographique* of the 1881 reprint done at Brussels; in the most recent edition of the *Index* available on the open shelves of the British Library – it was published in 1948 – Mirabeau's book is still listed and with the date 1804 by the entry, when the prohibition was re-inforced or reaffirmed, it is to be imagined, but without the Latin title. A further edition was ordered to be destroyed in 1826 by the Royal Court of Paris, and for 'outrages against public morality and good manners' there were two other prosecutions, in 1865 and 1868.

The reason for this great interest in the *Erotika biblion* by the authorities seems obscure. As a compendium of curiosities culled from the pages of ancient writings it is possibly one of the most peculiar books ever put together, and shows vividly the sort of eccentric bypaths that erudition and emotion can sometimes take when strangled by the confines of prison. But it is not an erotic or pornographic book, or even strictly speaking a blasphemous one although there are those of a pious disposition who might well be disagreeably surprised to learn, for example, of the many veiled references in the Bible to haemorrhoids.

Mirabeau has been credited with the authorship of two other works of a questionable character. These are *Le Rideau levé, ou l'Éducation de Laure* ('Cythère' [Alençon: J.-Z. Malassis], 1786), which hinges on the idea that the heroine believes her sexual tutor to be her father, and *Hic et hec, ou l'Élève des RR. PP. jésuites d'Avignon*. If Mirabeau were really the author of this, which seems highly improbable, the manuscript must have been in circulation for a number of years prior to publication because the earliest known edition is the one dated 1798 and bearing the probably false place of origin 'Berlin'. It concerns the adventures of a young student or trainee of the Jesuits at Avignon who, when the order is disbanded, takes a position as a sort of tutor to a well-to-do middle-class family. Sections of the book were plagiarized by the anonymous author of *Milord* [sometimes *Mylord*] *Arsouille, ou les Bamboches d'un gentleman*, a pornographic work that appeared about 1850 despite having the date '1789' on the titlepage of the first edition. *Hic et hec* is rather a poor work as such things go, but it does contain

Qui sçait, lorsque le Ciel nous
frappe de ses coups,
Si le plus grand malheur n'est
par un bien pour nous?
Ed. ch. Admète.

some spirited scenes – like the one where a character paints the face of an elephant on his stomach and waves his penis about like the animal's trunk – which are not without their charms.

Whether Mirabeau wrote *Le Rideau levé* or not has been the subject of much speculation. The only other serious candidate for the honour is a certain Marquis de Sentilly – 'a gentleman of lower Normandy' – as yet unlocated. According to the authors of *l'Enfer* (1919; no. 142), this nomination has its origins with Louis Dubois, a person '*bien au fait des mystères de la typographie alençonnaise clandestine*', who discovered the ascription in a note belonging to Léon de la Sicotière. On the other hand 'Helpey, Bibliographe poitevin' [i.e. Louis Perceau], in a well-argued *notice* to a reprint of *Le Rideau levé* secretly published at Paris by Maurice Duflou about 1925, defends the ascription to Mirabeau and dismisses the claim, and even the existence, of Sentilly.

The other really major figure of this school of erotic writing was André-Robert Andréa de Nerciat who, either anonymously or under the nom-de-plume *le Docteur Cazzoné* – 'membre extraordinaire de la joyeuse Faculté Phallo-coïro-pygo-glottonomique – was responsible for five novels and as many volumes of miscellaneous stories, dialogues and similar short pieces to say nothing of some perfectly respectable military and amorous verses, at least one play and an opera for which he wrote not only the libretto but the music as well. Since details of his life are sparse, and he is not well known outside France or the rarified circles of erotica collectors, it may be useful to summarize what little is known of him.

He was born in April 1739 at Dijon, where his father was a lawyer attached to the local parliament. The family came originally from Naples. His early life was spent in travel and in acquiring an education, and he seemed to prove particularly adept at languages, for he rapidly achieved fluency in German and Italian. As a captain in the infantry he served the King of Denmark, later returning to France where he joined the royal household at Versailles as a member of the *corps des gendarmes de la garde*. It was about this period of his life, from about 1770, that he first turned his hand to writing and he composed three novels, *Félicia, ou Mes fredaines*, *Les Aphrodites* and *Le Diable au corps*. *Félicia* was published in 1775, but the other two did not appear until some while later. Also in 1775, a play that he had written entitled *Dorimon, ou le marquis de Clairville* was performed at the theatre at Versailles but it failed miserably, a circumstance made all the worse by his regiment being disbanded the same year and its officers finding themselves pensioned off.

Andréa de Nerciat resumed his travels once more, visiting Switzerland, Belgium and Germany, during which wanderings he seems to have been employed for at least part of the time by the French secret service. He settled for a while in Prussia where he found employment as adviser and sub-librarian to the eccentric francophile Friedrich II, the Landgraf of Hessen-Kassel. Here Andréa de Nerciat achieved considerable success with a comic opera entitled *Constance, ou l'Heureuse témérité*, but following some irregularities in the cataloguing of the library – for which he took the blame for mismanagement of the project by his patron in

Hessen-Kassel, the Marquis de Luchet – he was obliged to move on once again, becoming director of building works to the Duke of Hessen-Rothenburg before returning to France and resuming his career in the secret service with trips to Holland and Austria in 1787. Presumably for services to espionage, he was awarded the *croix de Saint-Louis* in 1788. It was during this period that he wrote a short *galante* work called *Le Doctorat impromptu* (1788), and two erotic novels, *Mon Noviciat, ou les Joies de Lolotte* and *Monrose, ou le Libertin par fatalité* neither of which were published until 1792, the former at Berlin and the other at Liège by the printer and bookseller F. J. Desoer.

In 1793, *Les Aphrodites* was printed for the first time, also by Desoer at Liège, and its author was acting as the agent of Charles-Maurice Talleyrand-Périgord and his somewhat dubious diplomatic activities. In 1797, he went to Italy in order to keep an eye on Madame Buonaparte and a little later travelled to Naples where, not content with acting for Talleyrand-Périgord, he did a bit of spying for Queen Marie-Caroline as well. For this he was dismissed from his job, but Marie-Caroline, who took a liking to Andréa de Nerciat, entrusted him with a secret mission to the Pope in Rome. Here he was captured by French troops under the command of General Berthier and thrown into the prison of the Castel Sant'Angelo. As the new century dawned, he was released and made his way back to Naples, but the effects of imprisonment had left their mark on him and he died in poverty and extreme ill-health at the end of January 1800.

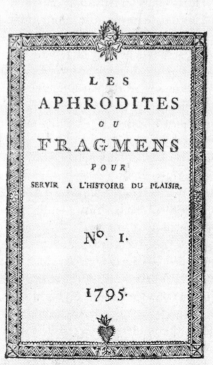

FAR LEFT Titlepage of the rare first edition of Andréa de Nerciat's *Les Aphrodites*

LEFT The front wrapper showing a different date of publication

Critical opinion does not favour Andréa de Nerciat's non-erotic works very highly, and of his erotic novels *Mon Noviciat* is not liked too much either. According to *Gay* (vol. 5, p. 107), it formed the basis of an English work called *How to Make Love*, first published at London in 1823 by John Aschem, and a sequel – presumably the balance of the translation or adaptation – is supposed to have appeared in two volumes in 1828 as *How to Raise Love*, from the same publisher. The history of this English version is traced in some detail by *Ashbee* (vol. 3, pp. 147–9) who fails to note its alleged connection with *Mon Noviciat*. This is probably accounted for by an entry in James Campbell Reddie's manuscript *Bibliographical Notes* (vol. 2, p. 122 [orig. p. 107]) in which any relationship between *How to Make Love*, its sequel and *Mon Noviciat* is emphatically denied. Ashbee certainly knew of this entry in Reddie's manuscript since he provides a footnote to that effect at the bottom of page 147; but whether Gay or Reddie is correct is unlikely to be determined until copies of the books that Aschem published are located.

Because it is not particularly outrageous, *Félicia* is the most accessible of all Andréa de Nerciat's 'clandestine' writings and has been reprinted many times. Likewise *Monrose*, a sequel to *Félicia*, in which the adventures of a character from the earlier book are recounted. The original manuscript of *Félicia* must have strayed from its author's possession at some point because the first edition ('Londres' [Paris?], 1775), and a reprint of this the following year, seem to have been both unauthorized and full of mistakes. A definitive edition, printed under the personal supervision of Andréa de Nerciat, probably by Desoer at Liège, came out in 1778; and fourteen years later in 1792, when he supervised Desoer's printing of the first edition of *Monrose*, he had a 'companion' edition of *Félicia* run off at the same time.

Without a doubt, however, it is *Les Aphrodites, ou Fragments thali-priapiques pour servir à l'histoire du plaisir* – to give the book its full title – and *Le Diable au corps* that are Andréa de Nerciat's masterpieces, and which must rank very high indeed on any list of erotic classics. Little is spared the reader by way of sexual description, and indeed something seems to be going on most of the time, yet for all the orgies and bizarre fancies there is an underlying conviction that we are reading about real people who have chosen to escape reality by shutting themselves away in a fantasy world all of their own. This is particularly evident in *Les Aphrodites*, which is about an expensive club or super-bordel that evidence suggests actually existed but which, like similar establishments that catered for more specialized tastes, was put paid to by the Revolution.

As *Les Aphrodites* proceeds, the rules and regulations of the society are explained. We learn, for example, that one of its basic tenets is a commitment to egalitarianism; one member, the pompous Duchesse de l'Enginière, who refuses to read Mirabeau's *Ma Conversion* on the grounds that its author is 'a turn-coat destroyer of the noble and titled', is tricked into believing that she has been made pregnant by a member of the lower orders – a *'vil petit bourgeois'* – and promptly throws a terrific tantrum. It is explained to her later that the ruse was to punish her for her 'damned arrogance' and if possible to cure her of it. There are committees and subcommittees, financial reports, arguments as to whether pederasts should be admitted to the ranks and discussions on whether existing members should be struck off for arrears in subscriptions or substandard performances on the couch. Grotesque characters and incidents are introduced; the Chevalier de Trottignac who, at a sort of initiation ceremony, succeeds in breaking the record for supporting an ever-increasing number of weights hung from his erect penis; Madame Valcreux who after driving a husband to an early grave with her sexual demands, exhausts her confessor and thirty-seven monks (by Papal dispensation of course) and is finally subdued by a simply enormous dildo – 'a *chef-d'œuvre* of Italian workmanship ... decorated in silver ... and built to last!'; and the heroic Madame don Conbanal, who expires on an 'electric bed' in the arms of eight Carmelites.

Le Diable au corps is, if anything, even more extravagant. The first part of the novel appeared in Germany in 1785 – with the usual false imprint 'À Londres' – as *Les Ecarts du tempérament, ou le Catéchisme de Figaro*. It was published without the author's permission, as was a pirated reprint entitled *Les Ecarts du libertinage et de tempérament* ('À Conculix', 1793). The first true edition appeared in 1803, three years after the author's death, in three volumes. It was published at Mézières by a printer named Frémont who also issued at the same time a reimposed version in six volumes. There have been a number of reprints since; two German translations, one of which was called, appropriately, *Pandämonium* (n.p., c. 1925); and an indifferent English rendering as *The Devil in the Flesh* published in 1970 by Holloway House of Los Angeles who also issued, the following year, a translation of *Les Aphrodites*.

Like *Les Aphrodites*, *Le Diable au corps* is a novel in dialogue form, not unlike a play and complete with stage directions. The text is preceded by an '*avertissement necessaire*', written by the author in 1789, in which the unauthorized piracy in 1785 of the first part of the book is condemned and an account given of how it came to be printed in the first place. This is followed by an '*argument du docteur*', a sort of *dramatis personae*, and then the text proper.

The plot, if it can be described as such, concerns the adventures of an unnamed marquise and her insatiable friend, the Comtesse de Motte-en-feu. These two belong to a club or society which, although remaining anonymous in the body of the work, is evidently meant to represent the *société des Aphrodites*. A footnote to the first, integral edition of 1803 points this out, but it is possible this was added by the publisher Frémont rather than the author. The marquise and her friend involve themselves in a progressively more epic and whimsical series of debauches and conspiracies that culminate in a monster orgy at which everyone is in fancy dress. Before this point is reached, however, there are a number of hilarious 'set pieces': the episode when the marquise is conducting business with a *colporteur* or travelling salesman named Bricon, for example. After a few innocent sales – although one of these is a monkey – he is compelled by the marquise to unveil his 'medical' merchandise, which he does with a great pretence of embarrassment.

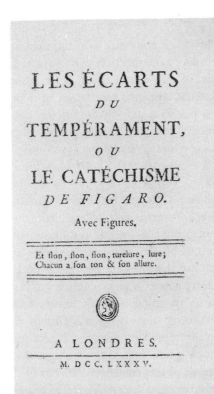

LES ÉCARTS
DU
TEMPÉRAMENT,
O U
LE CATÉCHISME
DE FIGARO.
Avec Figures.

Et flon, flon, flon, turelure, lure;
Chacun a fon ton & fon allure.

A LONDRES.
M. DCC. LXXXV.

LE
DIABLE AU CORPS,
ŒUVRE POSTHUME
Du très-recommandable Docteur CAZZONE,
Membre extraordinaire de la joyeuse Faculté
Phallo-coïro-pygo-glottonomique.

AVEC FIGURES.

TOME PREMIER.

1803.

RIGHT The pirated first part of Andréa de Nerciat's *Le Diable au corps*

FAR RIGHT The first integral edition of *Le Diable au corps*

These include specimens of Mrs Phillips's celebrated English condoms – about which more will be learned in the pages of Mr Peter Fryer's book *The Birth Controllers* (London, 1965) – and a whole range of dildoes, including a double one, the purpose of which has to be explained to his customer. The marquise has been eyeing Bricon speculatively throughout all this, and when his explanation of the double dildo inflames him it is only token resistance that she offers when he falls on her. At the height of this, a cupboard door flies open and out steps the 'extremely disgusting and scandalous' Abbé Boujaron. 'Good morning, every-one,' beams the newcomer and proceeds to instruct the marquise in the theory of sodomy, his great weakness. At length she is sufficiently convinced to put theory into practice and enjoys the simultaneous embraces of Bricon and Boujaron. 'It was in the stars and had to be,' sighs the marquise, 'nevertheless it is curious. . .' Afterwards the abbé returns to his hiding place with the words: 'another convert!'

All this sort of thing is rather silly of course, but like a lot of frivolous things does no harm. The quality of the writing is very good, and beneath the excesses of the characters, the extremes of licentiousness gone to for comic effect, there is a portrait of a certain type of society and environment that is accurate enough in its way; and making allowances for Andréa de Nerciat's literary indulgences it is possible to learn much about the prejudices, tastes, habits and feelings of his peers, which is rather more than can be said of most erotic writing.

*   *   *   *   *

Two other authors who have been considered as 'not quite nice' – as opposed to 'totally unspeakable' – should be mentioned briefly in connection with a brace of novels that if better known to the general reader of 18th-century French literature would do little to enhance the already somewhat tarnished reputation of their authors. These two novels are *Tableaux des mœurs du temps dans les différens âges de la vie* by Claude-Prosper Jolyot de Crébillon (1707–77), known as Crébillon *fils* and already mentioned above in connection with the 'transformation' novel *Le Sopha*, and *L'Anti-Justine, ou les Délices de l'amour* (1798) by Nicolas-Edme Restif (or Rétif) de la Bretonne (1734–1806).

If the *Erotika biblion* of Mirabeau is one of the most peculiar books ever written from the point of view of content, then *Tableaux des mœurs du temps* must take the laurels for peculiarity of production and history; not for nothing is it known as *le merle blanc de la fantasie érotique* ('the *rara avis* [rare bird] of erotic fantasy'). It was written by Crébillon to the order of Alexandre, Jean-Joseph Le Riche de la Poupelinière (1693–1762), an extremely wealthy *fermier général* – literally a 'tax farmer' – who was well known for his lavish spending, love of luxury and general dissipation. Together with a less interesting story entitled *L'Histoire de Zaïrette* actually by La Poupelinière – who attempted to take the credit for Crébillon's work as well, historically without much success – a calligraphic manuscript was prepared that included a portrait of the *fermier général* engraved by Jean Georges Wille. The manuscript appeared at an auction in March 1837 and was briefly described in the catalogue of the sale, after which it disappeared until about 1910 when it was rumoured to be in the collection of the poet and bibliophile Pierre Louÿs. It did not, however, feature in any of the six volumes of the sale catalogue of his library that were published between 1918 and 1930, and its present whereabouts remain a mystery.

At some point between 1750 and 1760, La Poupelinière decided to have the manuscript printed, which he did in an edition of just one copy. The volume is a large, morocco-bound quarto of 321 pages with the coat of arms of La Poupelinière on the covers and the false imprint 'Amsterdam' on the titlepage. (It was actually printed at Paris.) Originally it included twenty miniatures on vellum showing the author of *Zaïrette* in amorous positions with, it is said, the wives of men who owed him money. The likenesses of these ladies are reputed to have been excellent and the fact that at least two of the miniatures are wanting from the book has been attributed to action by relatives of the ladies concerned trying to protect the family honour. Who painted these miniatures is not known; they have been ascribed variously to Philippe Caresme, Marolles and Chardin among others. But whoever it was, Mr G. Legman in *The Horn Book* (p. 107) writes that the artist concealed himself behind a screen in the tax collector's bedroom and sketched the action therein from life. True or not, this is a good story, although in questionable taste; nowadays, as Mr Legman has pointed out elsewhere I believe, these things are more conveniently accomplished with Polaroid cameras.

Because of its uniqueness, the history of *Tableaux des mœurs du temps* after the death of La Poupelinière is rather like a roll-call of some of the most celebrated

TABLEAUX

DES

MŒURS DU TEMP

DANS LES DIFFÉRENTS AGES DE LA VIE

A AMSTERDAM

The first reprint of Crebillon's *Tableaux des mœurs du temps,* published at Brussels about 1863, possibly by Jules Gay. The original edition appeared as a single copy, privately printed, *c.* 1750–60

book collectors of the past two hundred years or so. It was first in the possession of Louis XV, who had confiscated it, and then passed through the cabinets of the Duc de la Vallière, the Marquis de Paulmy and the Russian prince Michel Galitzin. In 1844 it crops up in the catalogue of the library of J[ules] G[allois] when it was sold for 5000 francs to Baron Jérôme Pichon. It then belonged to the sadistic English bibliophile Frederick Hankey, who was resident at Paris, and from him it passed into the *Grenier* of Charles Cousin and was sold in 1891 for over 20,000 francs. For a short while it is supposed to have been in the collection of Henri Bordes and about 1912 was bought by Louis Deglatigny of Rouen. It was sold to an unnamed collector in Normandy in June 1937, and the book last surfaced in the 1970s when it changed hands yet again for a reported 30,000 dollars.

The first reprint was published secretly at Brussels in 1863 by Jules Gay, who presumably borrowed the original from either Jérôme Pichon or Frederick Hankey for the job. It was limited to just 150 copies. About two years later, Gay published another edition and in 1867 Auguste Poulet-Malassis published an edition with twelve plates by Félicien Rops that was prosecuted successfully the following year. Such is the notoriety of the book that the most recent reprint that I am aware of, published at Paris in 1959 by the *Cercle du Livre Précieux* [Claude Tchou], felt obliged to omit the few 'indecent' passages, incorporating them instead at the conclusion of the text in a section all to themselves where they appeared in Greek.

As a novel, *Tableaux des mœurs du temps* is constructed in the form of a series of seventeen dialogues that deal with the adventures of a young girl named Thérèse who is first encountered getting up to some very unecclesiastical games in a convent. Later she undergoes an arranged marriage set up for her by her mother, and the remainder of the book concerns the love affairs of the various characters. Coming as it does from the pen of Crébillon *fils*, the dialogues are not without charm, wit and force as might be expected; but it is not one of his happiest productions and in truth if it were not for its colourful history – on which all accounts of it concentrate – it would have little to recommend it over the many other *galante* novels of the period.

Restif de la Bretonne's *L'Anti-Justine*, on the other hand, is an erotic novel cast in the epic tradition, or at least in a potentially epic one since the author was unable to finish it. In an epilogue to the first part of the book, Restif writes: '*L'Anti-Justine* will have in all five, six or seven parts like the one preceding.' Since in the first edition the number of pages in part one runs to 204, the complete work would have been somewhere in the region of 1400 pages in length. Unfortunately – or fortunately, depending on one's point of view I imagine – only two parts were printed, the second incompletely since it ends abruptly with the words 'Je sors; elle...' ('I went; she...'). 'Helpey' [i.e. Louis Perceau], in a bibliographical note that he wrote for a clandestine reprint of *L'Anti-Justine* published at Paris about 1930 by Maurice Duflou, proposes that in fact Restif had written the whole of the work but that the activities of the police prevented him from finishing the printing, which he did himself. By 1803, when the book was officially suppressed, it was already scarce and when in the same year the First Consul, Napoleon, ordered all copies found in the brothels and bookshops to be confiscated and destroyed, it rapidly became one of the rarest of all erotic books.

Until recently, the whereabouts of just four copies of the first edition of *L'Anti-Justine* were known for certain, all in the *Enfer* of the Bibliothèque Nationale, Paris. One of these is unique and appears to be the copy Restif himself was working on in the print shop. It contains three illustrations, two of which are original designs of extreme obscenity and the other a perfectly respectable engraving by Louis Binet, together with tissue-protected blank leaves intended for further plates, proof pages corrected by Restif himself, and a manuscript note on the history of the work.

A fifth copy, however, has long been rumoured to exist. As with *Tableaux des mœurs du temps*, this fabled volume may be traced almost from its inception on Restif's printing press by a succession of celebrated collector-owners, starting with Armand Cigongne, then the Duc d'Aumale and finally to Frederick Hankey, who died in 1882. What happened to the book after that is not clear. A note in the Apollinaire/Fleuret/Perceau catalogue of the *Enfer* (1919; no. 492) says that it was in the United States. This tends to substantiate the suggestion that it was purchased by the elder J. P. Morgan and stayed for a while in America until it was shipped back to France along with his other erotica for resale by descendants of the old boy who failed to share all his tastes in literature. But what actually happened to the book after Hankey's death will probably never be discovered.

What is certain, however, is that for over twenty years this mythical fifth copy of *L'Anti-Justine*, in a superb binding and two cases, has been lying quietly on a shelf in the library of Cambridge University where the present author and a colleague, Mr Peter Mendes, discovered it purely by chance one morning in the autumn of 1981. The entry for it in the catalogue is brief, giving just the short title and the date 1798, and at first we both thought that it might be a reprint, but curiosity got the better of us and we called for it, and there, to our amazement, it was. Carrying the bookplate of Louis Colville Clarke, it was bequeathed to Cambridge University Library in December 1960. The pressmark is *Arc. d. 79. 14.*

Most authorities state that reprints of *L'Anti-Justine* began to appear in 1863, when a manuscript copy of the work formed the basis of an extremely poor edition printed at Brussels. In 1864, the first reprint to conform with the original printed edition was published also at Brussels by Poulet-Malassis after, it is assumed, the copy containing the corrected proofs and illustrations, mentioned above, which did not reach the Bibliothèque Nationale until after 1860, in which year it was still in the library of the Comte de La Bedoyère, its last known private owner. All subsequent editions stem from this.[21]

In English, the work first appears as *The Double Life of Cuthbert Cockerton*. It was published at Paris in 1895, probably by Charles Carrington. The only known copy of this is in the library of the Kinsey Institute for Sex Research attached to the University of Indiana. *The Double Life* is more of an adaptation than a translation, since the story has been updated, the characters made English and the action

relocated to, of all places, Sheffield. The translator is unknown; Mr G. Legman
has proposed the mysterious John Stephen Farmer (1854–1916), an occultist who
later became interested in erotic folklore and lexicography, but the location of
the story to Sheffield might just point a finger in the direction of Leonard Smithers,
a solicitor and something of a linguist, who with a shady individual named H. S.
Nichols came to London from Sheffield and they worked together on many publishing and bookselling ventures that were dubious to say the least. A much more
correct English version was translated by 'Pieralessandro Casavini' (Austryn
Wainhouse) and published at Paris in 1955 by the Olympia Press as *Pleasures and
Follies of a Good-Natured Libertine*. A German translation, by 'Dr Martin Isenbiel'
[Richard Fiedler], was published privately in 1905.

Restif's declared purpose in writing *L'Anti-Justine*, as his title implies, was to
counteract the influence of the works of his enemy the Marquis de Sade. 'No
one has been more incensed than I', he writes in the Preface, 'by the foul performances of the infamous Marquis de Sade – I refer to his *Justine*, to *Aline* [*et
Valcour*], to *la* [*Philosophie dans le*] *Boudoir, la Théorie du libertinage*, which I read
while languishing in prison . . . my design is to write a book, sweeter to the taste
than any of Sade's, and which wives who would be better served will bring to the
notice of their undiligent husbands.'[22]

For the most part this design is carried out, yet it is still one of the most outrageously pornographic works ever written. Its main theme is that of incest,
which it carries to astounding lengths, and readers of Restif's other, more respectable, novels will not be surprised to learn that there is a great deal of shoe fetishism
as well, these peculiarities always having featured in his writings, although never
so openly. Like Henry Miller's, Restif's books are largely autobiographical and
realistic – he was called by his contemporaries 'the Rousseau of the gutter' among
other things – and these characteristics are not absent from *L'Anti-Justine* either,
despite the sexual extremism and fantasy. As 'Cupidonnet', for example, he
plays the central role in the book himself. His sisters Beaucousin and Geneviève
figure as 'Beauconin' and 'Jenovefette', while his hated son-in-law Charles-Marie
Augé, who is vilified in one of Restif's earlier novels, *Ingénue Saxancour* (1789),
is really given a bad press in *L'Anti-Justine* where, first as 'Vitnègre' and later as
'Guaé', he is portrayed as a most appalling beast.

For all Restif's good intentions, however, the horrors that he associates with
Sade manage to creep in, and nowhere stronger than in chapter fifteen which is
entitled, ominously, 'Concerning a fucker à la Justine'. In the space of barely five
pages just about every perversion imaginable is crammed together, including
necrophilia and cannibalism. Even being charitable and supposing that Restif
intended a parody or burlesque of Sade, it fails; he does not have the conviction
to make it truly 'sadistic' and neither has he the temperament that made Apollinaire's novel *Les onze mille verges* (1907) such a rollicking satire. It winds up
being merely rather horrible, and Mr Legman tells an understandable tale about
a collector who enjoyed having his mistress read to him from *L'Anti-Justine* as a
sort of aphrodisiac, but who carefully taped up the pages of chapter fifteen so

that she might not see them. (See *The Horn Book*, p. 114.) Other Sadeian influences appear in the book too, and with equal lack of success. In chapter forty-five, Vitnègre's wife recites an obscene prayer which in its extremes of blasphemy and cynicism easily matches the adaptation of Piron's *Ode à Priapus* that Sade composed and included in volume eight of his *La Nouvelle Justine* (1797). Sade's piece though reads like it means business, whereas there is a feeling of half-heartedness, childishness almost, about Restif's offering. Reading *L'Anti-Justine* it is impossible not to wish that he had kept to incest and shoe fetishism; at least he was on home ground with those two.

One other obscene publication has been ascribed to Restif, although on extremely flimsy evidence. This is *Dom Bougre aux États Généraux, ou Doléances du Portier des Chartreux*, a pamphlet of sixteen pages that was published in 1789. It was one of three pamphlets that his son-in-law Augé accused him of writing to the authorities. Augé's charges concerning the other pamphlets, which were political and not obscene, were later withdrawn, but the charge that Restif was the author of *Dom Bougre* he stoutly maintained. The paternity of the pamphlet is given on the titlepage as being by the author of *La Foutromanie*, an obscene poem in six 'chants' or cantos that was originally published in 1778. The poem has generally been attributed to Gabriel Sénec de Meilhan (1736–1803), with whom Restif seems to have been acquainted. On the slightly irrelevant grounds that *L'Anti-Justine* is ascribed on the titlepage to a lawyer named Linguet against whom Restif had a grudge, the authors of the *Enfer* (1919; no. 631) argue that Restif must also have written *Dom Bougre*, since that is credited to someone other than him as well. A further proof they muster in support of their claim is that on page eight of *Dom Bougre* there is a favourable mention of one of a series of books that Restif wrote on themes of social reform. The work referred to is *Le Pornographe* (1769) in which details are given of a grand scheme to institutionalize brothels, so that they run on a more humane, healthy and discreet basis.

It seems extremely unlikely, however, that Restif did write *Dom Bougre*. The attribution is dismissed by both C. R. Dawes and A. Tabarant in their biographies of him, and in the standard bibliography of Restif, written by J. Rives Childs, it is not dealt with except in passing reference. It seems more probable that it is merely another of the very many anonymous, obscene pamphlets that circulated in France before and during the Revolution. Some, like *Bordel National sous les auspices de la reine* (1790) and *Fureurs utérines de Marie-Antoinette* (1790), had clearly defined targets; others, like *Dom Bougre*, were less specific. But they all helped shape the Revolution and the directions it took.

*　　*　　*　　*　　*

As the 18th century drew to a close, there emerged a writer who, moulded by the experiences of both revolution and imprisonment and driven by some unique inner fire, was to influence profoundly the thinking of the generations that came after him and created in those generations almost as much passion and controversy

OPPOSITE Plate from a typical illustrated pamphlet attacking the Queen issued at the time of the French Revolution. Possibly re-drawn

BELOW Titlepage of plate illustrated opposite

FUREURS UTÉRINES
DE
MARIE ANTOINETTI
FEMME DE LOUIS XVI.

*La mère en proscrira la lectu
à sa fille.*

AUX THUILERIES,
Et dans tous les Bordels de Par

1790.

OPPOSITE A further plate from the pamphlet attacking the Queen. See pages 90 and 91

as a major political or religious figure. This is not a trivial or ill-conceived analogy either, for the writer was Donatien Alphonse François, Marquis (actually Comte) de Sade (1740–1814). Apart from imaginary or allegorical portraits by such artists as Man Ray, H. Biberstein, Clovis Trouille and Beresford Egan – or deliberately denigrating ones such as the illustration to Restif de la Bretonne's *Les Contemporaines* by Louis Binet entitled '*L'Atroce extase*' – there is no record of what Sade actually looked like, other than for brief descriptions in police files and the testimony of one or two people like Charles Nodier and Ange Pitou who met him in later life.[23] Curiously, this anonymity makes the man more of an enigma; even with an indifferent likeness of someone it is possible to divine something of their character and temperament, but with Sade there is only the evidence of his own books and the opinion of critics, psychologists and other founts of knowledge, some of whom may actually have read them.

The limitations of a book of this sort preclude a detailed examination of someone as complex and paradoxical as Sade. Between the extremes of Jules Janin, who in a memorable article in the *Revue de Paris* (1834, pp. 321–60) declared that Sade's books had murdered more children than twenty Maréchaux de Retz could and that his readership was recruited from madhouses and prisons, and the uncritical adulation of some of the early Surrealists, there has to be some midpoint where he can be looked at coolly and without prejudice. Unfortunately, that mid-point must be elsewhere. Although the critical and biographical literature on Sade is immense, Gilbert Lély's *Vie du marquis de Sade* (Paris, 1952–7, 2 vols) and Lorna Berman's monumental and apparently privately printed *The Thought and Themes of the Marquis de Sade* (Ontario, 1971) – dedicated 'only to those who seek to understand' – provide the most thorough keys to his life and work we have to date. Mention should also be made, however, of C. R. Dawes's biography of Sade and Guy Endore's *Satan's Saint* (1965). Dawes's book, published at London in 1927, was the first serious attempt by an English writer to deal at length with a difficult subject, and until Lorna Berman's book appeared almost fifty years later it was the only source of detailed plots and analysis of Sade's work in the English language. *Satan's Saint* is a strange book, part novel and part biography, that combines genuine documents and fictitious ones in such a way that reality and fantasy merge uneasily together. Despite these devices, however, Guy Endore provides a warts-and-all portrait of Sade that nevertheless displays an understanding and sympathy for the subject. For the purpose of the present work, however, a short account of his clandestine writings and the circumstances of their composition and publication will have to suffice.[24]

Sade's most famous book of all is the novel *Justine, ou les Malheurs de la vertu*, first published 'En Hollande' – actually at Paris by J.-V. Girouard – in 1791. But this was really the second of three distinct versions of the work, the first having been written in 1787. During June and July of that year, while a prisoner in the Bastille, he completed the manuscript of a short philosophical story called *Les Infortunes de la vertu*, which he intended to include in an anthology of his short pieces entitled *Contes et fabliaux du XVIIIe siècle*. The following year he abandoned

JUSTINE,

O U

LES MALHEURS

DE LA VERTU.

O mon ami ! la prospérité du Crime est comme la foudre, dont
les feux trompeurs n'embélissent un instant l'atmosphère, que
pour précipiter dans les abîmes de la mort, le malheureux qu'ils
ont ébloui.

EN HOLLANDE,
Chez les Libraires Affociés.

1791.

this plan. Instead he worked the story into the novel that was to appear in 1791 as *Justine*.[25]

'They are printing a novel of mine,' wrote Sade to his lawyer Reinaud in June 1791, 'but it is too immoral to be sent to you, a pious and decent man. My publisher wanted it *well peppered*, I was short of cash, so I wrote it fit to corrupt the Devil. It is called *Justine, ou les Malheurs de la vertu*. If it by chance falls into your hands, burn it rather than read it. I disown it.'[26] If Sade was concerned at the effect that the 1791 *Justine* might have on the 'pious and decent' Reinaud, it did not prevent him from reworking the book a third time, for in 1797 appeared, possibly from the publisher Nicolas Massé, the final and definitive version which was called *La Nouvelle Justine*. In ten volumes, this monstrous work tells the story

ABOVE Titlepage of the first edition of Sade's *Justine*. See colour plate opposite page 81

94

first of Justine (vols 1–4) and then of her sister Juliette (vols 5–10). It is illustrated with a frontispiece and 100 unsigned engravings, almost all of which are obscene and usually missing when the book crops up at auction or in booksellers' catalogues. It has been said of Sade that he was not a particularly good writer and that he had trouble with plots. If he were a novelist in the conventional sense, even one who wrote pornography, then criticism of that sort would be justified, but he was not a conventional novelist and one might just as well level the charge of poor writing and bad plot development at Karl Marx or Wilhelm Reich. The point with Sade is that he was more interested in content than form; ideas were what fascinated him and if he is to be criticized it is his philosophical theories that should be looked at, not the framework upon which they are hung. He did not invent philosophy, nor was he the first man to question the world in which he lived, but he did throw himself headlong into areas of inquiry that had seldom, if ever, been looked into before. His ideas on property, for example, or the supremacy of the individual brilliantly anticipated the anarchists P.-J. Proudhon and Max Stirner, while in his approach to sexual matters he demonstrated an understanding of psychology and analysis that was a century ahead of his time. This does not excuse the horrors of some of his books, of course, but it does go some of the way to reconcile the apparent contradiction between the orgies and depravities and what are generally considered to be 'the boring bits'; Sade had the ability to question and wonder, but he had no way in which to do so scientifically or to apply practically what theories he devised. For one thing such methods had not been devised yet, and for another much of his life was spent either in prison or asylums. He was rather like a man who has invented a light bulb before electricity has been harnessed. In a sense, then, his books were an attempt to prove his ideas in a way that was both empirical and theoretical at the same time. He had an idea, for instance, that there might be a connection between crime and sexuality, so in *La Nouvelle Justine* the character Dorval delivers a long and far from uninteresting exposition on the subject of crime and its relationship with lasciviousness, and later in the same book Noirceuil declares that 'crime is the soul of lust'. It seems as though Sade, with neither freedom nor a thorough scientific tradition to make use of, deliberately makes his characters do disgusting things in order that the survivors can sit around and discuss it afterwards.

La Nouvelle Justine presents two sides of a coin, and one of Sade's major themes: that of vice and virtue, the former rewarded and the latter persecuted. This cynical but far from unreasonable view of life is illustrated through the lives of the two sisters who, choosing different paths, suffer or profit accordingly. Justine determines on a life of goodness and purity, and the outline of her story is hardly different from the original 'draft' of 1787 and the first published version of 1791, but in the edition of 1797 the whole thing is enormously expanded by the insertion of new characters and incidents, and greatly enlarged philosophical discussions or monologues. Some of the new characters tell their stories in great detail, in one instance at such length that it was published separately at Paris in 1936 as *Histoire de Jérôme*. But throughout it is Justine who is the central figure, and despite her commitment to piety and decency, all is not beer and skittles for her. She suffers appallingly at the hands of a whole series of ever more dreadful villains and lunatics, including Bressac, a shameless pederast who regales her with an extended and vitriolic critique of the Bible, and the infamous Rodin who, when he is not flagellating and otherwise abusing the children in his care – he runs a school in partnership with his equally repellent sister Celestine – potters about indulging in his hobby of amateur-status surgery. At the conclusion of volume four of *La Nouvelle Justine*, a chance encounter reunites the two sisters once more and Juliette is prevailed upon to tell her story.

Juliette, while still in the convent with Justine where we first met them at the beginning of the book, falls under the influence of the abbess, Madame Delbène, who initiates her into the mysteries of debauchery and instils into her a philosophy based entirely on the precepts of crime and ruthlessness. Armed with these edifying principles and a thorough grounding in depravity, she embarks on the road to fame and fortune. Juliette participates with joy and fervour in the sorts of schemes her sister tried so desperately to avoid, with the result that she grows rich and powerful. The one hiatus in her life of enormity occurs when the minister of state Saint-Fond, who is obsessed with a hatred of mankind in general, except for Noirceuil and one or two other maniacs of his stripe who are central to the book, confides to her a plan he has conceived to starve two-thirds of the population of France to death. This is too much even for Juliette. A brief expression of horror on her face causes Saint-Fond to fly into a rage and order her death. At Noirceuil's prompting, she flees to Angers where she marries a respectable man named Lorsange and assumes the role of devoted wife and mother. For two years she puts up with this until, bored to tears and concerned at reports that Saint-Fond is still after her, she poisons her husband, leaves her child in the care of a cleric and travels to Italy in the company of a maid and a flunkey. Here she resumes her life of dissipation and crime, meeting the King of Sardinia, Pope Pius VI – who delivers a lecture on torture, holds orgies and satanic rituals in St Peter's, and who is robbed by Juliette – and King Ferdinand I of Naples.

After many incidents, she learns that Saint-Fond has been murdered and that France is now safe for her. In company with Noirceuil and other of her cronies who, like herself, have grown enormously wealthy through robbery and other iniquities, she returns once more to her château and there, as at the beginning of her story, she meets Justine. The timidity and purity of the girl finds scant favour with Juliette or Noirceuil – whose cruelty may easily be judged by the fact that they have already murdered their own children during the course of their orgies – or with the other three libertines present at this family reunion. Arguments as to what to do with Justine are proposed, but eventually it is Noirceuil who has the final say. ' "My friends," quoth he to the jovial company, "I have often had occasion to remark how instructive it proves in such adventures to tempt fate. A mighty storm is brewing, let's expose this creature to the thunderbolts and lightning; if she escapes unscathed, I'll dedicate the rest of my days to God." ' This idea is enthusiastically accepted by everyone, and Justine is accordingly thrown out into the storm where she is almost at once struck down by lightning and killed. What follows is unpleasant, but in keeping with its general tone.

> Our four libertines crowd round the cadaver; and though horribly disfigured, the knaves can still form gruesome designs upon that very bloodied hulk. They strip off her clothes; our infamous Juliette goads them on. The bolt, entering through the mouth, had departed by way of the vagina; several bawdy jests are cracked concerning the itinerary chosen by heaven's wrath, its entrance and its exit.
>
> 'How wise they are who praise God,' Noirceuil observes. 'You see how fundamentally decent he is; he respected the ass and gave it the go-by. 'Tis still very lovely, this sublime ass, that caused such rivers of fuck to flow in its day; does it not tempt you, Chabert?'
>
> Our wicked Abbé's only reply is to infiltrate up to his bollocks in that lifeless mass. His example is soon followed; all four, one after the other, affront the mortal remains of the wretched girl; our execrable Juliette frigs herself happily as she watches them go about their business. They retire, leaving her where she fell, refusing her even the last rites. Sad, unhappy creature; 'twas written that even in death thou shouldst not be spared man's perversity.[27]

Juliette and the other debauchees, we are told, continue in their evil ways and find success, wealth and power as a result, but this final scene involving the violation of Justine's corpse is the end of the story as presented by Sade. His point has been made, and the challenge to God to choose between good and evil is the ultimate proof of the argument.

Of Sade's other two remaining clandestine works, the most important is *Les 120 Journées de Sodome*. This extraordinary novel was written during 1785, in a period of thirty-seven days commencing 22 October, onto sheets of paper that were pasted together into a roll about twelve metres in length and eleven centimetres wide. Ten days before the Bastille was stormed and destroyed in 1789, Sade was hurriedly evacuated from his cell and moved to Charenton lunatic asylum; in the confusion, the manuscript was apparently left behind and its author never saw it again. It has been suggested, by Gilbert Lély among others, that the famous 'tears of blood' letter written by Sade to the lawyer Gaspard Gaufridy in May 1790 was a reference to his loss of this manuscript in particular and that the enormous novel *Les Journées de Florbelle, ou la Nature devoilée*, destroyed at his death before it was published, was an attempt to rewrite or recreate the original.

But Sade should not have worried. The manuscript was discovered in his cell by Arnoux de Saint Maximin, one of the revolutionaries who took part in the attack on the Bastille, and from him it passed to the Villeneuve-Trans family with whom it remained until about 1900, at which time it found its way into the library of a collector in Germany. In 1929, the great Sade scholar Maurice Heine succeeded in negotiating for its return to France where it now is. It is perhaps interesting to add that the first reliable description of this very remarkable manuscript occurred as early as 1875, in the first volume of Henry Spencer Ashbee's bibliographies.

Shortly after the manuscript reached Germany, a printed edition appeared at Berlin. It was published secretly in 1904 by Max Harrwitz, with the false imprint 'Paris: Club des Bibliophiles', and edited by the psychiatrist Iwan Bloch who employed the pseudonym 'Eugène Dühren'. Being full of mistakes, however, this edition is of little but historical interest and the one that is considered to be the first true and faithful edition appeared at Paris between 1931 and 1935 under the editorship of Heine, the man who had brought the manuscript back to France.

Towards the end of the reign of Louis XIV, the Introduction of *Les 120 Journées de Sodome* tells us, four enormously wealthy degenerates lock themselves away in an isolated château deep in the Black Forest. These four, who have acquired their money through murder and theft and bound their association securely by marrying each others' daughters, are the Duc de Blangis, his brother, who is a bishop, a banker named Durcet and the Président de Curval. Accompanying this quartet, apart from catering staff, cleaners and other domestics, are sundry relatives, sixteen children – eight of either sex – who have been kidnapped from their parents, and eight sodomistic 'fuckers' who rejoice in names such as 'Arse-splitter' and 'Skyscraper'. In addition there are four *servantes* or ladies-in-waiting, and four bawds.

The personnel once listed are described in some detail, and of these portraits Maurice Heine has drawn a comparison with Balzac. The following is the description of the lady-in-waiting named Fanchon:

> ... six times she had been hanged in effigy and not a crime exists in this world she had not committed. She was sixty-nine, she was flat-nosed, short and heavy, she squinted, had almost no forehead, had nothing but two old teeth in her stinking maw, and they were ready to cave in, an erysipelas blazed all over her ass and hemorrhoids the size of your fist hung from her anus, a frightful chancre consumed her vagina and one of her thighs had been entirely burned. She was dead-drunk three-quarters of the year and in that condition, her stomach being very weak, she vomited over everything. Despite the batch of hemorrhoids adorning it, her asshole was by nature so large that all unawares she perpetually blew driblets and farts and often more besides.[28]

The point of this gathering was that each of the bawds would, by monthly rotation, narrate 150 tales of perversion from their personal experience. These tales are segregated into four distinct categories: passions that are designated 'simple', of the 'second class or double', 'criminal', and 'murderous'. Following these narrations, discussion will take place and not infrequently a re-enactment of the perversion in question. In order that things do not get completely out of hand, strict rules are laid down which everyone is obliged to adhere to or otherwise suffer the most dire penalties.

After the preliminaries have been got rid of, the characters introduced and rules and regulations itemized, the action begins with the portentous words: 'And now, friend reader, you must prepare your heart and ready your mind for the most impure tale that has been told since our world was born, a book the likes of which are met with neither amongst the ancients nor amongst us moderns.'[29]

And Sade, not being one for understatement, indeed presents a catalogue of horrors that is quite without parallel, but there is reason to suspect that the book that has come down to us is not wholly complete. The first part, the 'simple' passions, is worked out in considerable detail; there are discussions and digressions, although these are not nearly so frequent or extended as they are in *La Nouvelle Justine*, and time is taken off from the business at hand for such mundane activities as coffee breaks, afternoon naps and the odd mutilation that has been occasioned by trifling infringements of the by-laws. Parts two, three and four, on the contrary, become progressively more fragmented until by the end of the book the passions are little more than short-hand notes, hints at what might have been perhaps, with passages like: '137. A notorious sodomist, in order to combine that crime with those of incest, murder, rape, sacrilege and adultery, has himself embuggered by his own son, a host in his ass, rapes his married daughter, and kills his niece.'[30]

The survivors of these orgies and massacres return home and the reader is left to ponder on the point of it all. It is of course extremely difficult to fathom the mind of someone like Sade, but it is evident that whether or not the book is complete as it stands, in no way can it be described as erotic or pornographic; what was his intended audience if it were? There are far too many aberrations to make it a satisfying read for any one individual, something which likewise rules out the possibility that Sade wrote it for his own amusement while languishing in durance vile. The most obvious solution, and the one most generally accepted, is that *Les 120 Journées de Sodome* is an attempt systematically to itemize all known sexual deviations. Given that there was no real precedent for this sort of venture it lacks the scientific approach that research like this would employ today, and yet for all its lack of sophistication it is a remarkable precursor of Richard von Krafft-Ebing's *Psychopathia Sexualis*, which first appeared almost exactly 100 years after Sade had put the final flourish to his own compendium of perversity.

The third and final work of Sade's requiring examination is *La Philosophie dans le boudoir* (À Londres [Paris]: aux dépens de la compagnie, 1795). It is the shortest of his clandestine texts, and in a feeble attempt at throwing the authorities off his trail he added as a sort of subtitle to the book that it was a posthumous work by the author of *Justine*. There is an opening address directed 'To Libertines', after which are a series of seven dialogues in which is traced the gradual sexual initiation and corruption of a pretty 15-year-old girl named Eugénie de Mistival at the hands of a group of debauchees. Some of the advice or tuition given to Eugénie is, for Sade, remarkably light in tone, as when Madame de Saint-Ange explains to her the purpose of the testicles: 'The technical word is *genitals, male genitals ... testicles* belongs to art, the *balls* contain the reservoir of this abundant semen I have just mentioned and which, ejaculated into the woman's *matrix*, or *womb*, produces the human species – but we will not place emphasis upon these details, Eugénie, for they relate more to medicine than to libertinage. A pretty girl ought simply to concern herself with fucking, and not at all with engendering.' And on the matter of the act of sodomy: '... it is a pleasure incontestably preferable to all those procured by introduction of this member into the cunt. And, besides, how many dangers does not a woman avoid! Less risk to her health, and none at all of pregnancy.'[31]

This rather jolly approach does not last, however, and although *La Philosophie dans le boudoir* is the least cruel of his clandestine books, there is a dreadful episode in the final dialogue in which Madame de Mistival, who has popped in to see what her daughter is getting up to, is raped by a servant who suffers from a particularly virulent strain of syphilis, has her anus and vagina sewn up and is kicked out into the street. Although unpleasant, this scene is psychologically interesting for the character of Madame de Mistival has been interpreted as representing Sade's mother-in-law Madame de Montreuil, whom he loathed. Other characters in the narrative are thought to represent real people too: the cynical libertine Dolmancé, Sade himself, and Eugénie his sister-in-law Louise, whom he loved far more than his wife. The fact that Sade conceived the notion of fictionalizing his 'sister-in-law' happily being a party to the infibulation and infection of his 'mother-in-law' may have something to say concerning his attitudes.

One of the most absorbing parts of *La Philosophie dans le boudoir* is the fifth dialogue in which Dolmancé reads aloud a pamphlet that he has purchased on the street. Entitled *Yet Another Effort, Frenchmen, if you would become Republicans*, it contains a good abstract of Sade's ideas on such subjects as religion, morality and the nature of political power and the state. These ideas are curiously contradictory, to each other within the 'pamphlet' and to similar ideas expressed elsewhere in his writings. Yet they also serve to explode the popular conception of Sade as a monster. All thinkers are prone to contradiction and weakness, even those fortunate enough to be able to do their thinking in comfortable surroundings. Sade was doubly unfortunate; he usually had extremely uncomfortable surroundings, and was ahead of his time. But in an admittedly clumsy and ill-conceived way, which won him few friends then or now, he tried to explore the darker recesses of man's heart and mind, and challenged many of the accepted conventions of his day at times when it was far from safe to do so: as when, during one of his rare tastes of liberty, he opposed the excesses of the Revolution and was accused of 'moderatism'. It is tempting to think that the 20th century would have been more tolerant of his ideas and allowed him the freedom and understanding to develop them along more rational lines. But then one recalls another and recent sexual radical, Wilhelm Reich. He died a victim of state repression and ignorance as well.

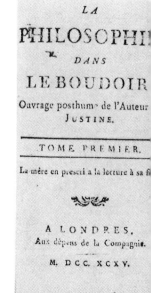

Titlepage of the first edition of Sade's *La Philosophie dans le boudoir*. See frontispiece

CHAPTER THREE

THE 19ᵀᴴ CENTURY

BESPOKE HACKERY

Then the right trusty Master
Went at him like mad,
And loud were the prayers
And shrieks of the lad,
Said Arthur, 'You coward!'
Said Redgie, 'Keep cool!'
Your bottom's a credit
To Whippingham School!

A. C. Swinburne *Frank Fane – A Ballad*

If erotica were to be considered in geographical terms, its atlas would resemble closely those political maps so favoured by history teachers at one time. The red bits though, instead of being the British Empire, would represent where the centres of the pornographic book trade lay at any given time. Police activity and fear of imprisonment being convincing arguments in favour of a nomadic mode of existence, publishers moved from one country to another, always on the look-out for a safe haven with a convenient printer attached. Thus Jules Gay, for example, who began his career in erotica publishing during the early 1860s after being earlier associated in England with the social reformer Robert Owen, was pursued by the authorities through half the countries of Europe – which says a great deal for his stamina and dedication if nothing else. Later in the century most publishers seemed obliged to perambulate between Paris, Brussels or Amsterdam.

But all this frantic rushing about did not really get under way until well into the second half of the century, for in an interesting parallel with the preceding century there was a distinct decline in the volume of erotica published, even in France where the years 1775–1800 had been so fruitful. Louis Perceau in his *Bibliographie du roman érotique* (1930), the standard work on 19th-century erotic French prose, lists only twenty-six separate and original works in the period 1800–50, whereas in the following fifty years he records almost seven times that number. This does not take into account reprints of earlier works, collections of verse and so forth, but accepting Perceau's figures for prose material as a relative comparison it will be seen that there is an almost precise dividing line between the two halves of the century.

If France showed signs of backsliding, however, the situation seemed to be improving elsewhere. Germany, which had not been a country noted for a prolific erotic literature of its own – although pornography in other languages was often printed there and German translations of foreign 'classics' were quickly produced – did not turn out what may be considered its own first 'classic' until the late 18th century. This was *Denkwürdigkeiten des Herrn von H.* ('Rom' [Berlin or Hamburg], 1787), which has been ascribed to Friedrich Gustav Schilling (1766–1839) and reprinted many times, most recently in 1981 by Wilhelm Goldmann Verlag, Munich, in the enterprising 'Erotikon' series. The first edition is of extreme rarity, the only copy known to me being in the State Library, Vienna, as is noted in *Hayn/Gotendorf* (vol. 2, p. 29). The British Library has two late reprints from the 1860s or thereabouts, one published possibly at Altona, a suburb of Hamburg, and the other at Stuttgart.

Denkwürdigkeiten des Herrn von H. is a conventional erotic novel, very similar to the sort of thing that was appearing in France at about the same time. It concerns a young man named Karl, conceived in bastardy by a profligate but kindly nobleman and a '*schüchternes Barbiermädchen*' (a 'shy barber's daughter'). Karl is raised and educated by the nobleman, who has taken a more than usual interest in one of his offspring. His amorous adventures, following an early glimpse of his aristocratic father being profligate with yet another of the local girls, are recounted in great detail, although generally without recourse to obscenity.

Another important German work, which appeared early in the 19th century, was *Schwester Monika* ('Kos und Loretto' [Poznań or Leipzig?], 1815). The authorship of this is generally considered to be the handiwork of Ernst Theodor Amadeus (actually Wilhelm) Hoffmann (1776–1822), the romantic writer whose stories inspired Offenbach to compose *Les Contes d'Hoffmann*. Unlike Schilling's book, *Schwester Monika* remained practically unknown for almost a hundred years until 1910 when it was reprinted for the first time, at Vienna in a privately printed edition of 800 copies. This reprint, which was published by Dr Rudolf Ludwig for the great Viennese collector Gustav Gugitz, contained a long preface by the latter in which the first serious attempt was made to examine the bibliographical history of the original edition and, perhaps more to the point, whether or not Hoffmann was really the author of it. Gugitz was vigorously challenged on his views by several of the more conservative authorities on Hoffmann, in particular Hans von Müller, who seems to have become extremely agitated by the whole business, but although Gugitz's arguments were not completely satisfying they carried greater force than the more emotional objections of his opponents. In 1965, Gala Verlag of Hamburg published a reprint of the 1910 edition and included a most interesting Postface by the eminent scholar Dr Rudolf Frank who, in 1924, had edited an eleven-volume *œuvres complètes* of Hoffmann. Frank's approach to the question of authorship was considerably more thorough than Gugitz's had been. Being familiar with Hoffmann's work, he was able to draw stylistic comparisons between his established canon and the disputed *Schwester Monika*. His conclusions were the same as Gugitz's fifty-five years earlier, but to confirm them he was able to relate an interesting story.

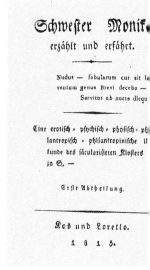

The rare first edition of E.T.A Hoffmann's *Schwester Monika*

It seems that on some unspecified date in the 1920s, Frank's sister Hildegard found herself sitting next to a Dr Ernst August Hauser at a dinner given by the S.A. Metallgesellschaft. For some reason, Hildegard Frank got talking to Hauser about Hoffmann, and about *Schwester Monika*. To her surprise, Hauser announced that he had the original manuscript of the novel which, he said, was a sort of family heirloom belonging to his wife, Susi. Susi's maiden name was Devrient, and she was a descendant of the actor Ludwig Devrient (1784–1832) who had been on good terms with Hoffmann and his circle of friends in Berlin, and participated in their drunken all-night get-togethers there in the Lutter & Wegener tavern. Manuscripts that had been written and read at these gatherings were apparently collected by Devrient and eventually they found their way into Susi Devrient's possession.

At the earliest opportunity, Hildegard told her brother of this and together with Wilhelm Jaspert, a director of the Reimar Hobbing publishing company, he went to Hauser's home at Munich to investigate the story. Hauser was extremely hospitable, and produced from a cupboard not only the original manuscript of *Schwester Monika* but other papers besides, manuscripts, drawings, caricatures, notes, and all unmistakably in the autograph of E. T. A. Hoffmann.

Jaspert conceived the idea of publishing these manuscripts, and of giving the task of editing them to Rudolf Frank. Unfortunately, before anything could be done Jaspert was murdered by the fascists and Hauser, under a cloud in 1927 as a suspect for the murder of his wife, was eventually cleared and left Germany for the United States, where he pursued a successful academic career until his death in 1956. His house in Munich was destroyed in an air raid during the war, and the Hoffmann manuscripts have never been seen again.[1]

Schwester Monika is very much a book of the 18th century, and as such is a little out of step with the direction that erotica elsewhere in Europe was taking. It combines the familiar libertine trappings of eroticism, philosophical digression and anti-clericalism – Sister Monika is of course a nun – and throughout the text there occur erudite notes and references to mythology, contemporary books and authors. Although a brief work – barely 140 pages in the edition published at Munich by Wilhelm Heyne Verlag in 1980 – and out of the mainstream of other erotica of its time, it nevertheless commands an important position in the development of the genre in Germany.

* * * * *

In England, after the excitement of Cleland's *Memoirs of a Woman of Pleasure* and Wilkes's *An Essay on Woman* had died down, there was a period of relative calm until the early years of the 19th century when there began a whole series of successful prosecutions for what had become known as 'obscene libel'. Isaac Aldrich (for *The New Rambler's Magazine* in 1801), Edward Rich and John Duncombe were all found guilty and received terms of imprisonment. One of the most colourful of these characters, however, was a former lawyer's clerk named

George Cannon who pursued a career in erotica publishing that spanned almost forty years, from about 1815 until his death in 1854, after which his widow carried on the business for a further ten years or so until she too died, killed in a fire about 1864.

One of Cannon's last books was *The Adventures of Sir Henry Loveall* (1853), a reprint of a work entitled *The Voluptuarian Museum* that Edward Rich had been prosecuted for in 1806, but his most peculiar venture was a French-language edition of Sade's *Juliette, ou les Prospérités du vice*, for which he was tried in 1830. The sort of market that such a publication was aimed at is hard to imagine; was it printed in England at the expense of a French publisher for foreign distribution? Or were there enough scholarly Englishmen with minds like sewers to justify the gamble? Whichever it was, the most interesting aspect of the case is that the prosecution was obliged to translate some passages of the book into English for the benefit of the jury, and these are preserved in the records of the trial kept at the Public Records Office in London. One such passage is extracted from the second volume of *Juliette*:

The Girl of Eighteen Years placed herself on her knees before her; Clairwill rested her Cunt upon her face, rubbing with all her might the lips of her vagina and her Clitoris on the Nose, the Mouth and the Eyes of that Girl to whom she enjoined to lick it. One Girl posted on the right, the other on the left, flogged vigorously my Friend who, holding a handful of Rods in each Hand, avenged herself on the two Bottoms for the Lashes she received. [Hoisted?] upon the head of the one who was licking the Cunt, I presented her [*Clairwill*] mine to be sucked; on this the whore spent, but with Cries, convulsions and blasphemies which characterized one of the deliriums the most lecherous and the most luxurious which I had ever observed in my days. The pretty face against which the Tribade (*meaning and intending thereby a woman polluting another woman*) had been working was inundated with Sperm. 'Come sacred God, let us do something else,' she cried out, without giving herself time for breathing. 'I never rest whilst my Sperm is in train to flow; work me, whores, shake me, suck me, whip me, frig me in the hardest manner.' The Girl of Eighteen Years lays herself down on the Ottoman. I set myself upon her face, Clairwill clasps her [*self?*] upon mine. I was being sucked; I returned it, raised above me the youngest of the Girls [*and*] offered her Buttocks to kiss to Clairwill, whom another Girl buggered with a Dildoe. The smallest of the four Girls being Cunt frigged with her Fingers the Clitoris of Clairwil[l] almost fixed upon my Mouth and presented during that time her Cunt to the same pollutions exercised by the hand of my Friend. By this means, our Libertine was frigging a Bottom with her Tongue, her Cunt was being sucked, she was being buggered and she was having her Clitoris frigged. (*Public Record Office*, K.B. 28/515/13; with an attempt to do something with the spelling and punctuation.)

The view of the jury on reading these lines is not recorded but it may be imagined since Cannon was gaoled for six months and fined £100. That Sade should enjoy his first appearance in English at the expense of the British government is not an irony to escape Mr Donald Thomas, who discovered the details of

OPPOSITE ABOVE and OPPOSITE BELOW and OVERLEAF LEFT ABOVE Three lithographs from the first edition of *The Pearl*

OVERLEAF LEFT BELOW The frontispiece illustrating *La Grotte Rouge* in *The Erotic Casket Gift Book* for 1882, a supplement to *The Pearl*. 'La Grotte Rouge', wrote Ashbee, 'seems to have been written up to the frontispiece, and is founded on an original idea, albeit as revolting, as it is impossible'

OVERLEAF RIGHT ABOVE Frontispiece to *Le Nouveau Merdiana*

OVERLEAF RIGHT BELOW Frontispiece from the first issue of *The Cremorne*, another erotic Victorian periodical. Although dated '1851' on the masthead, it was actually published in 1882

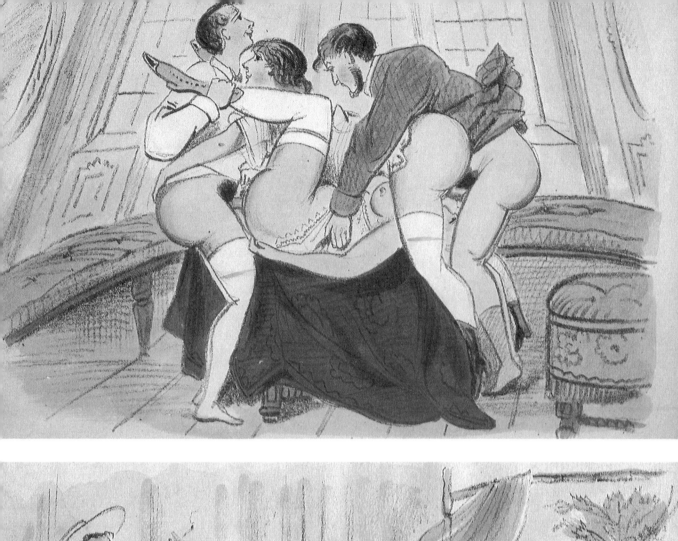

OPPOSITE The frontispiece
to the only known copy of
Edward Sellon's memoirs,
The Ups and Downs of Life

the prosecution during the course of his research for his book *A Long Time Burning*. 'The prosecution', he wrote, '... marks the entry of De Sade into the history of English censorship. This is one of the earliest English references to De Sade and, probably, the earliest of all to *Juliette*. It certainly suggests that his work was better known and more generally available in England during the early nineteenth century than has been supposed.'[2]

Mr Thomas was correct. In the same year that George Cannon was prosecuted for his edition of Juliette, a rival publishers named John Benjamin Brookes (*d.* 1839) brought out *The Inutility of Virtue*, a thoroughgoing imitation of Sade without, however, the philosophical content. This barely literate book, which purports to be a translation from the French, is cast in the form of a letter recounting the experiences of a 23-year-old girl who, like Justine, is constantly frustrated in her efforts to lead a virtuous existence. 'My Dear Friend,' she commences, 'You have often requested me to write the history of my life. I now comply with your request. By it you will see the danger, the virtue of us women is always in, even when we think ourselves the most secure. It also will shew you what man can effect by opportunity alone.'[3] Thoughtfully, she adds the hope that her friend's modesty will not be shocked by what follows.

Our heroine it seems was born of poor parents in Naples, and was 'educated for the Opera'. After numerous attempts on her chastity, including six tries at forcible abduction, she is betrothed to a Count Torso. On her way to be married to this 'noble Roman' she falls into the hands of a gang of brigands led by a man called Caesaro Barto who, after experiencing objections to his advances, delivers an ultimatum: ' "If you do not permit me quietly, I shall proceed to tie you down, then after having enjoyed you, shall turn you over to the rest of the gang, so make up your mind either to submit to my desires, which will make you my mistress alone, or resist and become the common property of all." ' To keep the tension up – we are still only on page twelve – there is further resistance. ' "Let me entreat you not to proceed in your wretched design"; "Yes, you may entreat, but to spare you would be folly ... Come, come, open your things [*sic*]"; and he forcibly stretched them. . .'

Her things safely stretched, the rape is achieved – to the accompaniment of 'impious prayers' of course, this being an imitation of Sade. Pornography being what it is, at least on this level, she afterwards takes a liking to the bandit chief and the way in which he makes her 'contented with my ruin'. Unfortunately, all good things must come to an end. Count Torso, himself captured by another group of the brigand gang, has contrived to escape and arrives with a company of soldiers under the command of a Frenchman named Captain de B***. In the ensuing skirmish, both Torso and Barto are killed and our heroine is carried to safety by the gallant captain with whom she falls in love. The two eventually marry, but after a while their relationship seems strained by boredom and the frequent absences of the captain so a plan is adopted whereby each of them draws up a list of friends or acquaintances whom they can visit or receive as guests. Their social circle immediately widens as they are introduced to friends of friends, but at each new encounter Madame de B*** finds herself inevitably raped or ill-treated in some fashion.

The influence of Sade on *The Inutility of Virtue* is unmistakable, but in another novel of the same period, and one that is far better written, the influence is from another quarter. *The Lustful Turk*, a work in two parts that was first published in 1828 by J. B. Brookes, tells in a series of letters from Emily Barlow to Silvia Carey what befalls the former who, while *en route* to India, is captured by Moorish pirates and given by their captain, an 'English renegade', as a gift to the Dey of Algiers. The long central letter, which occupies most of the first part of the book and the first few pages of the second, concerns the fate of Emily, whose defloration is described in great detail, the life stories of two other occupants of the Dey's harem and an account of what happened to Emily's maid, Eliza Gibbs, who after being captured with her mistress was packed off as a present to the Bey of Tunis. There then follows a brief letter to Emily from Silvia who expresses both dismay and disgust at her friend's 'account of the libidinous scenes acted between you and the beast whose infamous and lustful acts you so particularly describe'. What neither of them know is that the Dey has discovered that Silvia is staying at Toulon and has dispatched agents there to abduct her.

In the meantime there occurs an exchange of letters between a Father Angelo and one Pedro, the Abbot of St Francis, concerning a girl named Julia Mezzia who has been forced to enter an Ursuline convent and take the veil. Julia, having been apprehended in the process of trying to escape, is condemned to be buried alive but help of a sort is at hand in the form of the Abbot who, as luck would have it, possesses a convenient secret passage from his apartments to the underground vaults where recalcitrant nuns are interred. 'Help is nigh,' says the Abbot, 'but let not joy deceive you with hopes that may not be fulfilled, your release from death depends entirely upon your submission to certain terms.' These terms are eventually accepted, and a re-run of the same sort of thing that happened to Emily takes place. Interesting as all this doubtless is, its connection with the rest of the book is not apparent until toward the end of this exchange when it is revealed that these two men of the cloth are in partnership running a white-slave racket to the Dey of Algiers and other North African customers.

The final missive in the book is from Emily to a new character altogether, Maria Williams. In this we learn that Emily is far from happy, being pregnant by the Dey and ignored by him on that account, and depressed by the tone of Silvia's 'unfeeling letter'. A rumour that the Dey has in his clutches another English-woman arouses Emily's curiosity and jealousy – most heroines in pornographic books seem to end up in love with their ravishers – and with the assistance of a friendly eunuch manages to catch the Dey and his new woman in *flagrante delicto*. 'The first object that met my eyes was a naked female half reclining on a table, and the Dey with his noble shaft plunged up to the hilt in her ... Imagine to yourself, dearest Maria, what must have been my emotions on my beholding in his arms my friend Silvia. ...' The shock proves too much for Emily and she faints dead away. On being revived, the Dey tells her at length the story of how he had

Silvia kidnapped from Toulon, brought to Algiers and subjected to the inevitable defloration. The two girls are then united again and for a while are happy to share the embraces of the Dey to whom they have both become attached. Then disaster strikes. A new recruit to the harem, a Greek girl, draws the line at buggery, turns nasty and with a knife she has been hiding cuts of the Dey's penis, after which she commits suicide, With surprising presence of mind under the circumstances, the mutilated potentate calls for a doctor who is ordered to complete the castration, after which the girls are given their freedom, the Dey's testicles pickled in 'spirits of wine in glass vases' and the story draws to a close.[4]

The chief influence at work in *The Lustful Turk* is, of course, in literary terms a romantic one. Since Sade's writings are very much a part of the Gothic tradition, he is a romantic as well; but the difference between his cruelty – or rather the cruelty of his imitators since he is rather a special case – and the cruelty to be found in the pages of *The Lustful Turk* lies in motivation rather than method. The cruelty of *The Inutility of Virtue* is deliberate and calculating, whereas in *The Lustful Turk* it is almost incidental. The mania for deflowering virgins that runs like a thread through English erotica, especially of the Victorian period, is certainly curious but not exactly sadistic. It is probable that some underlying peculiarity of the time, either psychological or social, was the cause of its fascination, and its decline in popularity as a theme in itself among readers of erotica in the 20th century tends to confirm this theory. But the specific influence in *The Lustful Turk* is Byron. This is apparent from the first, when Emily is captured by that most powerful Byronic image, the 'English renegade' corsair. And later, in the sub-narratives that recount the lives of Honoria Grimaldi and Adianti, two of the other girls in the Dey's harem, there are strong Byronic elements, particularly in Adianti's story which in part concerns the excesses of the Turks during their occupation of Greece.

Aside from the interest that the book has in its influences, there is also a stylistic trick or device that is rather attractive; the letters are so arranged that there is sometimes an 'overlap', thus allowing the same incident to be viewed and described by more than one character. While hardly used as effectively here as it was in Tobias Smollett's novel *The Expedition of Humphrey Clinker* (1771), this device does nevertheless give a suggestion of depth to the story; this, together with the 'exceedingly voluptuous' nature of the adventures as Ashbee describes them, has made *The Lustful Turk* one of the most frequently reprinted erotic novels in English.

* * * * *

If the first thirty years of the 19th century were dominated by publishers of the stripe of Cannon and Brookes, the next thirty were the almost exclusive domain of William Dugdale (1800–68). Born at Stockport in Cheshire, he was at the age of 19 involved on the periphery of the Cato Street conspiracy, which was a plot devised by a revolutionary named Arthur Thistlewood, among others, to blow up the government of the day while they were tucking into a cabinet dinner. The plot failed, and its ringleaders were executed.

Dugdale seems to have begun as a publisher of erotica, or semi-erotica, as early as 1827, in which year he issued under his own name *Memoirs of a Man of Pleasure* which was actually a reprint of *The History of the Human Heart*, a sadly neglected picaresque novel of Dutch and English low life that had first appeared almost sixty years earlier in 1769. In 1832, he brought out an edition of Cleland's *Memoirs of a Woman of Pleasure*, illustrated with twenty-five coloured engravings, after which he rather let his standards slip and published little else but badly printed rubbish, in such profusion though, and between so many prison sentences – he ended up dying in prison – that his life takes on a fascination simply by virtue of its complete dedication to filthy literature and its vicissitudes.

His main centre of operations was the maze of narrow alleyways and passages that used to exist in that part of London now occupied by Bush House and its immediate environs at the eastern end of the Strand. Here, in Holywell Street, Russell Court or Wych Street, he would trade under such uninspired aliases as Turner, Smith, Young or Brown. To confuse matters, his younger brother John who was in the same line of business but on a much more modest scale worked from premises in the same area and employed the same aliases. It was partially the activities of these two in the 1850s and '60s that led to Holywell Street being renamed later in the century as Booksellers' Row in a vain attempt to give it some semblance of respectability. In the event, it was the demolition gangs of the Aldwych Development scheme in 1900 that finally exorcized Dugdale's ghost. A vivid and entertaining portrait of a Holywell Street publisher very similar to what Dugdale must have been like – complete with facsimiles of some of his advertising leaflets – will be found between pages 410 and 422 of Michael Sadlier's splendid novel *Forlorn Sunset* (London, 1947); and Donald Thomas tells a good story of Dugdale barricaded in his shop in early September 1851, feverishly burning his more spectacular stock to the background racket of the police and agents of the Society for the Suppression of Vice trying to beat the door down.

Dugdale was a rogue and a pirate, and he would stop at nothing in order to make a quick profit. For as much as two shillings and sixpence – most other publishers charged only sixpence or a shilling for the same sort of thing – it was possible to buy little booklets of bawdy music hall songs with titles like *The Wanton Warbler* or *The Tuzzymuzzy Songster*. For young lads of limited means and less experience, there were wretchedly printed and innocuous pamphlets with lurid titlepages or, if they were lucky, a copy of M. G. Lewis's *The Monk* dressed up in the wrappers of something more salacious but which at least gave them a taste of real literature. Then there were the semi-erotic periodicals such as *The Exquisite* which ran from 1842 until 1844, 145 issues in all which sold for just fourpence each. In its pages could be found woodcut or lithograph portraits of the principal actresses of the day, in classical settings to justify their *déshabille*, and translations of French erotica, memoirs of famous whores, arguments for and against contraception and much else besides.

But all this was the head on the beer; the real stuff lay underneath, and very cloudy it was. Dugdale's main stock-in-trade was the reprint – there being no author to pay – and at this he was the master of trickery and deception. One such reprint was *The Battles of Venus*. This started life as a brief work of thirty-six pages and first appeared, if the titlepage of the original edition is to be believed, in 1760 and was ascribed absurdly to Voltaire. Dugdale reprinted this between 1850 and 1860. His text was slightly altered and occupied sixty-four pages, and offered as 'A handsome pocket volume . . . Price Two Guineas'. A little later he added a few extra flourishes, split the book into two volumes and sold it for three guineas. With *La Rose d'Amour; or, the Adventures of a Gentleman in Search of Pleasure* (1864) the customer happily went on his way thinking that he had a translation of a French work since it said just that on the titlepage; actually it had appeared originally in Philadelphia in 1849.

With his original books, Dugdale behaved a little like his Grub Street predecessors and kept around him where possible a small clique of authors who could be relied on to turn in a publishable manuscript at short notice. One of these was James Campbell Reddie, Ashbee's friend and fellow collector who preferred to be known simply as James Campbell.

Without the advantage of a university education, James Campbell's acquirements were considerable [wrote Ashbee]. He read with ease Latin, French and Italian, and although not familiar with German, few erotic books in that language were unknown to him. So thorough indeed was his knowledge of this particular branch, that hardly an obscene book in any language had escaped his attention. His industry was unflagging. Each book, or different edition, as he acquired it, was at once collated, confronted with every available authority upon it, and compared page by page, word by word with any other procurable issue of the same work. Of very scarce books, which he might not be able to acquire, he frequently made copies with his own hand ... His collection of books was extensive – more extensive than choice, for while he by no means disdained a copy containing extra illustrations, or in an artistic binding, it was the book itself that he coveted, not the adornments, and, as he was not a rich man, he preferred more books and less embellishment.[5]

In between all this collating and copying, Reddie somehow found the time to provide Dugdale with most, if not all, the translations of French and Italian erotica that appeared in *The Exquisite*, and a number of pieces of pornographic fiction that were published separately. Only one of these can now be identified – thanks to a manuscript note in Ashbee's own working copy of his *Index Librorum Prohibitorum* in the British Library – and that is *The Adventures of a School-Boy; or the Freaks of Youthful Passion* (1866), a work of 125 pages illustrated with eight coloured lithographs. In his usual verbose and semi-literate style, Dugdale describes it in one of his catalogues as: 'A very natural and powerfully written tale, describing in vivid colours the seduction of two young and delicious creatures by two sprigs of fashion, Eaton [*sic*] scholars, and the gradual transition from the most refined voluptuousness to the grossest sensuality are [*sic*] richly and lusciously depicted.'

However, at least two other works by Reddie – or rather, one and a third other works – were issued after his death in 1878; he is known to have written the final forty-seven pages of *The Mysteries of Verbena House* (London: 'Privately Printed,' 1882), an above-average flagellation novel left unfinished by the journalist George Augustus Sala (1828–96) whose interest in such matters as the birch and corporal punishment was greater and far more perverse than his biographer Ralph Straus felt able to admit. Reddie was also the author of *The Amatory Experiences of a Surgeon* ('Moscow [London]: Printed for the Nihilists [Edward Avery?]', 1881), a feeble offering whose only point of interest lies in a reference to the use of ginger as an aphrodisiac. The opening pages, however, contain some brief adventures of a pederastic nature, and since schoolboys figure in his earlier novel of 1866, it may not be out of place to reproduce here the opening lines from a 'Memoranda from Mr. P –' which appeared in *The Pearl*, a pornographic periodical published at London between July 1879 and December 1880 by the mysterious W[illiam?] Lazenby, otherwise known as 'D. Cameron':

Mr. Reddie used to call me Petro, as a short familiar name; but whilst he lodged with me at my house, Brecknock Crescent, Camden Town (N.B. – This is where I first was introduced to Mr. Reddie), I was continually afraid he would bring himself or both of us into serious trouble.

Once, I remember, we went to Margate for a few weeks at the seaside, and the landlady of the house where we stopped, had a very good looking son, a youth not

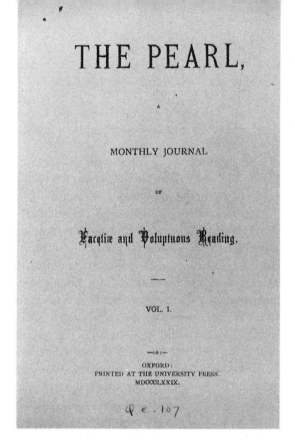

THE PEARL,

A

MONTHLY JOURNAL

OF

𝔉𝔞𝔠𝔢𝔱𝔦𝔞𝔢 𝔞𝔫𝔡 𝔙𝔬𝔩𝔲𝔭𝔱𝔲𝔬𝔲𝔰 𝔕𝔢𝔞𝔡𝔦𝔫𝔤.

VOL. I.

OXFORD:
PRINTED AT THE UNIVERSITY PRESS.
MDCCCLXXIX.

Titlepage and lithograph from the first edition of *The Pearl*

over fifteen, if quite so old. Mr. Reddie was in love at once, but how to win the boy over was the difficulty.

'Petro,' he would say, 'I must fuck that boy or go out of my mind from frigging myself as I lay in bed and think of him. How can we manage it, old boy?'[6]

OPPOSITE Plate from the 'D. Cameron (Lazenby)' reprint of Edward Sellon's *The New Epicurean*

The 'memoranda' continue with an account of the boy's seduction by Reddie, the landlady's by 'Petro', who seems to have been bisexual, and finally a homosexual orgy on the rug in front of the fire.

Homosexuality as a theme in Victorian erotica was extremely uncommon, which makes this piece, short though it is, quite remarkable. It is, of course, conceivable that the Reddie referred to in it is not the same person who wrote *The Adventures of a School-Boy*, but circumstantial evidence suggests that it is; the blunt and sudden introduction of Reddie's name in the opening sentence implies that somebody – perhaps some of the readers and almost certainly the publisher/editor of *The Pearl* – knew him by name if not personally. He was also familiar to erotica collectors and publishers, as Ashbee's account of him verifies. And, of course, he died just before *The Pearl* began publication, a time when salacious gossip concerning a fellow erotomaniac would prove most topical. If, then, this is the same Reddie, it is just possible that he may have written, or ghost-written, *The Sins of the Cities of the Plain; or The Recollections of a Mary-Ann* (London: 'Leicester Square,' 1881). This purports to be the memoirs of Jack Saul, who is almost certainly the same person as John Saul – known as 'Dublin Jack' at home in Ireland – who was later to figure as a witness in the trial that followed the so-called Cleveland Street Scandal of 1889–90 in which Lord Euston, among other notables, was accused by the *North London Press* of frequenting a homosexual brothel. During the course of the trial, Saul admitted that since leaving Ireland for London he had led 'a grossly immoral life'; the time limit he put on this dissolute existence was fifteen years, but in fact it must have been closer to twenty since in his 'memoirs' he mentions having seen Boulton and Park, a pair of transvestites who were prosecuted in 1871, and spending a night at their rooms. Since Reddie died in 1878 'at a ripe age' he would clearly have had time to know Saul quite well and 'ghost' the latter's experiences for him; it is, however, interesting that Saul allowed his real name to be used.

A sequel or 'Appendix' to *The Sins of the Cities of the Plain* appeared in 1883 under the title *Letters from Laura and Eveline*. This deals with two hermaphrodites and their sex lives with their respective husbands. It is not by Reddie since, as Ashbee observes, it was written by the publisher. 'The work,' he adds with his familiar disapproval, '. . . is mainly remarkable for its gross obscenity both in idea and language, and possesses no literary merit whatever.' (*Ashbee*, vol. 3, p. 403.)

Another of Dugdale's hacks was the unfortunate Edward Sellon (1818–66), who seems actually to have been possessed of considerable intelligence and promise. Among his more respectable literary efforts may be included a partial translation of Boccaccio's *Decameron*, a book on Indian temples and a novel dealing with army life in India entitled *Herbert Breakspear, a Legend of the Mahratta*

64

OPPOSITE Another plate from the 'D. Cameron (Lazenby)' reprint of Edward Sellon's *The New Epicurean*

War (Brighton, 1848). He is, however, more famous among the *cognoscenti* of erotica for two pornographic novels. *The New Epicurean; or, The Delights of Sex, Facetiously and Philosophically Considered, in Graphic Letters Addressed to Young Ladies of Quality* (London, '1740' [1865]) and *Phoebe Kissagen; or, the Remarkable Adventures, Schemes, Wiles, and Devilries of Une Maquerelle; being a sequel to the 'New Epicurean'* (London, '1743' [1866]); a well-written and extremely rare erotic autobiography; and the obscene illustrations to *The Adventures of a School-Boy*, already mentioned, and *The New Lady's Tickler; or The Adventure of Lady Lovesport and the Audacious Harry* (1866), all published at London by Dugdale.

Sellon's dealings with Dugdale came during the last two years of his life, and may be seen as a final attempt to stave off poverty and, in view of the fact that he committed suicide, probable depression. Raised from an early age by a widowed mother, he entered the army at 16 and spent the next ten years in India where he rose to the rank of captain. On leave in England, he made the disagreeable discovery that his mother had arranged for him to be married. This was not to his taste at all, but on learning of the reputed fortune that his betrothed was supposed to be an heiress to, he eventually went along with the plan. His future in-laws objected to their only child going to India, so Sellon resigned his commission and the marriage took place in the early 1840s. Things did not go well from the start, especially when it was learned that his wife's fortune was merely an allowance of £400 a year. The two separated not long after the honeymoon, and for a couple of years Sellon lived with his mother in London and amused himself with a girl he kept in a 'suburban villa'. At the end of this period, there was a reconciliation between Sellon and his wife. After a promising start, he was caught out in an alliance with the maid and a terrible fight took place during which his hands and shins were so badly lacerated that he fainted from loss of blood and was seriously ill for a month when his wounds became septic. There was another family argument between the two while he was convalescing at Hastings, and once again they parted.

For the following six years, Sellon was obliged to work for a living because his mother became impoverished through the machinations of a firm of crooked solicitors. For two of these years, he drove the Cambridge Mail Coach, but the advent of the railway made him redundant so he opened some fencing rooms in London. Then his wife materialized again, and there was yet another reconciliation which this time lasted for three years, years that proved to be idyllic for the pair of them until his wife became pregnant. Sellon began to feel more and more ignored, at length leaving her and going to London where he told his story to a titled relative. Six months after the birth of his child, his wife came to London, paying a visit to Sellon's relative and giving him her account of what had happened. Sellon received a short, sharp note from 'Lord E – ' which told him to return at once to his wife. Fearing to offend his wealthy relative and put in jeopardy any spare cash that might be coming his way, he complied but it was a half-hearted gesture. Before long he was debauching the pupils at a local girls' school. Caught in the act one day by his wife, he was forced to flee to London. . . .

THE
NEW EPICUREAN

OR

THE DELIGHTS OF SEX

FACETIOUSLY AND

PHILOSOPHICALLY CONSIDERED

IN

GRAPHIC LETTERS

ADDRESSED TO YOUNG LADIES OF QUALITY.

« Domi maneas paresque nobis
» Novem continuas fututiones. »
CATULLUS CARMEN XXXII.

A NEW EDITION.

LONDON, 1740 (Reprinted 1875).

φ.f. 100

PHŒBE KISSAGEN

OR THE

REMARKABLE ADVENTURES, SCHEMES

WILES AND DEVILRIES

OF

UNE MAQUERELLE

BEING A SEQUEL TO

« THE NEW EPICUREAN »

SIR TOBY. — « Do'st think that
because thou art virtuous, there
shall be no more cakes and ale ? »
CLOWN. — « Yes! by St. Anne,
and ginger shall be hot i'the
mouth, too! »

Twelfth Night, or What you will.

LONDON, 1743 (Reprinted 1875.)

φ.f. 102

This account of Edward Sellon's history is condensed from *The Ups and Downs of Life. A Fragment* (London: Printed for the Booksellers [William Dugdale], 1867), his autobiography. At the beginning of his essay 'Benefit of Clergy' George Orwell observes that 'Autobiography is only to be trusted when it reveals something disgraceful.' There is much that is disgraceful about Sellon's *memoire*, and for that reason there seems little point in disagreeing with Ashbee when he writes '... allowing for a little colouring, [it] portrays truthfully enough Sellon's career.'

The Ups and Downs of Life is one of the very few genuine erotic and autobiographies. It is also one of the rarest. No copy of the first edition was thought to exist until the mid-1970s when a young American *amateur* discovered a beautiful copy in its original paper boards and with all eight illustrations in a Paris bookshop. It is now, along with the remainder of the American's collection, in the library of a great German collector. A reprint with the new title *The Amorous Prowess of a Jolly Fellow* (London [Amsterdam]: Privately Printed [Auguste Brancart], 1892) is, like the original edition, known only to exist in a single copy, again in Germany.

*   *   *   *   *

LEFT Titlepage from the 'D. Cameron (Lazenby)' reprint of Edward Sellon's *The New Epicurean*. See colour plates opposite page 112 and 113

ABOVE The '1875' (i.e. 1876) reprint of *Phoebe Kissagen*, Edward Sellon's sequel to his own novel *The New Epicurean*

After Dugdale died in 1868 – of syphilis one might surmise since on the death certificate the cause is given as 'Paralysis' – attempts to plot the further course of erotica publishing in England become markedly more difficult for the simple reason that the main source of information dried up. Ashbee, although he describes many post-Dugdale books, is restrained from saying too much about their publishers and authors since many of them were still in business. There are, however, one or two shadowy figures who emerge blinking from their self-imposed anonymity into the bright lights from time to time in newspaper reports of court cases or in the occasional, tantalizing notes in Ashbee's books in the British Library. Chief among these are 'D. Cameron'/Lazenby and Edward Avery.

Of the former, practically nothing is known at all. 'D. Cameron' is clearly a pseudonym, a play on 'Decameron', but there is no certainty that Lazenby is genuine either. The earliest printed reference to him that I am aware of occurs in the 1913 catalogue of the *Enfer* of the Bibliothèque Nationale, compiled by Apollinaire, Perceau and Fleuret. At no. 169, the notice for the obscene periodical *The Pearl* already mentioned above, the authors of *L'Enfer* state that '[t]he first edition of *The Pearl* was done by Cameron (a borrowed name) at London'. It is not known how the compilers of *L'Enfer* obtained this information, but one possibility is that they got it from Charles Hirsch. From about 1889, Hirsch ran a bookshop in Coventry Street, London, called the *Librairie Parisienne* from which he sold respectable French books – if the works of Zola and others could be called respectable in the London of the 1890s – as a cover for a presumably more lucrative trade in erotica. About the turn of the century, he moved his business back to Paris where he settled on the rue de Rivoli. He is mentioned several times in *L'Enfer* in connection with erotic books that he printed – *The Initiation of Aurora Trill* ('London', 1903; no. 180), for example – so the compilers presumably knew him, and may well have consulted him concerning English erotica; it is not beyond the bounds of possibility that among his customers during his years in London was Ashbee, and he knew all the answers.

'Cameron' again puts in an appearance in two manuscript notes in Ashbee's working copies of his own bibliographies, kept in the British Library. These notes refer to a reprint of Wilkes's *An Essay on Woman*, and to a new edition of Sellon's *The New Epicurean* that was printed at Brussels for a London bookseller named 'D. Cameron (Lazenby)' in 1875. Although there is no allusion to either Cameron or Lazenby, Ashbee's printed notice of *Phoebe Kissagen*, the sequel to *The New Epicurean*, mentions a reprint of that as well, done in 1876, and it is possible that it appeared under similar circumstances.

Finally, there is what may be a cryptic reference to this elusive fellow in Ashbee's notice of a work entitled *Curiosities of Flagellation*. 'The book is being printed at Brussels, for a London bookseller, and has reached at present [i.e. 1875] the completion of the first volume.' (*Ashbee*, vol. 1, p. xlii, footnote.) The parallels between this and the reprint of *The New Epicurean* – the printing in Brussels, the London bookseller and the date 1875 – may be nothing more than a coincidence, but there is one other small item which, although not conclusive, tends to support the idea that these two books are from the same publisher. In 1875, *Curiosities of Flagellation* never got beyond the first volume, although according to the title-page there were to have been four others. Four years later, in 1879, this volume was reprinted and in 1880 a second volume added, completing publication in two rather than five volumes as originally projected. Of *this* work Ashbee wrote: 'The publisher is also the author; his initials, W. L., terminate the address to the reader on the verso of the titlepage of the first edition of vol. I.' (*Ashbee*, vol. 3, p. 252.) W. L.? Could this be William or Walter Lazenby?

In comparison with Cameron/Lazenby, Edward Avery, the other half-glimpsed figure in late 19th-century erotica publishing in London, was practically an exhibitionist. His name is frequently seen, sometimes even in erotic books that he himself sold, and like John Camden Hotten (1832–73), who combined a thriving business publishing Swinburne and pirating Bret Harte with an equally thriving sideline in flagellation pornography, Avery managed for the best part of twenty-five years to run a successful second-hand bookshop as a 'front' for his more dubious activities.

Avery would seem to have begun in bookselling and publishing in 1879. This may be deduced from an advertisement in Clegg's *Directory of Second-Hand Booksellers* (5th edition, 1899, p. 9) in which he states that he established himself in that year. Earlier advertisements in the same publication show that he was in the 'remainder' business, which is to say that he bought up the sheets of other publisher's failures, had them bound with a new titlepage of his own added, and sold them off cheap. Several of these are listed in the various advertisements in Clegg's directories, such as W. Russell's *Eccentric Personages*. That he was also a publisher and vendor of erotic books did not become public knowledge, however, until the autumn of 1900 when a police *agent provocateur* went to his shop and, posing as a customer, purchased a book later described as being of a 'grossly obscene nature'. Justice was swift. A warrant was issued on October 1900, and Avery's premises were raided. The minutes of the *Joint Select Committee on Lotteries and Indecent Advertisements* (London, 1908) include the evidence of Chief Inspector Edward Drew who was, apparently, present at the event: '... in addition to a large number of already elaborately bound books ... all in different sizes, and of the most grossly obscene character, there were also found nearly a ton of the letter press, all printed, wrapped up in separate large parcels, all ready to go to the binders to be bound ... In addition ... there were found thousands of the grossest and most obscene pictures and photographs that one could well imagine, as well as a number of beautifully carved models showing persons in the act of coition.'

Avery was sent for trial at Clerkenwell before W. B. McConnell Q.C. The counsel for the prosecution was Mr Laycester, and counsel for the defence was Horace Avory. Avory (1851–1935) was a big man in legal circles; by 1900 he had already received his baptism of fire in at least two spectacular trials, those of Oscar Wilde, when he appeared for the Crown, and the Havelock Ellis/*Sexual Inversion*/George Bedborough trial in which he appeared for the defendants. In

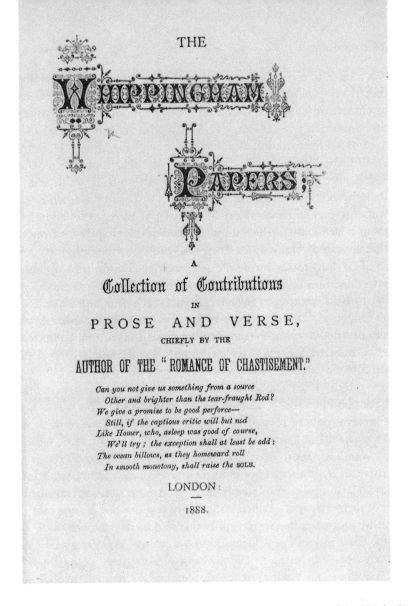

THE

Whippingham Papers

A

Collection of Contributions

IN

PROSE AND VERSE,

CHIEFLY BY THE

AUTHOR OF THE "ROMANCE OF CHASTISEMENT."

Can you not give us something from a source
Other and brighter than the tear-fraught Rod?
We give a promise to be good perforce—
Still, if the captious critic will but nod
Like Homer, who, asleep was good of course,
    We'll try ; the exception shall at least be odd :
The ocean billows, as they homeward roll
In smooth monotony, shall raise the SOLE.

LONDON :
—
1888.

ABOVE A source for students of Swinburne's less celebrated poetical offerings

1910 he was appointed a Judge of the King's Bench Division of the High Court and received a knighthood the same year. This was pretty heavy-calibre legal assistance for Avery to wheel out, especially when it is considered that he pleaded guilty and presented the most extraordinary plea for leniency based on the fact that in all his twenty-five years in the business, this had been the only time that he had been caught. He got six months, after which he disappeared completely.

Despite the Aladdin's cave of pornography found by Edward Drew and his *confrères* at the Greek Street shop – coincidentally, it is still a dirty bookshop today, although under new management of course! – only one clandestine book can with certainty be said to have been printed or published by Avery. This is *The Whippingham Papers*, an unappetizing farrago of bits and pieces whose sole *raison d'être*, as the title implies, is flagellation. One of the two copies in the British Library contains a manuscript note by Ashbee giving the information that it was limited to 250 copies, cost two and a half guineas and was published in December 1887 – the titlepage gives 1888. The titlepage also makes the claim that the contents are 'chiefly by the author of "The Romance of Chastisement"', a reference presumably to St George H. Stock, who published a book of that title in 1870, or to a different book altogether, but with the same title, published in 1866 by William Dugdale. The real reason, though, that *The Whippingham Papers* has acquired a reputation out of all proportion to its value as a work of literature is that it contains some unsigned verses by Swinburne, whose weakness for writing doggerel on the subject of schoolboys having the daylights beaten out of them is well known; the lines at the head of this chapter are from one such poem that appeared originally in *The Pearl*, and unfortunately their tone sums up much of English erotica during the 19th century. Swinburne's obsession went so far as to cause him to compose a full-length epic poem or verse drama called *The Flogging Block* written in twelve eclogues, each with titles like 'Prelude to Charlie's Flogging'. This exists only in manuscript in the British Library and is therefore not strictly within the scope of the present work; the interested reader, however, is referred to Jean Overton Fuller's *Swinburne: A Critical Biography* (London, 1968) in which an entire chapter is devoted to it.

Aside from *The Whippingham Papers*, there is evidence to suggest that Avery might have published the 'Rochester Series of Reprints'. This was a short series of quite nicely produced revivals of English *galante* titles. One of them was John Cleland's pleasant but hardly erotic *Memoirs of a Coxcomb* (1885), which shows that they were little more than cover items. He also imported French pornography; there are a number of books in the Private Case of the British Library of Dutch or Belgian origin that have 'sold by E. Avery, London' stamped on one or other of their endpapers, which leads one to suppose that he was catering for a fairly well-educated customer, certainly one able to read French.

But the most interesting information concerning Avery may be found in a unique copy of William Laird Clowes's pseudonymously compiled *Bibliotheca Arcana* (London, 1885) which is interleaved and annotated throughout in an unknown hand. Until late 1971 or early 1972, this was in the collection of Mr. G. Legman of Valbonne in the South of France. Subsequently it passed via an American collector to its present home in Germany. In the course of the annotations to *Bibliotheca Arcana*, there are some ten references to 'the Avery gang' or 'Avery and his gang'. Another of the notes alleges that Avery was the chief distributor of Ashbee's bibliographies, although the British Library received its first copies of these, on publication, not from Avery or even, perhaps a little surprisingly, from Ashbee himself, but from a bookseller named George Rivers. What was meant by 'the Avery gang', and whether it actually alludes to some sort of pornographic Dr Mabuse-style criminal organization, is not known. It seems unlikely unless one concocts an elaborate conspiracy theory that involves Ashbee, Horace Avory and others, but somehow this does not ring true.

* * * * *

Titlepage for *Country Retirement*, a typical flagellation novel of the late Victorian period

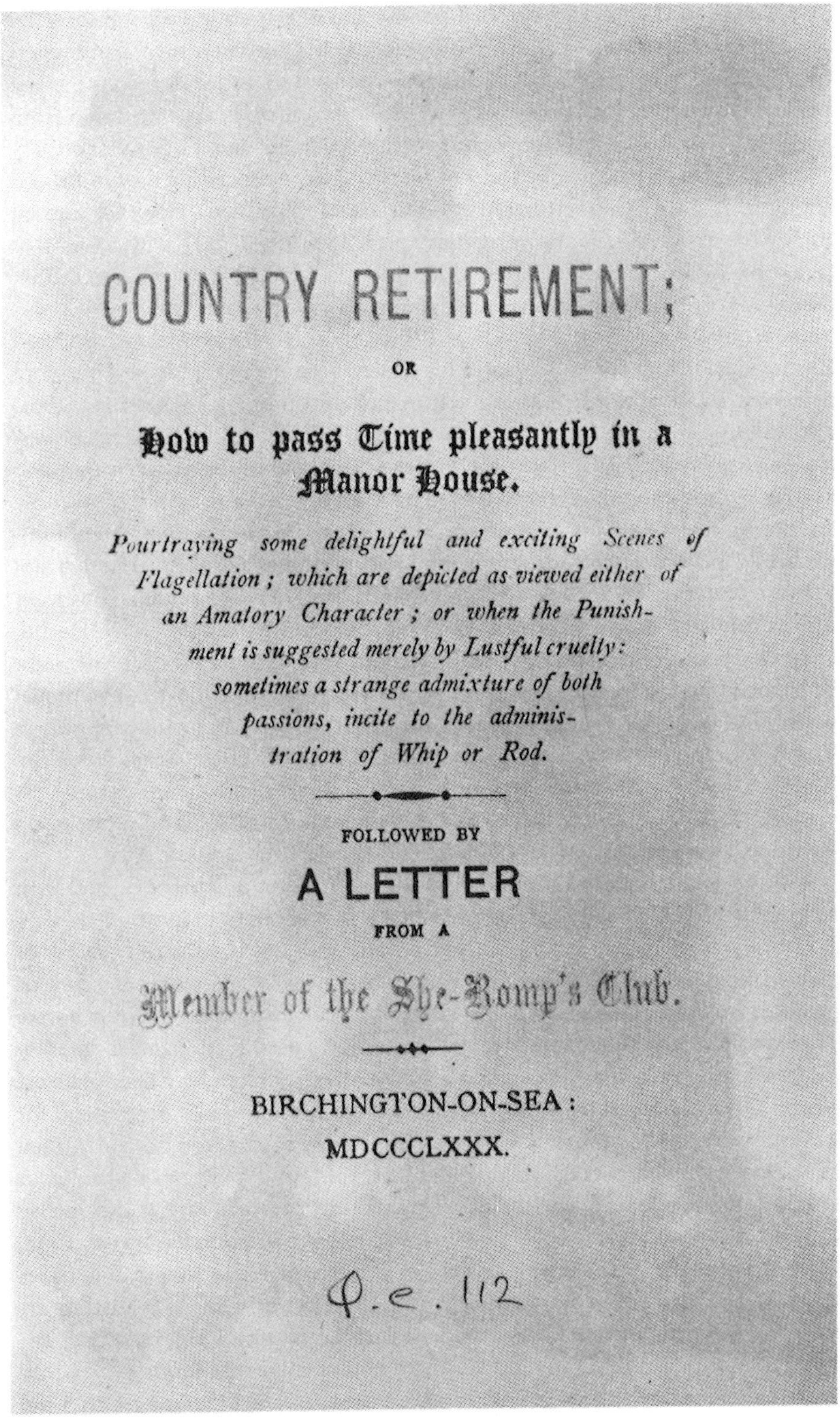

COUNTRY RETIREMENT;

OR

How to pass Time pleasantly in a Manor House.

Pourtraying some delightful and exciting Scenes of Flagellation; which are depicted as viewed either of an Amatory Character; or when the Punishment is suggested merely by Lustful cruelty: sometimes a strange admixture of both passions, incite to the administration of Whip or Rod.

FOLLOWED BY

A LETTER

FROM A

Member of the She-Romp's Club.

BIRCHINGTON-ON-SEA:
MDCCCLXXX.

φ. e. 112

Toward the end of the 19th century, production of erotica in England virtually ceased, the scene shifting, especially after 1900, to France where several publishers who had originally started in London were obliged to settle. But from the late 1880s there was a brief flurry of activity from two men who came down from Sheffield to the capital. These were Leonard Smithers and H. S. Nichols. By training, Smithers was a solicitor, but one with pronounced literary tastes and linguistic abilities. After settling in London, he rapidly made a name for himself among the *fin-de-siècle* decadent set with a periodical called *The Savoy*, which was edited by Aubrey Beardsley after he left John Lane's *The Yellow Book*, and by publishing Ernest Dowson, Arthur Symons and – at a time when it was extremely unfashionable to do so – Oscar Wilde. He also collaborated with Richard Burton on *Priapeia* (1889), an anthology in translation of 'Sportive Epigrams' that is still of value to students of the fruitier Latin authors, *The Carmina* (1894) of Catullus, and between 1894 and 1897 several different editions of *The Book of the Thousand Nights and a Night*, the first of which, published between 1885 and 1888 in sixteen volumes, is rumoured to have involved the assistance of Nichols.

That Smithers was a pornographer in the Dugdale mould seems highly improbable; he was far too discriminating for anything like that, although not averse to putting on an act and hanging inflammatory and mischievous signs such as 'Smut is Cheap Today' in his bookshop window to twit the police. He did, however, publish, in association with Nichols, several volumes of what might be termed 'literary' erotica, which were just as filthy as the more conventional variety but with delusions of grandeur. Among these may be included *Teleny or The Reverse of the Medal* (1893), *Gynecocracy* (1893) and *White Stains* (1898) by Aleister Crowley (1875–1947), who churlishly affixed the name of his mother's brother, G. A. Bishop – described as a 'Neuropath of the Second Empire' – on the titlepage as author.

Teleny has been habitually ascribed to Oscar Wilde on no other evidence than its graphic homosexual theme and pretentious purple prose. In its original form, the story was set in London but Smithers, fearing to outrage the *amor patriae* of his customers, relocated the action to Paris, where homosexual orgies and curious practices involving soldiers and wine bottles might be thought more at home. The way in which the manuscript of *Teleny* was passed from hand to hand in London's homosexual milieu in the early 1890s has been told by Charles Hirsch, whose Coventry Street bookshop was used as the collection and 'drop' point for it. Wilde, a regular customer at Coventry Street, one day toward the end of 1890 gave Hirsch a sealed package and asked if he would hand it over to a friend who would call later and present the playwright's card. Hirsch agreed and in due course a young man arrived, showed Wilde's card and collected the package. Later, the package was returned and the business was repeated three or four times until on one occasion it was returned to the bookshop with its wrapping insecurely fastened. Hirsch, being understandably inquisitive considering the circumstances, examined the contents of the package which he found to be a 200-page manuscript bound in greyish paper covers on which he at first read the single word FELENY. A closer look revealed that what it actually read was TELENY. That evening, he read the manuscript through, finding a 'profoundly interesting work', a narrative written in a number of different hands of varying ability, with many corrections and additions and with numerous quotations from the Bible, Greek and Latin classical literature and borrowings from foreign languages. Once read, the manuscript was wrapped up again and given to the next caller who presented Wilde's card, and Hirsch lost sight of it for a while.

In 1893, Smithers published *Teleny* in two volumes with the false imprint 'Cosmopoli', and Hirsch once again had the opportunity of reading it. Several significant differences between the original manuscript and the printed version struck him at once. The story being set in Paris rather than in London has already been mentioned above, but missing were the many literary and linguistic touches and an entire Prologue in which the characters were introduced to the reader prior to the story commencing.

About seven years later, Smithers left the manuscript of *Teleny* with a publisher in Paris named Madame Duringe planning, according to Hirsch, to issue a definitive version of the novel once the original edition of 1893 had been exhausted. He never managed it. Luckily, Hirsch knew Duringe as well and acquired the manuscript from her to which he added a history of it – allegedly as part of a 'Notes and Mementos of an Old Book Collector' – which was included in a French translation published at Paris in 1934, probably by Marcel Seheur. This translation is in a sense the first integral edition, despite being in French, because as the titlepage claims it was actually translated from the original manuscript rather than the first English edition of 1893 or later reprints, and although the literary quotations are absent, the prologue has been restored as has the story's location in London.

Gynecocracy is one of those rare masochistic novels in which a man is the victim for a change, in this case 'Julian Robinson', the first-person narrator of the tale, who is so badly behaved at home that his parents pack him off to enjoy the tender care of Mademoiselle de Chambonnard, a strict French governess, who reigns supreme at a secluded country house near Stowmarket, Suffolk. In residence too are Maud, Beatrice – who later marries Julian – and Agnes, cousins of Julian's and who are also being educated by the young mademoiselle.

Needless to say, all the girls are in league against the hapless Julian and it is not long before he is being flogged, forced to wear women's clothes and tight corsets, locked in a cage and generally mistreated in a most shameful way. He grows to enjoy this enormously, but as if somehow to excuse himself to the reader he attempts to present his ill-treatment as a personal necessity, and even to infuse it with a kind of grotesque dignity. At the conclusion of the three volumes, there is an epilogue in which an attempt is made to summarize these things.

The petticoat, as administered by Mademoiselle and then by Beatrice, after all is said and done, I consider beneficial.

A woman can make a man. In the first place she has the monopoly of the making,

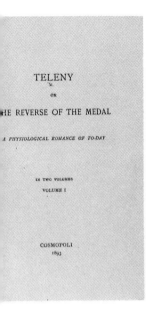

TELENY
OR
THE REVERSE OF THE MEDAL

A PHYSIOLOGICAL ROMANCE OF TO-DAY

IN TWO VOLUMES
VOLUME I

COSMOPOLI
1893

The homosexual novel *Teleny*, ascribed to Oscar Wilde

for she alone can conceive and give birth to him, and in the next place she can make him by discipline, by instilling her common sense into him, and by keeping him rigidly under her thumb. I do not believe that I should be what I am but for this education.

I confess – whether I shall be pitied for it or not – that I love my bondage and I love my tyrant. She has developed me intellectually and physically.

The physical compensations are so many and so great. There is a wonderful luxuriousness and sensuality in being made to bow down before a woman, and to perform her behests, which is not experienced when one takes the initiative one's self.

My lady's stockings and drawers upon me give me, whenever I am reminded that I wear them, an electrifying thrill through and through. And as for the management of affairs, well, they are much better managed by my wife than they could be by me.

Still there is something in me which assures me that man was made for more than the petticoat. This world is woman's earth, and it is petticoated all over. Their is the dominion, turn and twist the matter as you will. Therefore, I conclude there must be some other world where men will have a ruling part to play.

Still, I trust even there, it will not be without woman, her influence, and the great mystery of sex.

Is this the reason why it is written that into a certain kingdom the effeminate will not be admitted?

I wish the word defined. What is effeminate. Effeminacy cannot be the product of wholesome discipline.

'Julian, writing still!' It is Beatrice's voice. 'Go to my bedroom at once, Sir!' I tremble and go. I *must*.

In common with many novels concerning the more unusual aspects of sexuality that have been written by practitioners, so to speak, rather than mere pornographic hacks, *Gynecocracy* is a troubling and personal book to read. It deals with aberrations of the sort that are found hilariously funny by those who do not happen to share them – myself included I must confess – and it deals with them in a way that demands an end of laughter and a glimmer of understanding. Which is not to say that it is exactly a propagandistic book, but it is powerful and convincing enough to convey the impression of a man's private and tortured fantasies into which we, as readers, have been allowed as guests. What business we have there – the motive we had for reading the book in the first place – is our own concern, but once there we might have the courtesy to wonder instead of laugh.

Apart from its psychological interest, *Gynecocracy* is also quite well written. The emphasis on undinism – the hero is urinated on when he is particularly naughty – has led the book to be ascribed to Havelock Ellis, whose childhood experiences of having wet nappies pushed into his face are said to have created problems for him in later life. But the most likely candidate is proposed by the compilers of *L'Enfer* (1919) who at entry numbers 818–819 wrote: 'This strange and very well written novel, published at London for the first time by R.bson et C°, has for its author it would appear M. St.n.sl.s. de R.dès, a London barrister whom, it is said, also wrote *The Yellow Room* (an erotic novel published by G.u.ch.), *The Petticoat Dominant* and an unpublished work called *Fernand*.'

This sentence contains several challenging statements or suggestions. Thanks to the London Law Lists, it proved easy to establish that at the time *Gynecocracy* was published in 1893 there was indeed a barrister in London named Stanislas de Rhodes. But did he also write *The Yellow Room* (1891) and *The Petticoat Dominant*? This latter novel has no date on the titlepage of the first edition, but since it is ascribed to 'the author of Gynecocracy (Julian Robinson, afterwards Viscount Ladywood)' and is stated to be a sequel to *The Yellow Room*, it was presumably the last of the trio to be published. This puts them into chronological perspective and shows that they fall into a logical sequence. Stylistically, though, *The Yellow Room* and *The Petticoat Dominant* are totally at variance with *Gynecocracy*, the only point of similarity being in theme, and it seems on balance unlikely that all three books are from the same pen. *The Autobiography of a Flea*, another late-Victorian erotic novel, which was published at London about 1887, is ascribed in the *Galitzin* catalogue (no. 577) to 'an English lawyer, very well known in London'. Again the style, and this time the theme as well, do not suggest the same author as *Gynecocracy*.

The claim that *The Yellow Room* was published by 'G.u.ch.' is probably a reference to a man named Elias Gaucher, but it is improbable in the extreme that he was responsible for the first edition of *The Yellow Room* if it really was published in 1891. Gaucher was a fly-by-night operator who seems to have printed books for *colportage* – which is to say for hawking around bookshops in suitcases, or even at a pinch for selling at street corners. He appears to have been active in Paris from about 1910 and his chief money-spinners were piracies of other people's books, so what the compilers of *L'Enfer* may have written about was one of his *contrafaçons*. A chapter dealing with Gaucher will be found in John Glassco's *Memoirs of Montparnasse* (Oxford University Press (Canada), 1970; repr. 1973 by the Viking Press, N.Y.).

'R.bson et C°' is almost certainly an allusion to a firm of booksellers and publishers named Robson & Kerslake (or Carslake) who had premises in Coventry Street – the same street in which Hirsch had his *Librairie Parisienne*. The Welsh author Arthur Machen (1863–1947), who worked for them as a cataloguer, found them a genial couple and referred to them in his autobiography as 'The Brothers'; and it was they who had Machen's translation of Casanova printed in 1894 by Nichols. Before the arrival of Nichols in London, they also published a clandestine reprint of the Earl of Haddington's *Select Poems on Several Occasions* ('1824' [1883]) that was printed by J. H. Gaball, as a handwritten note by Ashbee in a British Library copy points out. It will be seen that Robson & Kerslake were no strangers to under-the-counter book production, but neither the Casanova nor Haddington's charming early 18th-century bawdry were in quite the same league as *Gynecocracy* and the suspicion arises that the compilers of *L'Enfer* were wrong and had been misinformed by Hirsch or whoever their source was. A Smithers-Nichols co-production is a far more believable publishing partnership for such a robust performance as *Gynecocracy*.

No such complications exist concerning Aleister Crowley's collection of

Baudelaire-influenced verses, *White Stains*: it forms part of the established body of his work and has long been recognized as having been published by Smithers, whose taste for decadence it certainly appealed to. Since the text of this otherwise scarce book has been made more readily available thanks to the good offices of Gerald Duckworth & Co., who published a reprint of it at London in 1973, a brief look at one of Crowley's other clandestine books might prove of interest. I am indebted to Mr Timothy d'Arch Smith for the information that on the evidence of typographical ornamentation *Snowdrops from a Curate's Garden* was probably printed by Philippe Renouard at Paris about 1904. Renouard also printed for Crowley *The Scented Garden of Abdullah the Satirist of Shiraz* (1910), a homosexual parody of Sir Richard F. Burton's translation of Nefzaoui's better-known *The Perfumed Garden* (1886), the *Sword of Song* (1904) and in 1906 a poem entitled *Alexandra*, the whole stock of which is supposed to have been destroyed by the British Customs for 'obscenity and *lèse-majesté*' in 1910. Of all Crowley's erotic books, *Snowdrops from a Curate's Garden* is the most outrageous, disgusting and cynical. In mitigation, though, it has to be said that it is also extremely funny, not at all badly written and reveals in the author a remarkable facility for coining new words. It is divided into four parts: a burlesque Introduction, a prose work entitled *The Nameless Novel* and two collections of shorter pieces, the first a brief selection of *Juvenalia* and the second a more substantial gathering called *The Bromo Book*.

WHITE STAINS

THE LITERARY REMAINS OF GEORGE ARCHIBALD BISHOP
A NEUROPATH OF THE SECOND EMPIRE

1898

Aleister Crowley's contribution to *L'Esprit décadent*

The Introduction purports to be an outline of the life of the author of the rest of the book, and is supposed to be written by a friend of his, an unnamed editor, who stole the manuscript from him. The author's real name cannot of course be divulged, and the 'editor' refers to him simply as 'K', and writes: 'It is the custom to study, even if briefly, the life of a great writer from the biographical standpoint. In this case it is impossible to follow the usual course, for I have no wish to blast the useful public career of the most talented artist of our day, and there can be no doubt that precision of allusion would cause his innumerable friends to recognise in the infamous blackguard who penned these abominations the saintly and delicate-minded hero of their dreams.'

After this Introduction begins *The Nameless Novel*. A prologue introduces us to the chief character, an archbishop whose habits and appetites are of Sadeian proportions. Detected by a reporter from the 'Daily M – ' while in the process of murdering a countess in a highly unusual manner – ' "There are more ways of killing a dog than choking it with shit," he mused, "but none are so economical ..." ' – and committing an act of necrophilia on the remains, he is persuaded to dictate his memoirs. Interspersed with orgies involving the reporter, these then follow and reach a surrealistic degree of indecency as the following passage from Chapter Five will illustrate:

It is a singular circumstance, continued the Archbishop, leading the way across the piles of dung with which the devoted camel had adorned the floor, that no poet has yet adequately sung the passion which exists in such luscious splendour between the Ship of the Desert and the wild Bedawi. Leila, the juicy-cunted nigger nockstress who took my first spunkings as I told you in Chapter III, used to see a great deal of the business when she was first brought up from her home by the Nyanza to serve the vices of George G[ordo]n at Khartoum. She had seen Mesrur, the famous eunuch of the Mahdi, violate the hairless cunnies of sixty virgins without losing erection. She had been present when Zuleika, the Queen of the Soudan, as they called her, under-took (to suck off, and swallow the spend of) fifty-seven men in the first hour, and seventy-two in the second, when she had got into her stride, as it were. Alas! all Europe knows the treachery which cost her life. In the third hour the infamous Selim bin Haroun presented himself disguised to her lips. As you know, this chieftain, desirous of checking his fertility without interfering with his pleasures, had bored a hole at the root of his life-preserver permitting the vital fuck-spunk to dribble away. Of course, when the unhappy Zuleika pulled at his vibrating tuning-fork and found no juice followed her efforts, she shrieked and fainted, suspecting magic. Recovering herself by a great effort, she caught hold of the traitor's bollocks, and went on. For three minutes and a half she continued to suck him with all her force: he reeled, fell, and expired. Zuleika was avenged. But for all her gallantry the Amir was adamant. Your engagement was to average over fifty cocks an hour (he said) and you have failed; the penalty is known to you. The unhappy woman groaned and acquiesced. The eunuchs stuffed a vast quantity of rice into her front and back paddy-fields, and with delicate enemata of boiling water caused it to swell. They stood away at the critical moment, and with a yell like ten thousand devils in torment the bowels of the wretched woman burst open and she expired in frightful agony . . . The recital of this scene of lust, said the Archbishop, always moves me to tears . . .

In comparison with the rest of the Archbishop's confession, this episode is rela-tively tame, but it indicates an approach to erotica that is closer to Apollinaire, who barely three years later was to publish his equally extravagant *Les Onze mille verges*, than to Sade as was suggested by one of Crowley's biographers.

Juvenalia comprises three pieces, two in prose and the third, entitled 'The Parson's Prayer', in verse, which are of rather less interest than *The Bromo Book* which follows them. This is subdivided into two sections. The first consists of a series of parodies of Shakespeare, Swinburne and Browning for the most part, and concludes with six limericks. The second part is called *Miscellaneous*, a col-lection of fourteen poems and songs and one epigram. In order to give some idea of just how gross Crowley could be, I will close this notice of *Snowdrops from a Curate's Garden* with the opening verse from 'Birthday Ode', a poem dedicated to 'Percy Bowles, Esq.':

> There was a young bugger named Percy
> Who let a most poisonous fart;
> He collected the spend of an intimate friend
> From the cunt of a twopenny tart.
> This notorious whore had a tertiary sore
> Half way from her bubs to her belly
> He licked up the pus and distilled it – for us!
> With the toe-jam of M[ari]e C[orell]i.[7]

MY SECRET LIFE.

VOLUME I.

AMSTERDAM.

Not for publication.

No discussion of 19th-century English erotica can be considered complete without mention being made of *My Secret Life*, yet in readily available sources – Steven Marcus's *The Other Victorians* (1966) for example – every aspect of this extraordinary and epic work has been examined. As with Cleland's *Memoirs of a Woman of Pleasure*, an equally well-documented erotic book, I shall confine myself to a bare outline of the known facts.

Between approximately 1885 and 1895, someone, presumably an Englishman of means, had printed on the Continent an eleven-volume sexual autobiography limited, or so he thought, to just six copies. Who the printer was has not been established but the most likely possibility is Auguste Brancart, a prolific publisher of erotica who began his professional career in the early 1880s in Brussels and toward the end of the decade moved to Amsterdam. Interestingly, the titlepage of

ABOVE The first of the eleven volumes of *My Secret Life*

My Secret Life has 'Amsterdam. Not for Publication' on it but in the *sub rosa* world of erotica publishing such indications are to be taken with a pinch of salt.

Volume one of *My Secret Life* opens with a brief Introduction in which, according to the traditions of these things, it is claimed that the real author of the book is dead and that it is being seen through the press by a friend to whom the manuscript was entrusted. In order to conceal the identity of the dead author, and those with whom he came into contact, names, dates and places will, where necessary, be disguised. 'If I have done harm in printing it,' the Introduction concludes, 'I have done none to him, have indeed carried out his evident intention, and given to a few a secret history, which bears the impress of truth on every page, a contribution to psychology.'

There then follows two Prefaces by the author, the second of which contains the following interesting paragraphs:

> I have read my manuscript through; what reminiscences! I had actually forgotten some of the early ones; how true the detail strikes me as I read of my early experiences; had it not been written then it never could have been written now; has anybody but myself faithfully made such a record? It would be a sin to burn all this, whatever society may say, it is but a narrative of human life, perhaps the every day life of thousands, if the confession could be had.
>
> What strikes me as curious in reading it is the monotony of the course I have pursued towards women who were not of the gay class; it has been as similar and repetitive as fucking itself; do all men act so, does every man kiss, coax, hint smuttily, then talk baudily, snatch a feel, smell his fingers, assault, and win, exactly as I have done? Is every woman offended, say 'no', then 'Oh!' blush, be angry, refuse, close her thighs, after a struggle open them, and yield to her lust as mine have done? A conclave of whores telling the truth, and of Romish priests, could alone settle the point. Have all men had the strange letches which late in life have enraptured me? I can never know this; my experiences, if printed, may enable others to compare as I cannot.
>
> Shall it be burned or printed? How many years have passed in this indecision? Why fear? it is for others' good and not my own if preserved.

The secret life itself then begins, and the reader is at once plunged into one of the strangest and most obsessive books ever written, the more so because it is clearly not a work of fiction. From his youth, the author kept a diary of his sexual life and would seem to have maintained it in one form or another for the following forty years. It is this diary, edited into a single narrative during the course of two serious illnesses that kept the author out of action, that is the basis of *My Secret Life*. To attempt to provide a synopsis of a book that extends to eleven substantial volumes is clearly impossible; Professor Marcus barely skimmed the surface in his two chapters on the subject which together run to over 100 pages, although to be fair he was as concerned with the thinking behind the book as with what it was about. It should be said, however, that *My Secret Life* is a document of the most profound importance; its authenticity, its painful, at times agonizing, insistence on absolute truth reveal more about London's low life and the cruel exploitation of women and young girls than a dozen or so Dickens or Mayhews could ever have achieved between them. In addition it gives an insight into sexual attitudes which, because the author felt presumably secure in his anonymity, has an interest and value born of honesty and lack of fear. It would require a similar work, written today, to discover whether these attitudes have altered.

The scarcity of *My Secret Life* has been overstated; it is certainly a rare book, but it is not unique like Sellon's *The Ups and Downs of Life* which, as we have seen, exists in just one copy. More than six copies, as ordered by the author or 'editor', were undoubtedly run off, but how many more? From the number that have been reliably recorded, or rumoured to exist, the total seems to have been in the region of twenty or twenty-five sets: Aleister Crowley was supposed to have had one, as was the silent film comedian Harold Lloyd and Marlene Dietrich's 'Svengali', film director Joseph von Sternberg; C. R. Dawes had two sets, one of which was destroyed by the British Customs with their celebrated disregard for the printed word, and the other eventually went to the British Library; Louis Mountbatten's brother, the 2nd Marquess of Milford Haven, certainly possessed a copy of it for it is now in a fine London collection and contains his bookplate; there is a copy in Switzerland, another in Germany and at least two in the United States, and the list could be extended. Some of the people who are said to have had sets may not actually have done so, or perhaps the same set was owned by several different collectors at various times and was thus counted more than once. Short of all the proud owners sticking up their hands and 'coming clean' the real number of extant sets can only be guessed at.

Fortunately for the interested general reader, a complete reprint was published at New York by Grove Press in 1966, from the original in Germany. This new edition contains a fascinating Introduction by Mr G. Legman (which was partially responsible, incidentally, for getting the present writer interested in erotica) in which he puts forward a persuasive argument in favour of *My Secret Life* being written by Ashbee. Several other authorities have disputed this, however, and although Mr Legman persists in his theory it is far from certain that he is correct. My own view, for what it is worth, is that Ashbee may have been involved in its publication. The Introduction, in which it is claimed that the real author is dead, could at a stretch of the imagination be genuine and along with the extensive Index in volume eleven be by Ashbee. And Ashbee had both the resources and the contacts to embark on such an extensive printing job. But even if this theory is correct it brings us no closer to who actually wrote the bulk of the book; his identity will have to await the outcome of a new researcher in the field, in Illinois, who is doing sterling work by painstakingly going through *My Secret Life* and collating recognizable names, dates and places into a pattern that might point to the author. I have no idea who he will unearth, but I will be very surprised if it is anyone we have heard of.

*   *   *   *   *

OPPOSITE Plate for *Country Retirement*, see page 119 and colour plate opposite page 129

OPPOSITE Plate for *Country Retirement*, see page 119 and colour plate opposite page 128

In France, the 19th century started well and promptly went into a decline for more than thirty years. Excepting *Le Diable au corps* (1803), which properly belongs to the preceding century and has already been dealt with in the appropriate place, the first important erotic work of the new century was *L'Enfant du bordel* (1800), a short, picaresque novel in two volumes concerning the adventures of what today would be called teenagers. It has been ascribed to Guillaume Charles Antoine Pigault-Lebrun (1753–1835), the author of *La Folie espagnole* (1799) and *Le Citateur* (1803), the latter being a virulent attack on the Bible which Napoleon had issued in enormous quantities during his difficulties with the Pope.

It is said that *L'Enfant du bordel* has been translated into English, but if it has no copy of it seems to survive. There is, however, an undated Portuguese translation entitled *O Cherubim ou O Filho de Paes Incognitos*. Ashbee notices this briefly and points out that it contains in its second volume a continuation of the story. 'This is very curious and interesting', he continues, 'because, although at the end of the second volume, of the first edition, of "L'Enfant du Bordel", a continuation is promised, no such continuation, as far as I have been able to ascertain, exists in French.' (See *Ashbee*, vol. 1, p. 160.) Unless this continuation is something that a hack in Lisbon cobbled together – which seems improbable because Ashbee would quickly have spotted any obvious change in style – the possibility exists that the Portuguese translation is, in part, a true first edition.

After *L'Enfant du bordel* there was a lull. Two slightly interesting novels attributed to Félicité de Choiseuil-Meuse appeared in 1802 and 1807, *Amélie de Saint-Far ou la fatale erreur* and *Julie ou J' ai sauvé ma rose*, but of greater importance, if in fact it ever existed at all, is the '1805' first edition of *Lettres d'un provençal à son épouse*, a series of letters concerning the brothels and *maisons auxiliaires* of Paris, and their occupants. The earliest edition of this to have been recorded with any authority was published at Brussels in 1867, possibly by Jean-Pierre Blanche, although it was a bookseller named Charles Sacré-Duquesne who was prosecuted for selling it in May 1868. No earlier edition has ever been seen or reliably described, and until one surfaces it seems safe to assume that the rumour of its existence arose from manuscript copies of the work that circulated in Paris during the early 1860s, when it may actually have first been written, which were falsely dated '1805'. One of these calligraphic manuscripts was sold at auction on 27 April 1971 in the Parke-Bernet 'Libertine Literature' sale (lot 112), and its description matches closely that given by Perceau, Gay and other authorities of a printed '1805' edition which, however, none of them had managed to see.

One pointer towards an answer to this puzzle lies in the fact that both the manuscript copies and printed editions give the author as being 'M. H....y'. J. Lemonnyer, in his revision of the *Gay* bibliography (vol. 1, 1897), suggested one candidate by filling out the gap in the name so that it reads 'Hankey' and adding a cautious mark of interrogation. Frederick Hankey, the person referred to by Lemonnyer, was a wealthy Englishman who lived much of his adult life, until his death in 1882, at Paris where he gathered about him a particularly fine collection of erotic books and prints, which he had sumptuously bound by

Trautz–Bauzonnet and other masters of their craft, and erotic artifacts that included ivory dildoes, antique chastity belts and statuary of marble and bronze. His friends and acquaintances included the Goncourt brothers, Octave Uzanne, who was the editor of the literary periodical *Le Livre*, the artist Félicien Rops and, inevitably, Ashbee. 'Hankey was in every respect an original'; wrote Ashbee, 'he never rose until after mid-day, and his hours of reception were after 10 o'clock at night, when he was to be found among his books. He had fair hair, blue eyes, and an almost feminine expression, and answered in many respects to the descriptions which have reached us of the Marquis de Sade, his favourite author. He told me he had on one occasion recovered from a serious illness by suddenly obtaining an edition of *Justine* which he had long sought in vain. He had a curious habit of repeating himself, which at times rendered his conversation tedious.' (*Ashbee*, vol. 3, pp. li–lii.)

The Goncourts were less generous in their estimation of Hankey. In a memorable entry in their *Journal* for 7 April 1862 the brothers wrote:

Today I visited a madman, a monster, one of those men on the edge of the abyss. Through him, as through a torn veil, I glimpsed something abominable, a frightening aspect of a blasé moneyed aristocracy, the English aristocracy which brings ferocity to love, and finds satisfaction only through the sufferings of women.

At the *bal de l'Opéra*, a young Englishman who had been introduced to [Victor de] Saint-Victor said to him, quite simply and by way of opening the conversation, 'that one could hardly find anything to amuse oneself with at Paris, that London was infinitely superior, that at London there was a very good place, the establishment of Mistress Jenkins, where there were young girls about thirteen years of age with whom one could first play the teacher, then whip them etc... At various times in the past a friend and I have hired a window for a large sum, in order to see a murderess who was to be hung, and we had some women with us that we could *do things* to', – his words are always extremely decent – 'at the moment she was hung, etc. . . .' And today Saint-Victor introduced me into the home of this terrible eccentric. He is a young man about thirty years old, bald, with temples swelling out like an orange, his eyes are blue and piercing, his skin extremely fine revealing the subcutaneous network of veins, his head – and this is strange – is the head of one of those emaciated and ecstatic young priests who surround the bishops in old pictures. An elegant young man with a little stiffness in the arms and the bodily movements, at once mechanical and feverish, of a person in the early stages of a disease of the spinal marrow, and together with all that, excellent manners, exquisite politeness and a particularly gentle manner of speaking.

He opened a large, breast high book-case in which is to be found a curious collection of admirably bound erotic works, and handing me a Meibomius, *Utilité de la flagellation dans les plaisirs de l'amour et du mariage*, bound by one of the leading book-binders of Paris with interior metal clasps representing phalluses, skulls and instruments of torture, for all of which he had supplied the original designs, he said: 'Ah! these clasps . . . no, the bookbinder didn't want to make them . . . then I let him borrow my books . . . now he makes his wife very miserable . . . he goes after little girls . . . but I have my clasps.' And showing us a book which was all ready for binding: 'yes, for this one I am waiting for the skin of a young girl, etc.' And looking at us all the while with a maniacal gleam in his eye, his fingers spread out before him, he spoke, he spoke continuously and his somewhat chanting voice, which would stop and then immediately start up again, seemed to pierce our ears with its cannibalistic words.

This portrait describes a man sufficiently familiar with brothels to turn up his nose at the ones in Paris in preference to those in London and who would, therefore, be eminently qualified to write a book on the subject. And as Ashbee has shown, Hankey was no stranger to literary flights of fancy either, for he had a hand in the composition of an erotic novel in dialogue form called *L'École des biches* ('Paris, 1863' [Brussels: J.-P. Blanche, 1868]) – if not another work, *Instruction libertine* ('Sadopolis, 1860' [Brussels: Blanche, 1870]) as well – both of which, like *Lettres d'un provençal à son épouse*, circulated in manuscript prior to being published.

None of this is certain of course, or anything more than circumstantial, but as G. Legman says at the close of his essay that attempts to establish Ashbee as the author of *My Secret Life*, 'a more likely candidate will not easily be found.'[8]

The first really important work in French to come from the clandestine presses of the 19th century, however, and one that is still reprinted, is *Gamiani ou une nuit d'excès*, a brief tale written largely as a dialogue between two tribades that is usually said to have been the work of Alfred de Musset (1810–57), one of the key figures in the Romantic movement. Until 1980, when a copy of the very rare first edition in a fine private Swiss collection was printed in facsimile by Slatkine of Geneva, the subtitle of the book has always been recorded as 'ou deux nuits d'excès', which is in actuality the subtitle of the book's second part. An earlier facsimile edition, done secretly in 1926, possibly at Paris, incorporated both these subtitles in their correct places at the beginning of each of the two parts, but strangely persisted in retaining the *'deux nuits'* for the main titlepage, perhaps for the sake of tradition. With the new Swiss reprint, *Gamiani* appears for the first time in almost 150 years with its true title.

Gamiani, as it was first published at 'Brussels' – really at Paris – in 1833, is a strange book, being as much an album of erotic illustrations as a short piece of fiction. And although a slim volume, amounting to less than thirty pages, it measures height by breadth approximately 340 mm × 265 mm – or nearly half as big again, overall, as a London telephone directory – which means that it does not sit too comfortably on the bookshelf. But despite its unwieldiness it is an attractive production that presages what has been called the 'golden age' of French erotic book production in the 1920s and 1930s. The text, which is printed in columns, is reproduced by lithography from a calligraphic manuscript and is illustrated with twelve very free plates, again lithographs, which have generally been ascribed to Achille Devéria and Henri Grévedon.[9] Certainly two artists would appear to have been at work, for the plates are uniform neither in style or quality, the four in part two being much less attractive.

Reprints quickly followed, the first in 1835 and at least thirty-nine others by 1928 when Perceau stopped counting in his *Bibliographie du roman érotique*. Not

L'ECOLE

DES BICHES

OU

MOEURS DES PETITES DAMES DE CE TEMPS.

PARIS

M DCCC LXIII

LEFT Titlepage of the first edition of *L'Ecole des biches* decorated with an original pen and ink drawing by Chauvet

OPPOSITE An original pen and ink drawing by Chauvet for *L'Ecole des biches*

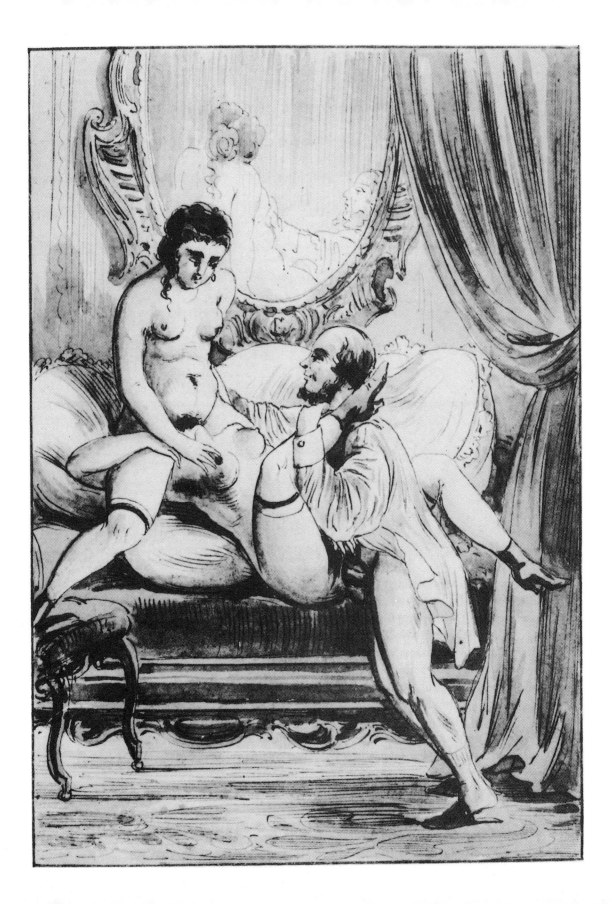

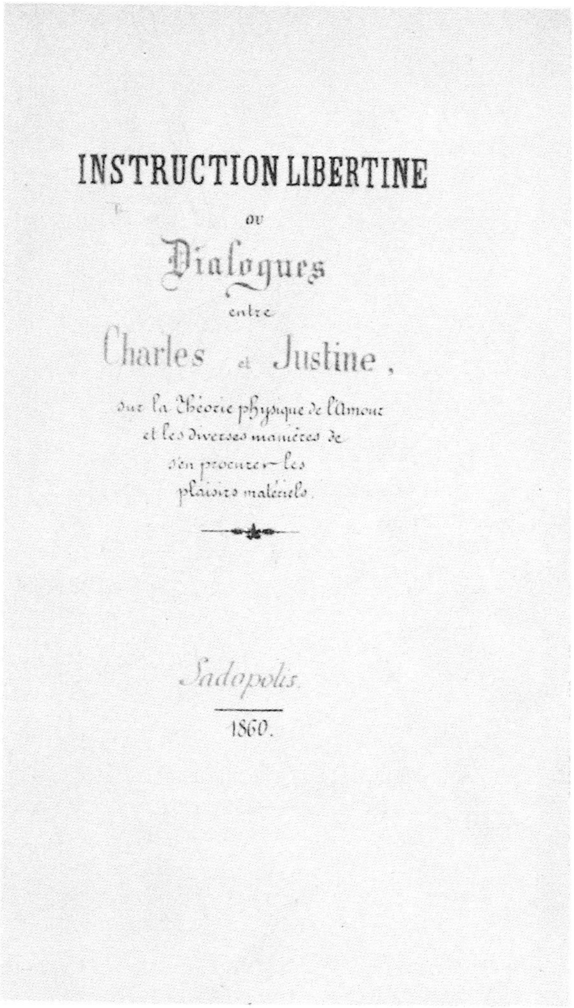

INSTRUCTION LIBERTINE

ou

Dialogues

entre

Charles et Justine,

sur la Théorie physique de l'Amour
et les diverses manières de
s'en procurer les
plaisirs matériels.

Sadopolis.

1860.

3.

toutes les ressources de l'Amour libre et heureux.
L'accord le plus parfait régnait toujours entre eux, mal-
gré le temps et la jouissance satisfaite, ils avaient l'un
dans l'autre une confiance absolue et méritée. Justi-
-ne trouvait dans Charles, outre un amant discret et
infatigable, un homme plein d'un esprit ferme,
juste et sensé, exempt de préjugés, mais les respec-
tant pour le monde.

Charles reconnaissait en Justine, une
femme peu capricieuse, d'un coeur excellent porté
à l'Amour et à ses plaisirs par un tempérament
de feu, mais réglé par un esprit raisonnable, pers-
picace autant que curieux d'apprendre! Ces deux
âmes devaient s'entendre.

Un jour Charles trouva à la chambrette
un avis de Justine, qui le prévenait que le soir mê-
-me elle y viendrait passer la nuit, la journée du
lendemain et la nuit suivante, ayant obtenu de son
mari d'aller passer deux ou trois jours chez une amie
à quatre lieues de Paris; elle se proposant de ne s'y
rendre que le surlendemain et de n'y rester qu'un jour
pour en donner d'abord un entier et deux nuits à l'Amour.

Les deux amants désiraient depuis long-
temps pouvoir coucher ensemble au moins une nuit,
et cela n'avait pas été possible jusques là.

Charles fut enchanté, il lui semblait qu'il

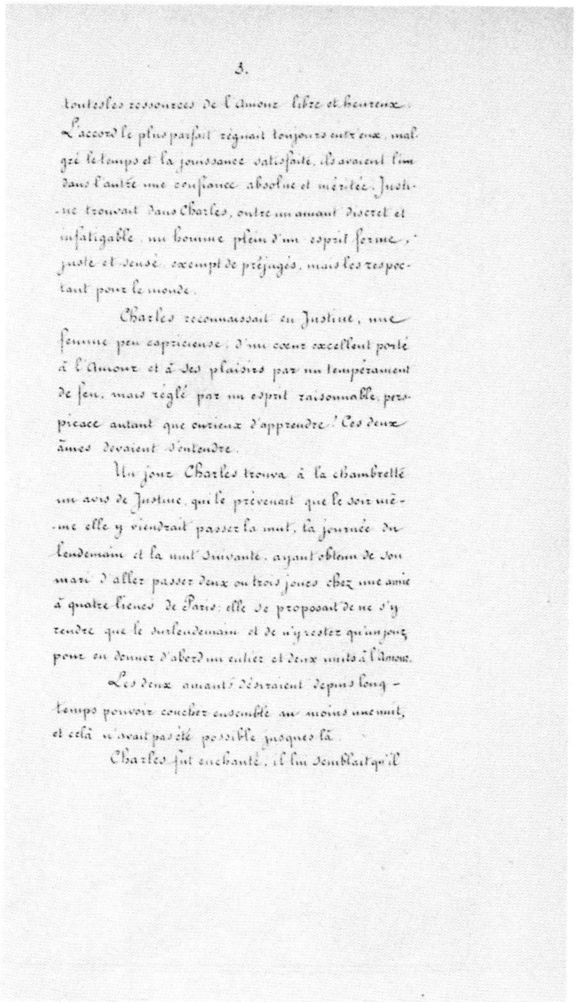

all of these reproduced the plates of the original edition. Some had no plates at all, while others were illustrated by Félicien Rops or Jules Adolphe Chauvet.

The ascription of *Gamiani* to Musset began with the second edition of the book in 1835, on the titlepage of which the author is given to be 'Alcide, baron de M***'. The initials of this name, A. D. M., were taken to mean Alfred de Musset and it has stuck ever since, some later editions merely printing the initials themselves to emphasize the point further. In 1864, three editions of *Gamiani* appeared in quick succession, the first two reinforcing the Musset ascription, although more by suggestion than by hard evidence. The first of these reprints – 'Amsterdam [Paris, Barraud], 1840' – included a Preface in which the old chestnut about the book having been written as a sort of a bet seems first to have been aired. Musset is not named – he is referred to as 'our young writer' – but a number of clues are provided that point to him indirectly. Following this Preface are some lines of verse, said to be by the 'young writer', that because of their appearance for the first time in an edition of *Gamiani* were later reprinted in the *Nouveau*

ABOVE Titlepage and specimen of text of the rare *Instruction libertine*, reproduced by lithography from a caligraphic manuscript

Parnasse satyrique (1866), a repertoire of erotic 19th-century poetry published by Auguste Poulet-Malassis as a supplement to his similar *Parnasse Satyrique* of 1864, where they were credited to Alfred de Musset. Elsewhere they have been credited to Gustave Drouineau. In the second edition of 1864 – 'Lesbos [Brussels], Institution Méry – Pavillon Baudelaire' – the publisher, Auguste Poulet-Malassis, added an anonymous but thinly veiled portrait of Musset which he extracted from *Adieux au monde* (1854), the dubious autobiography of the Comtesse de Chabrillan otherwise known as Céleste Mogador who, during the time that she worked in a brothel near Paris, entertained the poet. Musset does not fare too well in the Comtesse's memoirs, appearing as a petulant, drunken lout given to such boorish behaviour as pouring bottles of Vichy water over his companions at dinner.

The story of *Gamiani* is straightforward enough. A young man named Alcide takes an interest in the Comtesse Gamiani – who has been seen as a disguised 'George Sand' (Lucile-Aurore Dupin), Musset's lover – and manages to hide himself in her bedroom where he observes her and a young girl named Fanny engaged in a lesbian *affaire*. He becomes aroused and joins in, after which turns are taken at telling their stories in between which orgies take place. These stories and orgies involve rape in a monastery, bestiality with a variety of animals including a donkey and a horrible episode where a man strays into a convent and is debauched to such a degree by the inmates that he appears dead at the end of it. The nuns decide to hang him. Seeing that this has produced an erection in the unfortunate fellow, the mother superior climbs aboard him but their combined weight proves too much for the rope and the two crash to the ground, the nun's legs being broken in the process. The fall revives the man sufficiently to allow him to strangle the mother superior, after which he expires. The book finishes on an equally unsavoury note with Gamiani tricking Fanny into drinking a particularly mordant poison, and then taking some herself: '. . . I have known all the extremes of sensuality,' cries Gamiani. 'Understand that, fool! But I still have to know whether in the torments of the poison, in the agonies of another woman joined with my own, a still greater sensuality is possible! It is appalling, do you hear! I am dying in an agony of pleasure, an agony of suffering! . . . I can't stand it any more! . . .'

The relationship between death and sexuality that is touched upon here is developed more fully and with greater force and intellect by some of the 20th-century erotic writers, in particular Georges Bataille, as will be seen below. But the fact that it approaches the subject at all, and that as a piece of book production it anticipates the way that erotica will look a hundred years later, make *Gamiani* rather more interesting than if it were just another piece of commercial pornography, and despite its unpleasant aspects it deserves its continued fame.

* * * * *

To generalize, France, or at least French erotica, was dominated during the 1860s and 1870s by just two publishers, Auguste Poulet-Malassis and Jules Gay, and their output was almost entirely devoted to reprints of works from earlier times, usually the 18th century. Auguste Poulet-Malassis (1825–1878) was the grandson of Mirabeau's publisher, Jean-Zacharie Malassis, and the most cursory look at the output of the two men will show that Auguste was cast more in the mould of Jean-Zacharie than his father who was a respectable printer of police notices and similar legal and judicial documents. Today, Auguste is famous for just one book, *Les Fleurs du mal* (1857) of Charles Baudelaire which, following absurd attacks in *Le Figaro* and elsewhere, was prosecuted. Both author and publisher were fined, and six of the poems in the collection suppressed. In 1866, the year before Baudelaire's death, Poulet-Malassis reissued the six poems, together with some unpublished fragments of other works, in a small volume that he entitled with grim appropriateness *Les Épaves*, which can be rendered as either 'Strays' or 'Wreckage'. Although limited to only 260 copies, it was prosecuted with some other erotic books when copies were imported into France from Belgium and in May 1868 a bookseller named Charles Sacré-Duquesne, already mentioned in connection with *Lettres d'un provençal à son épouse*, was found guilty of 'outraging public morality, religion and good manners.' *Les Épaves* was not the only book published by Poulet-Malassis to get Sacré-Duquesne into difficulties; a short cycle of sonnets called *Les Amies* ('Segovie, 1868' [Brussels, 1867]) attributed to 'le licencié Pablo de Herlagnèz' was among them as well. 'These sonnets,' wrote Ashbee, '6 in number, are pretty, but display no great talent ... The author's real name is Paul Verlaine.' (See *Ashbee*, vol. 1, p. 42; he was noticing the second edition, also published at Brussels but probably by a man named Maximilian-Désiré-Vital-Puissant, if that was his real name.)

To *amateurs* of erotica, however, Poulet-Malassis is better known for his beautifully printed editions of such authors as Andréa de Nerciat, Pierre-Jean de Béranger (1780–1857) and Sade, and his fine reprints of earlier collections of satirical verse. Between about 1866 and 1869, he published these and others like them in collaboration with a printer named Briard and a third man named Alphonse Lécrivain, and the fruits of this collaboration produced some of the most exquisite erotic books ever seen, recognizable at once by their fine printing, paper and design and their intelligent and scholarly Introductions and annotation. In 1869, the trio split up, Poulet-Malassis carrying on by himself and the other two working together.

One of Poulet-Malassis' most interesting original publications was *Le Théâtre érotique de la rue de la Santé* which he first issued in 1864, and again in a more expanded form in 1866. Erotic theatre was not a new thing in France, and a number of extremely licentious playlets by such authors as Legrand, the Comte de Caylus, Bussy-Rabutin and Piron which had originally been published separately were gathered together and issued as *Théâtre Gaillard* ('Glascow', 1776). This was reprinted many times, once, apparently, by Poulet-Malassis in 1866, and in 1867 Jules Gay published a *Nouveau Théâtre Gaillard* in which was collected some pieces that had escaped or been overlooked by the editor of the earlier anthology. *Le Théâtre érotique de la rue de la Santé* was a similar collection, but by such contemporary writers as Henri Monnier, Albert Glatigny and Lemercier de Neuville. And whereas the 18th-century plays had been performed by real people, these were performed by marionettes, secretly and before a select audience of the authors and their cronies. Typical of these plays is *La Grisette et l'étudiant* by Henri Monnier. Set in a furnished room, it involves a series of love scenes between a student and his young girlfriend that are interspersed with arguments. Next door to the student's room lives M. Prudhomme, a dour and conservative *bourgeois* and Monnier's most famous creation in his more respectable writings, who is not seen but whose voice is heard booming through the wall at inopportune moments. One of these occurs when the boy and the girl are being particularly noisy in their lovemaking. Over the shrieks of passion from the girl, Prudhomme is heard to bellow out '. . . here, enough of that. If you don't stop I shall be forced to lay violent hands on myself!'

Another erotic play was *À La Feuille de Rose*, by Guy de Maupassant and

BELOW First edition of *Le Theatre érotique de la rue de la Santé*, with one of the two frontispieces by Félician Rops

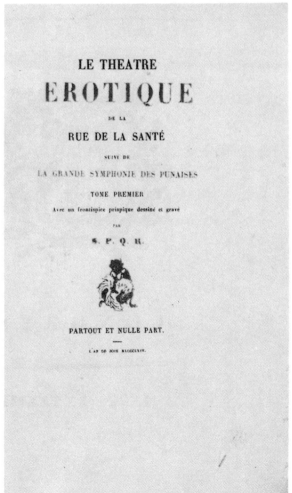

THÉATRE GAILLARD.

TOME PREMIER.

LONDRES.

M. DCC. LXXXVIII.

LEFT Titlepage of an edition of *Théatre gaillard* published at Paris by Hubert-Martin Cazin. See colour plate opposite page 145

G. de M.

A LA FEUILLE
DE ROSE

MAISON TURQUE

Comédie de mœurs (mauvaises)
en un acte en prose
représentée pour la première fois
à Paris en 1875

PARIS

1945

RIGHT First edition of an erotic play by Guy de Maupassant. It was published at Nice and not Paris

Robert Pinchon. This was performed twice in 1875 with live actors, the second sitting, so to speak, being attended by luminaries of the stature of Flaubert – who laughed all the way through – Edmund de Goncourt, Émile Zola and Turgenev. The action of the play takes place in a brothel done out with Turkish-style trappings. Into this establishment enters the respected mayor of a provincial town called Conville, M. Beauflanquet and his wife, who labour under the misapprehension that they are in an hotel. The mayor is seduced by two of the whores, while his wife is subjected to verbal indignities of the sort involving endless *double entendres*. Between times, other bits of business take place involving characters like a sort of scullion whose function is to wash out the condoms and who suffers with a dreadful stammer, particularly over words that sound vaguely suggestive at the best of times; and a poverty-stricken soldier who, unable to raise the cash to satisfy his lust in the conventional way, has to make do with a bottle of urine from one of the girls. It is not one of Maupassant's most outstanding literary achievements, but it is extremely funny in a schoolboyish way and deserves to be better known. The first printed edition of *À La Feuille de Rose, Maison Turque*, to give it its full title, appeared at 'Paris' (actually Nice) in 1945. Only 225 copies were run off, and it carried a Preface, unsigned, by Pierre Borel, the author of several studies of Maupassant including *Le Destin tragique de Guy de Maupassant* (1927). A second edition of the play was published in 1960 by Claude Tchou in his series *Au Cercle du Livre Précieux*.

Jules Gay, the other major publisher of erotica in the middle of the 19th century, was the archetypal nomad of his profession. He started his career with premises on the quai des Grands Augustins, overlooking the Île de la Cité in the centre of Paris, but harassment from the law forced him to leave France and settle for a while in Brussels, where he formed a partnership with a printer named Mertens. From Brussels he moved to Geneva in 1868, and to Turin in 1870, where he teamed up with the printer Vincent Bona, and in 1872 and 1873 divided his time between Nice and San Remo. After this he returned once more to Brussels where he formed a business relationship with a Mlle Doucé, and on their open publications will be found the imprint 'Gay et Doucé'. While he was in Turin, Gay founded the *Société des bibliophiles cosmopolites* under whose auspices he published a number of erotic works, most notably a series that he called the *Bibliothèque libre* which consisted mainly of reprints of obscene pamphlets issued originally at the time of the Revolution in France. Gay's impressive-sounding *Société* was, however, a bit of a sham since the only members were himself and his son, Jean.

Although Gay kept on the move for most of his professional life, and carefully disguised his identity on his more outspoken publications, he did not escape the inevitable hazards of his calling and was prosecuted several times. In 1863 he was fined and had his stock seized, and two years later was in trouble again, this time in company with Poulet-Malassis and others, when he was accused of publishing a considerable number of erotic or obscene books. Found guilty again, he was fined 500 francs and sentenced to four months' imprisonment. Not being one to avoid turning adversity to his advantage, Gay wrote up an account of these trials, including extracts from the prosecuted books and Gallien's defence speech, and published it in Italy, in a beautifully printed volume called *Procès des raretés bibliographiques* (1875) which was limited to just 100 copies. Unfortunately, somebody took exception to this as well – the French authorities presumably – for fifty copies were seized by the Italian police and destroyed, making it one of Gay's rarest publications.

Like Poulet-Malassis, as has been said, Gay concentrated primarily on reprinting books from earlier times, and it was not an uncommon thing for the two men to have editions of the same book available simultaneously. In one or two cases, where these books have closely resembled one another, problems have been created for book collectors in later years, but in general the publications of the two men are easily distinguishable.

Jules Gay published very little original material, but his son Jean was not at all averse to mixing reprints with any interesting new works that came his way. The exact date when the father and son team parted company, if it ever did completely do so, is not known but the earliest solo effort of Gay junior that I am aware of is a novel by the young Joris-Karl Huysmans (Charles Marie Georges) entitled *Marthe, histoire d'une fille* that was printed by Félix Callewaert and published by Gay at Brussels in 1876. Huysmans' first book had been a collection of prose poems very much in the style of Baudelaire and Bertrand. Called *Le Drageoir à épices*, it had been published at Paris by Dentu in 1874. But *Marthe* was a very different sort of book, being probably the first French novel to deal realistically with the life of a prostitute in a licensed brothel, and the author was obliged to think twice before trying to get it published in France, settling instead on Brussels. There is a tradition that Huysmans wrote an Introduction for an edition of *Gamiani* that Gay published in 1876, but since no edition of that date can be traced the story may be apocryphal.

Four years after *Marthe*, in 1880, Jean Gay – possibly in collaboration with his father – secretly published the first volume of *Les Cousines de la colonelle*, giving it the false imprint 'Lisbonne, chez Antonio da Boa-Vista' and the equally fictitious author 'madame la vicomtesse de Cœur-Brûlant'. Shortly afterwards, a second volume appeared together with a reprint of the first. All authorities have said that this two-volume edition was published in 1885 and that, like the original edition of volume one in 1880, it was published at Brussels by Gay in partnership with Doucé. Manuscript notes by H. S. Ashbee in British Library copies (shelf mark: P.C. 31. d. 6) throw these assumptions into doubt. According to Ashbee, volume one *was* published at Brussels in 1880, but by 'J. J. Gay' and volume two – and presumably the reprint of volume one as well – was published at Paris in 1882 by Doucé alone.

For many years this story of two sisters who enter into a lesbian relationship when their respective husbands die was attributed to Guy de Maupassant despite his strenuous denials. In reality the author was a certain Marquise de Mannoury d'Ectot, formerly Le Blanc, who in her younger days acted as host to poets and artists at her house near Argentan in northern France. Among those who visited her was Paul Verlaine. The manuscript of *Les Cousines de la colonelle* was first offered to another publisher of erotica in Brussels, Henri Kistemaeckers, who turned it down on the grounds, presumably, that it was insufficiently filthy. Kisemaeckers preferred fairly strong material for his clandestine productions, his 'open' ones being often anti-clerical and Republican in tone, or just a bit odd, as in the case of the celebrated and epic masturbation novel *Charlot s'amuse* (1883) of Paul Bonnetain. In effect, *Les Cousines de la colonelle* was too strong to publish legitimately and by virtue of its emphasis on metaphors rather than outright indecencies, not strong enough for the buyers of his clandestine offerings. Kistemaeckers, however, was a decent enough cove to introduce the author to the eventual publisher of her book.

Another novel with a strong lesbian theme that is generally thought to be by Mannoury d'Ectot is *Le Roman de Violette*. A claim on the titlepage that it is an 'Œuvre Posthume d'Une Célébrité Masquée' has led to a number of well-known, but dead, authors having the paternity of this novel foisted on their memories, chief among these being Alexandre Dumas *père*, Théophile Gautier and – although still just about alive – Victor Hugo. But all the indications suggest Mannoury d'Ectot to be the true author. *Le Roman de Violette* has the same false place of publication on the titlepage as *Les Cousines de la·colonelle*, but is falsely dated '1870'. In circumstances similar to those of *Les Cousines*, the second book was turned down by Gay to whom it was first offered, but thanks to representations by the poet Théodore Hannon, author of *Rimes de joie* (1881) and, as 'Monsieur de la Braguette', the clandestine *Les Treize sonnets du doigt dedans* (1882), it was taken up by a relative newcomer to the erotica field, Auguste Brancart, who published it in 1883 at Brussels.

Although little is known of Brancart, he was to become one of the most important, and prolific, publishers of erotic books of his time, first from Brussels, where he operated from about 1880 and later at Amsterdam. When he made this move from Belgium to Holland is not certain, but in 1886 he published a reprint of the *Mémoires d'un vieillard de vingt-cinq ans*, a novel originally issued in 1809 in five volumes, from Amsterdam so he must have left Brussels at least as early as 1886. Although not surviving as a publisher, so far as is known, much beyond about 1896, Brancart was in a sense a link between the 19th and 20th centuries, between the 'quality' publishers like Gay and Poulet-Malassis and the erudite Isidore Liseux, who never feared to place his name on his books, and sordid *colporteurs* like Elias Gaucher and others of his kidney who flooded the market with cheaply produced and largely illiterate rubbish.

Taking a leaf from Gay's book, Brancart founded his own pompous-sounding literary association which plagiaristically he christened the '*Société des bibliophiles cosmopolites*'. Under the portentous subheading '*Musée secret du bibliophile anglais*', he issued a series of translations, some of which are thought to have been done by Hector France, of English flagellation novels. Louis Perceau, in his *Bibliographie du roman érotique*, is of the opinion that this series began in 1880 but it is likely that he is in error. One of the titles in the series is 'Le Colonel Spanker', *Conférence expérimentale*, the first edition of which he dates 1880. It is true that this date appears on the titlepage, but in a copy of this edition in the British Library a manuscript note by Ashbee indicates that it was published in 1886 at Amsterdam. Ashbee's manuscript notes come to the aid of the researcher into erotica yet again concerning Brancart, in respect of an author he published who signed his works 'E. D.' Between 1887 and 1894 this writer turned out

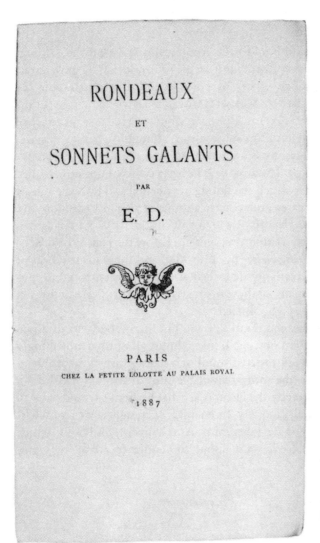

RIGHT The titlepage of
erotic verses by 'E.D.'

FAR RIGHT A manuscript
note in it by H. S. Ashbee
giving details of authorship

fourteen novels, a volume of plays and a collection of verse; a fifteenth novel, *Mémoires d'une danseuse russe* (1894), was ascribed to 'E. D.' on the titlepage but stylistically it may be by somebody else. In the catalogue of *l'Enfer* (1919; – no. 175), the compilers – who included Louis Perceau – identify 'E. D.' as a man named Dumoulin who was either a wine merchant from Bordeaux or a civil servant working for the Gironde. Seventeen years later, in 1930, Perceau seems to have come to a different conclusion for in his *Bibliographie du roman érotique*, published in that year, he states that 'E. D.' was a professor named Desjardins who had been attached to the faculty of the university of Montpellier. As it happens, Perceau and his fellow collaborators on *l'Enfer* had been correct in the first instance. A copy of 'E. D.'s' first book, *Rondeaux et sonnets galantes* (1887), is in the British Library and has a note by Ashbee giving not just the name of the author, which is Edmund Dumoulin, but his address as well.

Considering that Dumoulin managed to write sixteen books in seven years, it might be thought that Brancart could have comfortably lived off the earnings he made from them and their reprints, but it seems probable that he gave a start in life to an even more prolific writer of pornography, the remarkable 'Le Nismois' who has been identified by Martial Beauvais in articles he wrote for the *Dictionnaire des œuvres érotiques* (1971) as Alphonse Momas, a civil servant attached to the police who in later life took up spiritualism, although whether this was instead of or as well as pornography is uncertain. Momas's first book was an un-located work, *Un Caprice* (1891). The same year he had a two-volume novel called *Secrets de poste* published, after which the floodgates opened and by 1924 at least seventy-four other books appeared under one or another of his many pseudonyms, the last entitled *Un Lupanar d'hommes* by 'J. Le Wismois [sic]'. So far as it is possible to tell, Momas stopped writing at a point just before the First World War. In 1910 appeared *Dévotes et patronnesses* by 'L'Érotin,' and subsequent works of his noticed by Perceau are invariably described as being printed from an 'un-published manuscript'. And many of these manuscripts existed; Perceau lists ten of them, all in the possession of a bookseller.

What sort of person Momas was is not known, but for anybody to sit down and churn out almost a hundred obscene books, almost all of them appallingly badly written, implies either a disordered mind or a serious cash-flow problem. This latter explanation seems the more reasonable since if Momas had been a compulsive writer of pornography the chances are that his books would have all been on a similar theme: flagellation, say, or enemas, or straight sex even, whatever direction his fancy might have taken him. As it happens, his books, which include erotic plays as well, cover just about the entire spectrum of sexual

OPPOSITE One of the illustrations to the first edition of *Gamiani*

BELOW LEFT and RIGHT A typical 'Le Nismois' titlepage, together with a specimen of his handwriting on the envelope of a letter addressed to Louis Perceau

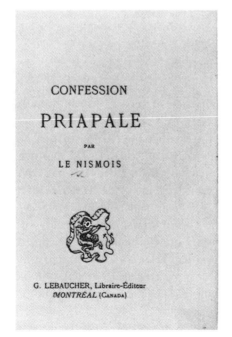

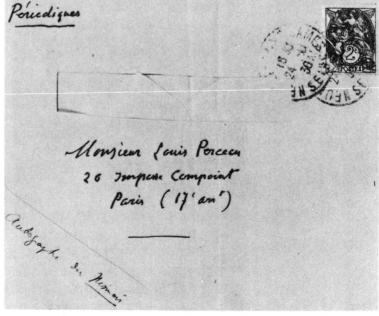

OPPOSITE Frontispiece of
an edition of *Théatre gaillard*
published at Paris by
Hubert-Martin Cazin.
See illustration page 138

experience and lead one to suppose that in his later career he was 'writing to order' for a bookseller who, sensing the market was about ready for a couple of incest novels for instance, would drop Alphonse a line and have him knock them out. This is very approximately what Henry Miller and Anaïs Nin and others were to do thirty years or so later when they wrote typescript erotica – at something like fifty cents a page after crooked agents had taken their cut – for the Oklahoma oil millionaire Roy Johnson. In their case, however, they retained their integrity for as Anaïs Nin relates in the third volume of her *Diaries* (1969) and, extracted from those, in *Delta of Venus* (1977), the first volume of her openly published erotic stories, the authors eventually rebelled against their patron's philistine complaints about the 'literary' quality of the material he was buying. This whole amazing story will be found admirably written up by one of the participants in Mr G. Legman's Introduction to the present author's *The Private Case* (1981).

But Brancart, who could only have published Momas for about five years, did not confine himself to rubbish of that sort, or even to the rather better novels of contemporaries of Momas like Edmund Dumoulin. He reprinted the classics of the preceding centuries – and those of his own, a practice that must have led to conflicts with his fellow publishers on occasion. Among these reprints were the *Joyeusetés galantes et autres* (1884), a collection of erotic pieces by 'Vidame Bonaventure de la Braguette' [i.e. the poet Albert Glatigny] which he published in direct competition to a very similar anthology published by Mlle Doucé at Paris in the same year, and Théophile Gautier's scabrous but jolly record of his sojourn to Italy in 1850, *Lettre à la Présidente*, which he issued during the same year that the first edition came out, 1890. Brancart also had an eye on the tourist trade, or booksellers in London like Edward Avery and Charles Hirsch, for he produced new editions of English works. The reprint of Edward Sellon's *Ups and Downs of Life* as *The Amorous Prowess of a Jolly Fellow* (1892) was one of these as we have seen above, and about the same time he also issued a reprint of *The Pearl* in three volumes which was itself pirated by a new publisher in Holland named P. Bergé who ran a concern called the 'Artistiek-Bureau' in Rotterdam until at least 1910.

Brancart was not the last publisher of erotica; while there are laws that prohibit literature, of whatever sort, there will be those who are prepared to break them, and this is as it should be. But Brancart was one of the last of a particular breed of publisher who convey the impression of men whose interest in what they do is not solely financial. He liked books for their own sake and while his publications were not so well produced as those of Gay or Poulet-Malassis before him, particularly the latter who almost bankrupted himself to maintain his standards of excellence, they were usually printed on Van Gelder or some equally good paper and were generally superior to the sort of books that by 1900 were beginning to emanate from the presses of people like Bergé. The French publishers of the 1920s and 1930s loved books too, but they were catering to an extremely narrow market of wealthy collectors who could afford to pay for fine paper, beautiful typography and design and illustrations by important artists. Brancart on the

OBSCENIA

LETTRE A LA PRÉSIDENTE

POÉSIES ÉROTIQUES

Édition illustrée de huit eaux-fortes
originales de Van Troizem et d'une singulière
planche de musique
et précédée d'un avertissement

PAR UN BIBLIOPHILE

———

BRUXELLES
—
CHEZ LES SUCCESSEURS DE POULET-MALASSIS
—
1907

other hand was catering to what by comparison was a mass market, and the risks that he took were correspondingly greater. Not all his books were masterpieces, either of the printers' art or literature, but enough of them were to show that he cared just a little for what he did; it is disagreeable to consider that today, printers and publishers in such places as San Diego who are able to operate in complete freedom, and who collectively have an annual financial turnover that could probably match the sort of figures associated with national defence budgets, are able to produce nothing but worthless junk. Perhaps people are really what they read – and publish – rather than what they eat.

ABOVE LEFT and RIGHT An edition of Gautier's *Lettre à la Présidente*, published together with his erotic poems, issued at Paris by J. Chevrel. The frontispiece (illustrated) and plates are by 'Van Troizem' – i.e. Martin van Maële

CHAPTER FOUR

THE 20ᵗʰ CENTURY

FAMILIAR LANDSCAPES, NEW DIRECTIONS

> Never ask a man of the world: 'Fancy a blow-job?' Only little street girls express themselves like that. Instead, whisper softly in his ear: 'Would you care to use my mouth?'
>
> Pierre Louÿs *Manuel de Civilité pour les petites filles à l'usage des maisons d'éducation* (1926)

This chapter will of necessity be short. There is still a little while to go before we reach the year 2000, and together Maurice Girodias and Jean-Jacques Pauvert hammered some of the first nails into the coffin of literary censorship by the century's half-way mark; Girodias with the formation of the Olympia Press at Paris in 1953, and Pauvert by having the courage to publish openly in France for the first time the works of the Marquis de Sade, commencing in the final days of 1947 with the *Histoire de Juliette*. Within the definitions that have been set for the present book, then, the history of erotic literature in the 20th century is really only the story of its first fifty years.

The beginning of the 20th century was a time of change for erotica yet again. Migration began once more, this time towards Paris, the city that still, even today, continues in the minds of many people to be synonymous with pornography despite what happened in Denmark, Holland and the United States in the mid-1960s. But the migration seemed to be exclusively in a southerly direction, from England, and as if taking their cue from this influx of foreigners new French publishers began to materialize, like the *frères* Briffaut, Georges and Robert, the uncle and nephew team Pierre and Jean Fort, and P. Brenet of the '*Librairie Artistique et Édition Parisienne réunies*', a publisher of dreadful flagellation novels by 'Aimé Van Rod' and others on the boulevard Magenta.

Some of these newcomers to the French capital were merely booksellers, agents for the publishers, who were in business selling pornography by post to English customers. From accommodation addresses, or perhaps shops, these dealers would flood London and other English cities with advertising leaflets, brochures and catalogues, usually unsolicited, on the presumable theory that for every ten sent out, one would result in an order for books. Thus in January 1901, a Member of Parliament named Ernest Flower arrived at his club in Pall Mall to discover a circular waiting for him from a certain H. Ashford of the passage de Harve, Paris, advertising indecent books for sale. Flower complained to the police at once. In the following month, the police received a similar complaint

OVERLEAF A typical publication by Jean Fort. The novel, *Petite Dactylo* ('The Little Typist'), is by Pierre Dumarchy, better known as Pierre Mac Orlan, while the frontispiece is by Louis Malteste, himself the author of flagellation pornography

Petite Dactylo

ROMAN

Suivi de : LES BELLES
CLIENTES DE M. BROZEN
et du : MAITRE D'ÉCOLE
avec un choix de lettres
concernant les faits curieux
touchant la flagellation
des Misses, et des Femmes

Jean FORT

Éditeur
73, Faubourg Poissonnière, 73
PARIS

from Lord Edward Spencer Churchill. Ashford did not send circulars to railway workers, for example, whose names he might have culled from street directories but concentrated on people who would be able to pay for pornography.

Almost a year later, another Member of Parliament, W. S. Caine, presented the police with five books that he claimed to have purchased from Ashford as a test of some sort, to determine the kind of books being offered. The Post and Home Offices went into action and between them obtained from the French Embassy the information that Ashford, who had lived on the rue de Verneuil, had died in January 1902 and that the business was being continued by his widow, whose name was Dolly. The police then set a trap. An officer calling himself 'Henry Douthwaite' wrote to Dolly Ashford from an address in Brixton and arranged to purchase for £15 'six dozen photographs, a certain article ... and four books', to be delivered care of a certain lady named Mason who lived in Wandsworth, South London. What the 'certain article' might have been can only be guessed at, but the probability is that it was one of those tickler condoms with spikes sticking out of them that look so ferocious in the wood-cut advertisements to be found in the turn-of-the-century clandestine catalogues.

When 'Douthwaite' was informed that his packages had arrived, the police descended on the hapless Mrs Mason who displayed 'intense surprise and disgust' when she was shown what the packages contained. Apparently she had acted for some while, innocently she maintained, as an intermediary between the Ashfords and their London clients. Subsequently, a warrant was issued for the arrest of Dolly Ashford who was informed that should she ever set foot in England again she would be taken into custody at once. Nothing more was heard from her.

A rather amusing case of a similar nature involved a man named Keary who about 1904 was distributing from the rue du Maubeuge pamphlets containing pictures of naked women that he was circulating to advertise a publication entitled the *Illustrated Artistic Encyclopaedia*. The British police complained to their French counterparts about this, with particular emphasis on the fact that the ladies in the pictures possessed pubic hair. The *Sûreté* rather stiffly replied that since in France pubic hair was not considered obscene, the most that they could do was to inform Keary that his wares were not finding favour with the English authorities. Those in Home Office and police circles who were privy to this communication doubtless felt that the British view of France as being morally beyond the pale had been justified.[1]

But English publishers and touts like Keary and the Ashfords who acted for them and their French colleagues did not all swarm across to France at once, on the same Channel ferry as it were. It was a slow process, and one of the last *emigrés* of this type was Jack Kahane from Manchester who, in 1930, founded the Obelisk Press under whose imprint he issued books like *Boy* by James Hanley and *The Well of Loneliness* by Radclyffe Hall, both of which had run into legal difficulties in England. He also introduced the reading public to Henry Miller and Lawrence Durrell, and published the remarkable but sadly almost forgotten *The Young and Evil* of Parker Tyler and Charles Henri Ford.

The collapse of erotica publishing in England was not an overnight event either, although by 1910 it had virtually ceased except for such privately printed vanities as *In The Outer Court*, a collection of erotic sonnets that appeared just before the First World War. They are said to have been the work of a highly placed government official, a claim made about much erotica to add something to its interest, but these sonnets are not badly written and were expensively printed, which suggests a more cultured hand at work than usual. A letter from the librarian of a northern university pointed out to me that three copies of *In The Outer Court* to his knowledge had been distributed through Arundell Esdaile, for many years closely associated with the British Library, but it is possible that Esdaile was acting on behalf of somebody else, or was simply doing his librarian's job of doling out to various deserving academic institutions copies of a book that had been donated anonymously to the British Library.

Probably the last original erotic novel to appear in England during the 19th century was *Crissie, a Music-Hall Sketch of Today* ('The Alhambra', 1899). Subtitled in some advertisements 'A Narrative of Music Hall Depravity', *Crissie* is an ill-printed but pleasantly written novel that seems to fit into the area of work produced by Smithers and Nichols by being featured in some of the promotional material of the 'Erotika [sometimes Erotica] Biblion Society' which the pair ran. Something seems to have frustrated the printing of *Crissie* in its entirety, for in an unpublished manuscript bibliography of erotica that surfaces from time to time in antiquarian book circles there is an interesting reference to a second part: 'At the end of [*Crissie*] is "End of Vol. I," and so far the work is completed in one printed volume. In the list of publications by the Erotika Biblion Society, however, it states that "owing to this work never having been completed, a few copies of vol. II have been typewritten, from the original MS., and nicely bound, for those readers and collectors who have read vol. I with appreciation." '[2]: I have never had a sight of one of these typescript copies of the second volume of *Crissie*, although the existence of one has been reported to me, but the reason for it not being printed together with the first volume may not be unconnected with Nichols's abrupt disappearance to Paris about 1900 while awaiting trial for books that he had published under the aegis of the Walpole Press at Charing Cross, one of which was *Kalogynomia, or, The Laws of Female Beauty* (1899), a primitive sexological work by a doctor named Bell that had first been published in 1821.

The relationship between Sidney Nichols and Leonard Smithers was to all intents and purposes at an end before the former decamped to France. Smithers liked erotica it is true, but despite his posturings as a smut fancier he believed in maintaining a veneer of civilization on what he published. Nichols on the other hand was less particular, and it is possible some of the more sensational books that have been associated with the two of them were actually run off by Nichols on the side. The publications of the Erotika Biblion Society included some splendid books, starting in 1888 (the summer of 1889 in reality) with *Priapeia*, a collection of Latin verses translated and annotated by Smithers and Sir Richard F. Burton. Shortly afterwards appeared a translation of *Les Tableaux vivants*, an anthology of short erotic pieces with titles such as 'On the Seat of a Close-Stool, or the Caprices of Nature', that had first been published in 1870. For many years ascribed to the journalist Gustave Droz, *Les Tableaux vivants* is now generally considered to have been written by Paul Perret. The Society also purchased from the Paris publisher Isidore Liseux the sheets of fifty copies of *Opus Sadicum* (1889), his historically interesting but whimsical English version of Sade's *Justine*, and had them bound up with a new titlepage and sold to subscribers.

But after about 1891, a change could be detected in the publications; the regularly used false place of publication, 'Athens', disappears from the titlepages and more frequently books are stated to have been issued 'in connection with' the Society. Whether the rift between the two men dates from this time is not certain. As we have seen, books appeared afterwards that are often said to have been published by the pair. *Gynecocracy* (1893) for example; but equally this might have been the book that finally ended the partnership, for in size – it was published in three volumes – and perversity of content it is like nothing else that Smithers had been associated with. Likewise, at the beginning of 'The Nameless Novel' in Crowley's *Snowdrops from a Curate's Garden* there is a cutting reference to Nichols being a swindler. By Crowley's own account, *Snowdrops* was composed in July and August 1904 as a diversion for his wife Rose who was recovering from the birth of their daughter, and it was published at Paris at either the end of the same year or early in 1905. Could this remark of Crowley's concerning Nichols have been inserted in a fit of pique after being offered unfavourable terms for publication by the latter, who was by then safely esconced in France? Or, rather more interestingly, could it have been a reference to Crowley's earlier book, *White Stains* (1898), implying that it was published at London by Nichols and not, as is generally believed, by Smithers?

By 1900 the question of who did what and with whom – to paraphrase the famous limerick – is academic anyway. Nichols was on the run in Paris, where he settled for a while on the place de la Madeleine before going to America with some preposterous forgeries of drawings supposed to be by Beardsley and eventually died, if the story is true, in the Bellevue Hospital, New York, sometime in the 1930s. The demise of Smithers was unpleasant, lonely and miserable. After being declared bankrupt in 1900, he entered an alcohol and drug induced decline that was to end in 1907 in a squalid room in Islington, North London, his only companions being two empty hampers and fifty bottles of chlorodyne.

But somebody was still at work in London publishing erotica, somebody who had either known Smithers and Nichols or was familiar with their publications. In 1902 appeared the first volume of *The Confessions of Nemesis Hunt*, and two further volumes came out in 1903 and 1906. In 1908 *Pleasure Bound 'Afloat'* was published, and in 1909 appeared *Pleasure Bound 'Ashore'* and *Maudie*. All four novels were clearly from the same author. In between times appeared *Harlequin Prince Cherrytop and the Good Fairy Fairfuck* (1905), a reprint of an engagingly obscene pantomime satirizing the Victorian 'disease' spermatorrhoea (viz. 'masturbation psychosis'), that had first been issued in 1879 and which has been attributed to the journalist George Augustus Sala and others. There were also translations of two novels that had originally appeared in French in 1894 and 1903: *Nadia* (1905) and *The Mistress and the Slave* (1906), the latter being a particularly dreadful sado-masochist work. With the exception of *Nemesis Hunt*, one volume of which displays signs of having been printed abroad, all these books have their origins in London. Their printing style has a certain uniformity which indicates the likelihood of a single press being used, and each of the books carries advertising matter for the others in which they are billed as having been published 'in connection with' the Erotika Biblion Society.

Who the publisher and printer of these books might have been, if they were not the same person, has not been established, but one possibility is the man referred to as 'Gerald N – ' in *The Early Life and Vicissitudes of Jack Smithers* (London, 1939), the memoirs of Leonard Smithers's son. According to Jack Smithers, after his father died he lived for a while with 'Gerald N – ' who had evidently been associated with Smithers senior for some while. Jack's account of his life as a 16-year-old in this singular household is not without interest:

> As one entered the front door of the house into the hall and passage, the first door on the right was the sitting-room, and in that sitting-room was a double-crown Wharfe press driven by an electric motor. In one corner there was a stack of unprinted book-paper; elsewhere stacks of printed sheets, and against one wall a single case-rack holding about twenty cases of book-type.
>
> Part of the floor had been removed by N- to put in silent foundations for the Wharfe and also to accommodate the motor. The whole thing was beautifully rigged up and ran silently and smoothly, turning out printed sheets, the next door neighbours never even suspecting that such a piece of equipment was in the street....
>
> Kate was the compositor; she would sit on an office stool all day setting type, as fast as light she would empty the cases ... She had been trained in some printing works in Scotland, and just how N- got hold of her I do not know; I think that she had been a chorus girl, and that Rosie [N-'s wife] had secured her....
>
> In this house, at least, the N-s turned out the most obscene books, the very crudest or lewdest it is possible to conceive. I read some of the sheets as they came off the press, and young as I was, I realised that it was, to say the least, tough.
>
> Rosie toured a lot, securing engagements here and there, but this was largely a blind, her job being to secure such customers for the books as she could ... She was a small, lightly-built, fluffy creature, full of life and fun and boldness. Friends of similar kidney came to the house, and there were parties which beggar description ... The low, abominable chanting of lewd songs that the neighbours might not hear, Rosie and Kate dancing nude for dear life on the dining-table, the photographing of women and men. (Jack Smithers, *The Early Life and Vicissitudes.* pp. 81–3.)

The author of the *Nemesis Hunt* group of books, and perhaps the translator of the French ones, may have been a man named George Reginald Bacchus (1873–1945), an Oxford graduate and journalist. Jack Smithers shows in his autobiography that Bacchus was a good friend of his father, and that he turned out 'foreign translations and bawdy books, at the same time that he was writing goody-goody stories for a weekly religious paper.' (Op. cit., pp. 40–1.) The theatrical background to *Nemesis Hunt* – and *Crissie* as well if he wrote it, which is not impossible – could well have been acquired from Isa Bowman (1874–1958) whom he married in 1899 and who, as one of the Bowman Sisters and also in her own right, pursued for many years a successful stage career. She also wrote a lively but fanciful biography of Lewis Carroll, with whom she had been friendly as a child. That Bacchus also did translating, as Smithers asserts, is confirmed by the existence of *Jim Blackwood, Jockey* (1910), an adaptation by Bacchus of a French work by Valentin Mandelstamm.[3]

Writing of *Nemesis Hunt*, its publisher opines: 'This book marks a new departure in English erotic literature. It has a definite and interesting plot, and is told in able and easy language, with a distinct literary style, and whilst being free from the banalities of the ordinary English erotic book it possesses a raciness and an intensely amusing and chatty manner, which places it far above the level of any modern work of that kind in our language.'[4] Making allowances for these lines coming from a person trying to sell something, their essence is not far from the truth. *Nemesis Hunt*, the *Pleasure Bound* books and *Maudie* are all quite well written, light and amusing. The characters possess a degree of conviction in the way they are portrayed, which leads one to suppose that some of them might be based on real people, a suggestion fielded by Lawrence Forster in his manuscript *Catalogus*. If Bacchus were the author of these books, which seems not unreasonable, then a number of interesting possibilities spring to mind. In *Maudie*, for example, there is a poet called Claude Lestrange who at a comfortable stretch of the imagination might be modelled on Ernest Dowson (1867–1900), the decadent poet best known for *Non Sum Qualis Eram . . .*, which has for its refrain 'I have been faithful to thee, Cynara! in my fashion'. Dowson was, along with Beardsley, Cyril Ranger Gull and others, part of Smithers's circle of writers and artists and would certainly have been known to Bacchus.

In chapter four of *Maudie*, the poet has an encounter with a soldier of the old school while attending a pre-weekend in the country get-together at a house near London's Barbican:

'Ah, General,' said the poet to the old officer, who was closely examining the life-size portrait of a fascinating young lady, and which particularly emphasised her vagina, 'ah, General, a tempting subject:
> 'How sweeter than the horrid clash of arms,
> The contemplation of those naked charms.'
The General sniffed: he did not like poetry, or poets.
'A dashed fine young woman, sir,' he snorted.
The poet persisted:
> 'Dost thou not yearn, oh, son of Mars, to thrust
> The vibrant signal of a lusting man
> Into yon fragrant arbour, there to place
> In form of sperm ambrosial, a fair child?
> Dost thou not – '

But the General turned on him.

'I don't know what the hell you mean, sir, by all that tomfool nonsense, but if you've the accursed effrontery to call my cock a "vibrant signal", I'd have you know that the word cock has been good enough for the Fitzhughs for generations, sir. "Vibrant signal", indeed, you'll be calling my arse-hole a railway tunnel next.'

'Oh, sir,' protested the poet, ''tis but poetic licence.'

'Then you ought to dashed well have your licence taken away – and look here, if by "fragrant arbour" you mean that young person's cunt, I'd have you know that the Fitzhughs call it cunt, sir, and always have. My father called it a cunt, my mother had a cunt, I came out of a cunt, and many a cunt have I stuck my good cock into.

'"Fragrant arbour!" there's a damned good stink attached to some of them, and I *like* it.

'And don't you refer to my good spunk as ambrosial sperm, or I'll toss myself off in your eye, and let you know whether it smells ambrosial or not.'

In Chapter VI, the poet is at Maudie's country house by the Thames near Staines, and is chagrined to find out that of all those present he has been denied a partner for the night:

Sorrowfully he undressed, regretfully surveyed his slim, naked form in the long cheval glass, and mournfully stared out at and over the moon-swept Thames valley. It was very beautiful, but the poet was *not* inspired, he was carnally mundane. His penis stood up in mockery; he gazed at the light of the windows of the opposite wing, and distinctly saw the silhouettes of two figures in close and rapt embrace. He could stand it no longer; firmly grasping his staff of love, he gazed wistfully at the moon, and brazenly tossed himself off on the lawn below.

Then with a sigh he got into his very elaborate flowered silk pyjamas, sprayed himself elaborately with some perfume which smelt like honey, and sank back onto the luxurious bed.

It was very comfortable. The lights were all that could be wished for night reading. Drinks were at his hand, and Maudie had given him a little key which she said opened a cupboard of erotic books.

He found a full selection. He felt that as a poet – and *several* society weekly papers had said so – he ought to have chosen Catullus or Verlaine, but he didn't. His fingers lingered for a while over a little brochure called *Fucksome Frolics*, but they ended up with that dear, delightful work, *The Confessions of Nemesis Hunt* ...

The tone of *Maudie* and the other books inspires a comparison with the libertine tradition of France in the 18th century. Although the writing in the English works is not so good, and they do not consciously spring from the same inspirational sources, there is a shared characteristic of frivolity, of fun. Ashbee's declared view of English erotica was that nothing worthwhile had been published since Cleland's *Memoirs of a Woman of Pleasure*. He died in 1900, before *Maudie, Pleasure Bound* and *Nemesis Hunt* were published; this is unfortunate, for I believe that he would have liked them.[5]

* * * * *

The Erotika Biblion Society had its imitators. If one is disposed to believe the titlepages of clandestine pornography, the Erotica Biblion Society of London and New York was the cover for a series of books all supposedly published about 1898 or 1899. A number of these were prosecuted in 1913 and 1914, which suggests that unless the books on trial were reprints, their publication was a good deal closer to the First World War than the South African War.

The productions of this new 'society' were published in France, a likely provider being Charles Carrington, another escapee from England. Of Portuguese origin, his real name was Paul Ferdinando and before leaving for France in the early 1890s was, according to Alec Craig's informant Vernon Symonds in *The Banned Books of England* (1962), alternately an errand boy, vanboy and lavatory attendant, and finally took to selling books from a barrow in Farringdon Market, London. From these lowly beginnings, he achieved considerable notoriety in Paris. 'During the past 14 years,' Chief-Inspector Edward Drew told the Joint Select Committee on Lotteries and Indecent Advertisements (1908), '[Carrington] has been a source of considerable annoyance to the police here, by the persistent manner in which he has been carrying on his business through the post in the shape of sending catalogues and books of a very obscene and vulgar character.' Indeed, but official English notions of what in 1908 was indecent were somewhat extreme; it was, after all, Edward Drew himself in the same testimony who brought to the attention of the Select Committee the difference in opinion of English and French authorities on the subject of pubic hair.

In fact Carrington had two sides to his business, the official and fairly respectable side and the clandestine side. Which of these it was that Edward Drew was complaining of is difficult to know because despite the interest of his evidence, and indeed of the whole Committee Report, the specimens of the 'obscene and vulgar' catalogues and books handed round to committee members are not identified. Since Carrington's name is so obviously associated with these specimens, though, it is likely that they were examples of his 'cover' items, pseudo-medical, historical and anthropological works in both English and French that skirted perilously close to the law courts. These would have carried his name and address. At the time Drew was giving his evidence in 1908, Carrington was doing business from 13 Faubourg Montmartre. In 1896, he was at 32 rue Drouot, as stated on the titlepage of *Marriage-Love and Woman ... otherwise entitled the Book of Exposition* – 'englished out of the Arabic by "Bohemian"' – and in 1912 he published at least one work from the rue de Châteaudun. The reasons for these moves might simply have been the result of business necessities – bigger premises required, or leases running out – but equally it might have had something to do with Carrington being expelled from France, as he was at least twice in 1901 and 1907 at the instigation of the British police. His absences made little if any difference to the rate of his book production, and it is possible that for the few weeks or months that he was under a cloud he simply cooled his heels in Holland – where he had dealings with a printer named Thieme – or Belgium, while an associate back home at Paris carried on the business.

The first edition of the alleged memoirs of Wilhelmine Schröder-Devrient

One of the more interesting of the books published by the Erotica Biblion Society of London and New York was *Pauline the Prima Donna, or, Memoirs of an Opera Singer*; dated '1898' this was one of a large batch of erotica condemned by the *cour d'assises de la Seine* two days before Christmas in 1914. A copy of this in *l'Enfer* of the Bibliothèque Nationale, Paris, is concealed within the wrappers of Jean Debrit, *La Guerre de la Balkan* (1914), which as well as showing the sort of knavish tricks publishers are capable of getting up to, tends to strengthen the theory that '1898' is a false date.

Pauline is a translation of *Aus den Memoiren einer Sängerin* ('Boston, Reginald Chesterfield.' [*c.* 1868; 1875] 2 vols), the first volume of which, at least, was published by August Prinz at the Verlagsbureau, Altona. Proposing to be the sexual autobiography of Wilhelmine Schröder-Devrient (1804–60), the mercurial opera singer who dazzled Beethoven with her performance of Leonore in the composer's own *Fidelio* (1822), and who took an active role in the revolution of 1848 at Dresden, this book has all the indications of having been written by two people, neither of whom, needless to say, was Schröder-Devrient.

The first volume deals with the singer's early life, up to the age of about seventeen when she loses her virginity to an Italian prince, and although far from free of erotic detail is considerably more believable than volume two. The following episode, extracted from chapter two, gives a flavour of the book and an insight into the use of dildoes not commonly to be found elsewhere.

... I did not at first notice an alcohol lamp on the table. It was lighted and some liquid was steaming on it. I suppose she had lit it before I came into the room. She dipped her liquid to see if it was warm enough, and when she removed it I saw that the liquid was milk. Then she took a bundle of linen out of her bag, and unwrapped a strange, curiously-shaped object, the use of which I could not imagine. It was black and almost the same shape as the part of my father I had first seen that morning. She dipped it into the milk and tried it on her cheek to see if it was hot enough. Finally, she dipped the end of it into the milk again, pressed the two knobs at the other end, and filled the instrument with hot milk. She sat down, put her legs on the bed right opposite me, so that I could see straight between her legs, pulled up her nightdress, and picked up the book in her left hand. I had just time to catch a glimpse of some pictures without really being able to see what they represented. She seized the instrument in her right hand and put the end of it in that admirable place which I was holding with both hands under my nightdress. She rubbed it slowly up and down and very gently on some particularly sensitive spot. Her eyes shone and seemed literally to absorb the pictures in the book. At last she found the entry for her instrument and slowly pushed in the whole of its barrel. Her thighs were now ever further apart, her abdomen, which advanced convulsively to the meeting, offered itself, and Marguerite uttered a sigh of pleasure. She pushed in the instrument as far as possible and the two round knobs buried themselves in the thickness of her hair. Then she drew it out again with the same care, and she was now repeating this movement more and more quickly, more and more feverishly, until the book fell to the floor. She closed her eyes and rubbed a finger across her lips. The movement of the instrument grew more and more rapid until her body seemed to swoon. She bit her lips cruelly as if to smother a cry which would have betrayed her. The supreme moment had arrived. She pressed the knobs with both hands and the milk flooded out inside her. She closed her thighs on the instrument, which was imbedded in her body, and remained without moving, only quivering slightly, profoundly shaken. At length she opened her thighs, withdrew the instrument, which was covered with foam, and when the milk flooded out she caught it in her cloth. She wiped everything very carefully, packed the instrument away in her bag, and came around to see once again if we were asleep. Then she got into bed and soon went to sleep herself, with a happy and satisfied expression.

The second volume has a distinctly different feel to it, the author evidently being influenced by erotic books, some of which are listed, and in particular Sade's *La Nouvelle Justine*. With this as a model it is hardly surprising that the orgies described take on a nightmarish and unreal quality in which cruelty and perversion are the staple ingredients. There is, however, in chapter five an unusual touch of realism for an erotic book in the form of an extended discussion of the various methods of contraception listed in a work entitled *The Art of Making Love Without Fear*.

Pauline the Prima Donna was probably the first German erotic work to appear in an English edition, and possibly in French as well for I am unaware of any earlier French translation of a German pornographic book than Guillaume Apollinaire's expurgated version of the novel which appeared in 1913 as *Mémoires d'une chanteuse allemande* in the 'Maîtres de l'amour' series of the Briffaut brothers. At the end of the same year, or the beginning of 1914, Apollinaire issued the complete text in a clandestine edition that he brought out in collaboration with the poet and novelist Blaise Cendrars. This edition has the false imprint and date 'Hamburg: A fond de cale, 1911'. Owing to a mistake during the printing and binding of the book, most copies were sold with about twenty or so pages out of sequence. When this was discovered the mistake was corrected and it is these that command the highest prices today, which shows how many faulty ones must have escaped.

French and English indifference to German erotica was to continue, with very occasional exceptions such as the translation of *James Grunert* (1908) that was secretly published in America in the 1930s, until the late 1960s when censorship of books all but collapsed. France led the way in 1960 with an open reissue of the '1898' text of *Pauline* in Maurice Girodias's Ophelia Press subsidiary of the better-known Olympia Press. Six years later, Eric Losfeld published his own translation of E. T. A. Hoffman's *Schwester Monika* under the '*Terrain vague*' imprint. In the United States, Brandon House among other publishers, which had taken immediate advantage of the new publishing freedom by resurrecting many of the Victorian and Edwardian English 'classics', began to commission translations of foreign works, among them novels of German or Austrian origin. The most important of these were *Josefine Mutzenbacher* (1906) and its interesting 'sequel' *Meine 365 Liebhaber* (c. 1943?), *Arabella's Opferung* (1927) and a very long novel called *Das Bildnis des Dorian Gray* (c. 1943) which seems to have been printed in

OPPOSITE One of Emil Satori's illustrations for the first edition of *James Grunert* (1908)

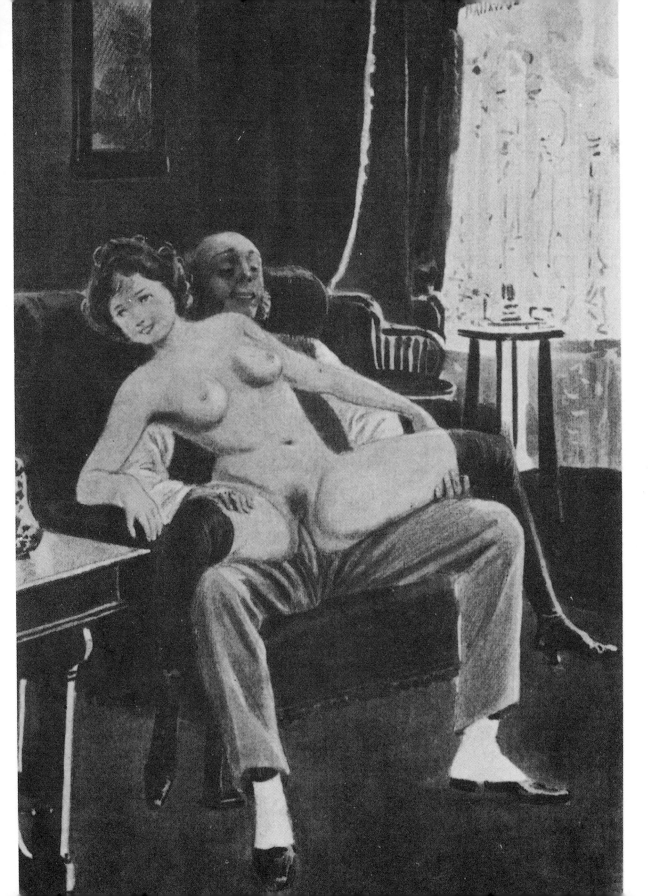

France for consumption by the German forces of occupation during World War Two and given its title as a subterfuge to fool the military censors. It has no recognizable connection with Oscar Wilde otherwise.

Josefine Mutzenbacher has the distinction of being ascribed fairly solidly to Felix Salten, the Austrian writer better known to readers in England and America for his children's book *Bambi*, and is the life of a Viennese prostitute told in extremely realistic terms. The so-called sequel is in fact a rather good pastiche by an unknown writer, the typewritten manuscript of which is supposed to have been found in the ruins of a bombed house in Vienna just after the end of the Second World War. Despite the apparent difficulty with the localized argot that non-Viennese German readers experienced, the original 1906 volume of *Josefine Mutzenbacher* was enormously popular, reprinting several times and inspiring a number of imitations, notably *Durchollte Nächte – durchjubelte Tage* ('Prag' [Berlin, Willy Schindler], 1908) that later appeared more familiarly as *Lore. Das Liebesleben einer kleinen Berlinerin* (1918, 1926, etc.).

Arabellas Opferung is a good, old-fashioned piece of commercial pornography, which in modern jargon would be called a 'fuck book'; it has no literary pretensions, no redeeming features, not even a claim to be particularly well-written. It does, however, possess one of those interesting background histories that sometimes livens up otherwise dull erotic books. The year it first appeared, 1927, another book with an identical title came out from a publisher in Berlin called Horodisch & Marx Verlag, with the authorship ascribed to a man named Alfred Frey. It is clear that the Berlin publication was an official or 'cover' version for the erotic, clandestine edition that is supposed to have been printed at Berne, Switzerland, by a presumably fictitious 'Arnold Meyer'. The story goes that *Arabellas Opferung*, in which the wife of a highly placed diplomat is persuaded to prostitute herself for political considerations to sundry foreign dignitries on official visits, was the true 'confession' of a member of the Prussian aristocracy, a countess it seems, who at the turn of the century had written it at the suggestion of the German psychologist Magnus Hirschfeld (1868–1935) by way of therapy. The reason for the appearance in book form of these memoirs was that an impoverished female relative of their by now deceased author saw the opportunity of making a quick *Mark* or two from their publication, and approached Frey, who happened to be Hirschfeld's private secretary, with the proposition. I have been unable to see a copy of the official version of the book, but assuming that there is anything resembling veracity in this yarn it is that the openly published Berlin edition was indeed the ramblings of one of Hirschfeld's patients, while the clandestine 'Swiss' version was a fantasy, a fabrication cooked up either by Frey or somebody else who knew about the memoirs.

*   *   *   *   *

As the new century began in France, so did a new school of erotic literature. 'Specialist' publishers and authors began to emerge who by 'de-sexing' their books

OPPOSITE Frontispiece of a late reprint of *Manuel de civilité*. The artist responsible for the illustrations to this edition is unknown, but is said to be Peter Schem

BELOW The first edition of *Josefine Mutzenbacher*, the 'life' of a Viennese prostitute written by Felix Salten, better known for the children's book *Bambi*

Josefine Mutzenbacher

oder

Die Geschichte einer
Wienerischen Dirne

von ihr selbst erzählt

Privatdruck.
1906.

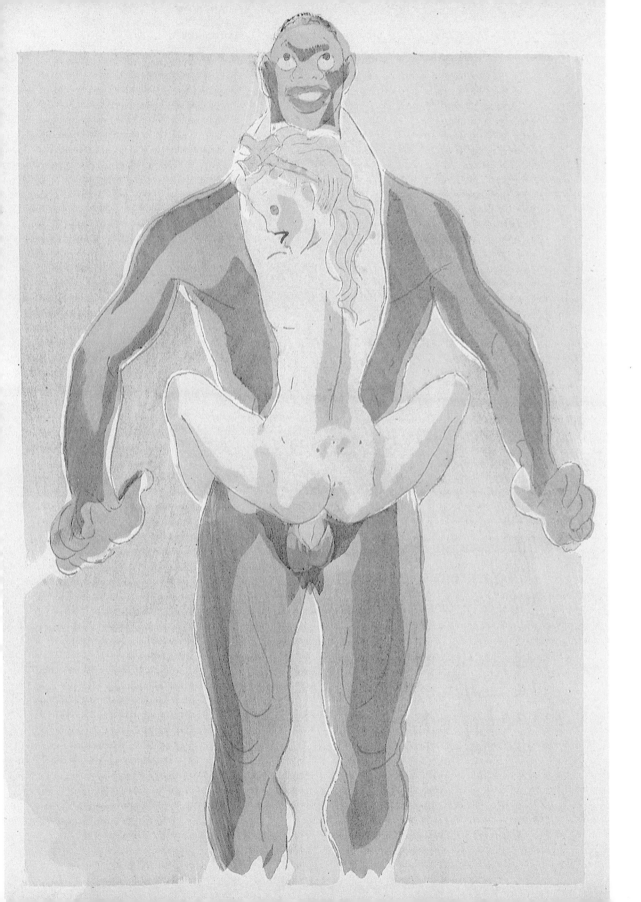

SAISON

Bilboquet dont je suis la tige
Sur laquelle est tombé ton corps,
Je comprends bien qu'un jeu pareil
Puisse te donner le vertige !

Aussi afin de satisfaire
Les désirs que loges en toi —
L'amour ne les veut qu'à l'étroit —
Rends-moi mignonne la pareille

were able to operate in many cases quite openly. An example of this sort of thing arose from one of Charles Carrington's publications, a novel dealing with slavery set against the background of the American Civil War that was entitled *The Memoirs of Dolly Morton* (1899). Written by Georges Grassal (1867–1905) using the pseudonym 'Hugues Rebell', this moderately well-written book contains a great deal of flagellation, but it also includes a healthy sprinkling of straightforward erotic episodes, and it was for these rather than the flagellation that the book was condemned by the courts in December 1914. In 1899 Carrington had issued the book quite openly, with his name and address clearly displayed on the titlepage; perhaps he felt safe publishing such a book in English since it is not a typical piece of hardcore pornography, and possesses points of interest that are unrelated to its sexual content. Two years later, in 1901, he evidently felt less secure publishing a French translation: in *En Virginie* by 'Jean de Villiot' he produced an expurgation that retained the sadistic elements but not the sexual encounters. Some years afterwards, about the time an edition of the original English text was being prosecuted in 1914, Jean Fort published *Dolly Morton* by 'Donovan Kipps' with illustrations by Louis Malteste, himself the author of flagellation pornography under the name of Jacques D'Icy. This purported to be the first French edition of Grassal's book but as it was similarly expurgated it may merely have been a new edition of *En Virginie*.

Neither *En Virginie* nor the 'Donovan Kipps' version seem to have fallen foul of the law, a striking illustration of how the perverse is so often protected at the expense of the normal. The absurd situation whereby books catering for the most sadistic and masochistic fantasies might legitimately be printed and sold was not lost on either publishers nor writers; and for many years such perverse series as *Les Orties blanches*, put out by Jean Fort, and the many books by 'Don Brennus Aléra' (i.e. Roland Brévannes) for the *Select-bibliothèque*, said to have been run by a man named Massy, provided hours of fun for those whose desires went in for such rare fancies as tight corsets, rubberwear, enemas, pony girls and women wrestlers. On occasion a book might go just a little too far and it would be prosecuted, but in general they would enjoy complete freedom and many of them will be found among quite respectable books listed in the *Catalogue Général de la Librairie Français* or similar equivalents to the annual 'What's in Print' indexes.

As usual, of course, even stronger fare lurked just below the surface. From the *Bibliothèque des Curieux*, their bookshop on the rue de Furstenberg, Paris, the Briffaut brothers issued 'sweetened' versions of 18th-century works for the general reader, and complete editions for the discreet *amateur*. To judge from the sort of books included in an '*extrait du catalogue de librairie générale*' which they issued as part of their catalogue for 1920, they also did a thriving side line in sadistic and masochistic books too, presumably from other publishers. Among them were works by 'Docteur Fowler' and 'Sadie Blackeyes', pseudonyms of 'Pierre Mac Orlan' under which name Pierre Dumarchey (1882–1970) became famous as a writer of adventure books and comic novels. Mac Orlan – it is the name he is best known by – wrote a number of indifferent flagellation novels for Jean Fort that were included in the *Orties blanches* series, as well as pseudo-sexological studies with titles such as *Le Masochisme en Amérique*, but for Fort's clandestine business he also wrote several much better books, erotic novels of some pretension. Two of them – *Aventures amoureuses de Mlle Sommerange* (1910) and *Mademoiselle de Mustelle et ses amies* ('1913' [1911?]) – were credited to 'Pierre du Bourdel'; *Petites cousines* ([1919]) to 'Sadinet'; and from 'Le Chevalier de X...' there came *Georges* (1908), the first – and only – volume of a projected trilogy with the general title *Femme du monde et sang bleu*.

Mac Orlan was not the only author whose career had a hidden aspect to it, and as the 20th century progressed others would join him, particularly in the 1920s and '30s. But two others of the pre-First World War period should first be mentioned, Alphonse Gallais and Guillaume Apollinaire.

Gallais – a '*très médiocre écrivain*' according to Pascal Pia – was a familiar figure in the Latin Quarter of Paris during the 1890s and the early years of the present century. He wrote at least one book under his real name for Jean Fort, *Aux griffes de Vénus*, but earlier, between about 1903 and 1906, he published several distinctly strange erotic books, and advertised five or six others that never materialized, all under the anagrammatical alias 'A-S. Lagail'. Best of those that did appear are *Les Paradis charnels ou Le Divin bréviaire des amants* (1903) and the extraordinary *Les Mémoires du Baron Jacques. Lubricités infernales de la noblesse décadente* (1904). The former is a sort of outspoken, eccentric sex manual which includes 136 different postures for various types of sexual activity. None of the postures is new of course, but they are all given the most imaginative names, the final section – titled *Les Clowneries charnelles* – concluding with '*Le jugement de Salomon*', a difficult piece of business in which the fellatrix, having brought her partner to an orgasm, re-ejaculates his semen through her nostrils.

Les Mémoires du Baron Jacques is one of the few books that caused Louis Perceau to vacate the detached, uncritical position he sought to maintain in his *Bibliographie du roman érotique*. 'The author is certainly not exaggerating when he says that this work is the most horrible of its kind,' wrote Perceau. 'These apocryphal memoires – of which the hero figured in a famous scandal in 1903 – accumulate revolting scenes. To give some idea of the author's imagination, it requires only to mention the incident in which Baron Jacques d'A- deflowers young boys on the skeleton of his mother! Scenes of truly bewildering bestiality are heaped up in this book.' (*Perceau*, 236.) 'Baron Jacques d'A- ' was actually Baron Jacques d'Adelswärd Fersen, the young homosexual poet, novelist and editor to whom Montague Summers dedicated his first book, a collection of decadent verses entitled *Antinous* (1907). Fersen is portrayed as 'Baron Robert Marsac Lagerström' in Compton Mackenzie's novel *Vestal Fire* (1927) – 'cruelly and ... outrageously caricatured' in Summers's view – and the scandal of 1903 referred to by Perceau, which involved erotic *poses plastiques* with small boys in Paris, is given a more sober treatment by Roger Peyrefitte in his book *L'Exilé de Capri* (1959), a fictionalized biography of Fersen.

Guillaume Apollinaire (1880–1918), the author of *Alcools* and *Calligrammes*,

and one of the central figures in Futurist and Cubist circles, is of sufficient importance to have had his life and works thoroughly sifted through a dozen times or
more and, in 1969, to have been the subject of a massive exhibition at the Bibliothèque Nationale, the catalogue of which is a handy reference work in itself.
With notoriety on this scale, it is evident that nothing new is likely to be discovered concerning his erotic writings at this stage, yet they are of sufficient
importance that some account of them must be given, even if only briefly.

Apollinaire's contribution to erotic literature may, for convenience, be divided
into two parts, the scholarly, pot-boiling editorial work that he undertook for the
Briffaut brothers, and compositions of his own that he had published secretly.
For the former, he compiled biographical and bibliographical Introductions to
their *Maîtres de l'Amour* and *Coffret du Bibliophile* series, reprints of texts, usually
from the 18th century, which he also expurgated when it was thought prudent
to do so. In 1964, these Introductions – less the bibliographical bits – were usefully
reprinted together in one volume as *Les Diables amoureux*, with an interesting
Preface by the Apollinaire scholar Michel Décaudin. In most cases Apollinaire
signed his own name to these pieces of editorial work, but he was not beyond
using false ones when it suited him, as for example 'Germain Amplecas' which he
applied to an anthology of 19th-century libertine poetry.

His labours for the Briffauts began in 1909; clandestine publication of his own
work started earlier, about 1900 with an unlocated novel called *Mirely, ou le
petit trou pas cher* which, according to Marcel Adéma's biography of the poet
Apollinaire le mal-aimé (1952), was commissioned by a 'specialist' bookshop on the
rue Saint-Roch. Apart from the fact that it was written strictly from hunger,
nothing is known about it.

In 1907 two more novels appeared, *Les Mémoires* [in subsequent editions,
Exploits] *d'un jeune Don Juan* and *Les onze mille verges*. The circumstances in which
these books were first published is obscure, and in the past there has been controversy on the subject among experts, particularly between Pascal Pia and
Louis Perceau who seemed unable to agree whether they appeared in 1907 or between 1910 and 1913. While not wishing to act as arbiter for the two authorities,
what seems to have happened – and this is pure conjecture – is that both books
were originally published in 1907 by Jean Fort, who may well have known
Apollinaire through the latter's friendship with Pierre Mac Orlan, and piracies
of these issued four or five years later, perhaps by Elias Gaucher whose habit of
reproducing in almost facsimile form the books that he copied makes it difficult
to tell the real thing from the fake.

Les Mémoires d'un jeune Don Juan is a pleasant, rather innocent book, cast in the
traditional mould of a young boy's growing sexual awareness and eventual
rampant maturity. Sodomy and incest are featured, and there is an element of
scatology that some might find upsetting, but it is all written up in an easy,
matter-of-fact way that softens what in less skilful hands would be offensive.
Les onze mille verges is a different sort of book entirely, a brilliant fantasy in which
all the demons of some insane, Sadeian hell are unleashed at once. The central

LES EXPLOITS

D'UN

JEUNE DON JUAN .

par

G. A.

Je suis jeune, il est vrai, mais aux âmes
bien nées
La valeur n'attend pas le nombre des
années.

CORNEILLE

PARIS

En vente chez tous les Libraires

LES

ONZE MILLE VERGES

PAR

G... A...

PARIS

En vente chez tous les Libraires

character, a Rumanian prince named Mony Vibescu, travels first from his native Bucharest to Paris and from there to Port Arthur in China where, in a most unlikely setting for a pornographic novel, he finds himself embroiled in the Russo-Japanese war of 1904. During this odyssey, no perversion or outrage is avoided if it can possibly be helped, and the book is in fact so extreme, so deliberately and self-consciously revolting that Apollinaire's purpose was clearly to parody the genre of ultra-sadistic erotic fiction by taking it to its furthest possible limits. And he succeeds admirably; those who approach the book in anything but the spirit in which it was written are understandably appalled. Once the idea behind it becomes apparent, it is less shocking and takes on the qualities of a surrealist farce. Certainly Apollinaire's fellow artists and writers thought highly of it. Robert Desnos (1900–45), himself the author of an erotic novel, *La Liberté ou l'amour* (1927), felt that with *Calligrammes, Les onze mille verges* was Apollinaire's most important work. Picasso went even further, declaring that it was the finest book he had come across. In France, it is available in the *Éditions J'ai Lu* pocketbook series; in America, the translation by 'Oscar Mole' [i.e. Alexander

ABOVE LEFT and RIGHT
The titlepage of Guillaume Apollinaire's earliest surviving ventures into erotica, in either their original editions or contemporary piracies

GUILLAUME APOLLINAIRE

Le Verger
des
Amours

orné de six pointes sèches

MONACO
1924

GUILLAUME APOLLINAIRE

LE
CORTÈGE
PRIAPIQUE

ABOVE LEFT The titlepage
to *Le Verger des amours*, a
collection of verses ascribed
incorrectly to Apollinaire.
The real author is thought to
be the late Pascal Pia. See
illustration page 166

ABOVE RIGHT A late (*c.* 1950)
clandestine reprint of an
authentic volume of
Apollinaire's erotic verses.
The vignette is by Mario
Prassinos. The original
edition of this work
appeared in 1925

Trocchi] that was originally published in Paris in 1953, is likewise on open sale. In England, however, a major work by an important modern author is available only in an expurgated version, a sad reflection of how English publishers in the 1980s are still at the mercy of those whose minds are firmly rooted in the 1880s.

Apollinaire's other clandestine writings were posthumous, and all collections of poetry. There are four of these: *Le Verger des amours* ('Monaco, 1924 [1927]'), *Le Cortège priapique* ('La Havane', 1925) and *Julie ou la rose* ('A Hambourg' [1927]) were all published at Paris by René Bonnel either alone or, as in the case of *Le Cortège priapique*, in association with the bookseller René Picart: and *Poèmes secrets à Madeleine* which was published at Paris by Georges Blaizot in 1949.[6]

Of the first three, which were reprinted together at Paris in 1978 by J.-J. Pauvert making them more easily accessible, considerable doubt has been expressed as to whether *Le Verger des amours* was really the work of Apollinaire at all. Marcel Adéma, in the bibliography to his life of Apollinaire, writes that a poet, whom he identifies only by the initials M. R. V., 'had occasion to see the dedication of a copy given to [Fernand] Fleuret by Pascal Pia, which leaves no doubt on

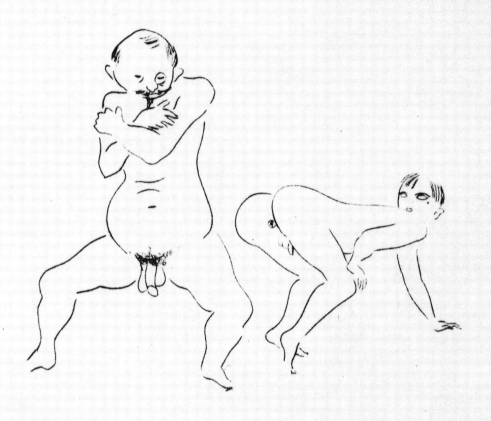

Faridondaine

Prends-moi l'as de pique en chantant

Je décharge comme une reine

Faridondaine

Le roi de Thune est mon amant

OPPOSITE One of Foujita's illustrations to *Le Verger des amours*. See illustration page 165

the matter.' This would seem to confirm the suspicions, and the likeliest person responsible for this 'very clever pastiche' – as Adéma refers to it – is evidently Pia himself who, as 'Léger Alype', had provided Bonnel and Picart with a brief Preface for *Le Cortège priapique* two years earlier.

Poèmes secrets à Madeleine is a brief and slightly sad little book. It was published on 9 November 1949 to coincide to the day with the thirty-first anniversary of the poet's death. Less than forty pages in length, and limited to just sixteen copies, it collects the poems that he wrote to Madeleine Pagès from the trenches in 1915, poems in which all the passion and sensuality of someone separated from the person he loves are expressed in vivid terms. Looking at the photograph of Apollinaire and Pagès taken at Oran in January 1916, it is difficult not to ponder on the wisdom of publishing these personal and very private verses.

*   *   *   *   *

Erotic book production, like everything else, suffered miserably as a result of the First World War and took its time getting over it. Such books as did appear during or shortly after these years were sorry affairs, printed on poor paper and usually with contents to match. One of the first books of interest to emerge from the post-war clandestine presses was *Le Keepsake Galante ou les Délassements du foutoir*, a scholarly anthology of erotic prose and verse that was edited anonymously by Louis Perceau, who devotes three and a half pages to a notice of it in his *Bibliographie*. The publisher of *Le Keepsake galant* was Maurice Duflou whose enormous output of *sub rosa* publications, many of them issued in association with Perceau, spanned a period of at least twenty-five years; one of his last, in 1948, was a reprint of an edition of Sade's *La Philosophie dans le boudoir* which he had published originally in 1923.

Le Keepsake galant came out in 1924, but it was in 1926 that the first rush of really fine books started to appear. Early in the year a bookseller named Paul Cotinaud published Pierre Mac Orlan's *La Sémaine secrète de Vénus*, with illustrations by Marcel Vertès, later reversing the situation by publishing *Entrée Interdite au Public* which is an album containing twenty erotic etchings in various states by Vertès with a short Preface by Mac Orlan. Another bookseller, Jean Budry, issued the delightful *Roger ou les à-cotés de l' ombrelle* ascribed to either Jean Bruyère or to the artist who illustrated it, Jean Lurçat; and René Bonnel, one of leading publishers of surrealist and *avant-garde* erotica between about 1925 and 1935, issued the first integral edition of Alfred Jarry's *Les Silènes*, parodies or adaptations of Christian Dietrich Grabbe's *Scherzi, Ironie, Satire* that had been partially printed in the *Paris-Journal* in 1923.

OVERLEAF The post-humously published *Les Silènes* of Alfred Jarry, with its erotic frontispiece engraved by Demetrius Galanis

The year 1926 also saw the first appearance in print of the erotic works of Pierre-Félix Louÿs who, at the age of 55, had died the previous year at Paris, a recluse suffering from worsening blindness, a nervous disorder and insomnia. Louÿs – his real name was Pierre Louis – was one of the most fascinating literary figures of his time, at once a graceful poet and novelist able to combine erudition

ALFRED JARRY

LES SILÈNES

Avec un frontispice gravé
à l'eau forte

PAPEETE
LES BIBLIOPHILES CRÉOLES

and languorous sensuality in a rich and heady mixture, and a savant bibliomane with a fine library of rare books and manuscripts. Of his openly published works, *Aphrodite, mœurs antiques* (1896), a novel dealing with courtesan life in ancient Alexandria, created the greatest impression on his contemporaries after the attention of the public had been drawn to it in a review by François Coppée. Another novel, *La Femme et le pantin* (1898), in which a man is destroyed by his passion for a scheming and worthless woman, was turned into a film vehicle for Marlene Dietrich, *The Devil is a Woman* (1935), directed by Josef von Sternberg.

But fame was not something that Louÿs sought, and he eventually withdrew to the solitude of his rooms on the rue de Boulainvilliers and a private world of his own to which few had access, a private world in which he worked out his secret fantasies in part through the medium of intensely erotic prose and verse, and in part by taking hundreds of photographs of naked little girls. When he died, enormous quantities of his papers were sold *en bloc* by his widow and her husband to be, Louÿs's last secretary, to a bookseller of doubtful reputation named Edmund Bernard, the publisher of *Anthologie Hospitalière & Latinesque* (1911, 13; 2 vols), a collection of erotic student songs. From Bernard these papers were in turn sold or otherwise disposed of to collectors or to other dealers, and some of them still appear to be in circulation almost sixty years later, for as recently as the autumn of 1981 a pretty little volume of *Pastiches et Parodies* was privately printed in an edition of two hundred copies, new material, never before published, and illustrated with four of the photographs of little girls.

The first of these manuscripts to be printed was *Manuel de Civilité pour les petites filles à l'usage des maisons d'éducation*, published by the bookseller Simon Kra in an edition of six hundred copies. As the title suggests, it is a book of etiquette for young girls in various social milieux – at church, in the classroom, at home, etc., etc. – and an obvious satire on the sort of genuine manuals of 'correct' behaviour that were in use at the end of the preceding century and earlier. Jokingly, Louÿs expects his little girls to know a thing or two already, and heads the text with a mock glossary:

> We have judged it to be a pointless exercise to explain the words: cunt, twat, quim, pussy, prick, cock, tool, balls, come (verb), come (noun), hard-on, wank, suck, lick, blow, fuck, screw, shag, stuff, grind, bugger, shoot one's cocoa, dildo, dyke, lez, sixty-nine, plate, gash, whore, knocking-shop.
> These words are familiar to all little girls.

A sample of the sort of etiquette recommended in *Manuel de Civilité*, which has been extracted from the section entitled *Pour sucer* – 'On sucking' – will be found heading the present chapter. Another, from the section 'With the President of the Republic', advises: 'If you recognise him as a regular at the whore house where you prostitute your pretty little mouth do not use his nickname there, "big boy", in the presence of his cabinet.'

Also in 1926 appeared what is probably Louÿs's best known clandestine book, *Trois filles de leur mère*, a novel about a student who finds himself living in a room

MANUEL

DE

CIVILITÉ

POUR LES

PETITES FILLES

A L'USAGE DES

MAISONS D'ÉDUCATION

MANUEL

DE

CIVILITÉ

POUR LES PETITES FILLES

à l'usage

des

maisons d'éducation

LONDRES
MCMXLVIII

ABOVE LEFT The first edition of Pierre Louÿs, *Manuel de civilité*, published at Paris by Simon Kra in 1926

ABOVE RIGHT Titlepage of a late reprint of *Manuel de civilité*. See colour plate opposite page 160

next door to a family of prostitutes, and which is particularly notable for its portrayal of the alienation of one of the daughters, Charlotte, whose only reliable friend is the finger with which she masturbates herself. It is a large volume, printed on specially made paper in which the watermark reproduces the name of the author in reverse, *Syuol Erreip*, and it was published by René Bonnel and Pascal Pia. The text is printed in facsimile of Louÿs's autograph manuscript, written distinctively in violet ink, and in general, erotic books ascribed to him that are not, in their first editions, reproduced from the original manuscript, or which do not include at least a specimen page from it, are usually viewed with some suspicion. One of these doubtful books is *Au temps des juges. Chants bibliques* (1933), a small collection of obscene verse, whose sole attribution to Louÿs rests on the presence of the initials 'P. L.' on the titlepage.

In 1927 four new works by Louÿs appeared: *Histoire du roi Gonzalve et les*

PIERRE LOUYS

PYBRAC

POÉSIES

CYTHÈRE

AU COQ HARDI

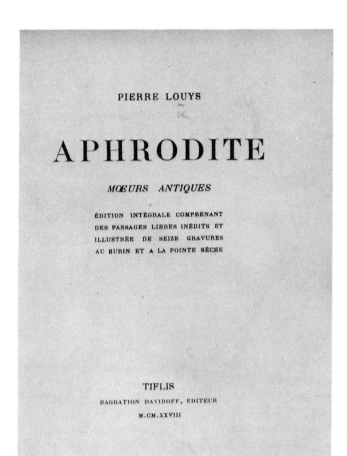

PIERRE LOUYS

APHRODITE

MŒURS ANTIQUES

ÉDITION INTÉGRALE COMPRENANT
DES PASSAGES LIBRES INÉDITS ET
ILLUSTRÉE DE SEIZE GRAVURES
AU BURIN ET A LA POINTE SÈCHE

TIFLIS
BAGRATION DAVIDOFF, ÉDITEUR
M.CM.XXVIII

douze princesses, a short novel, *Pybrac* and *Poésies érotiques*, all published by René Bonnel; and *Douze douzains de dialogues ou Petites scènes amoureuses*, from a bookseller named Robert Télin. The following year, a new edition of *Aphrodite, mœurs antiques* was published secretly in which an entire chapter, omitted from the original public edition of 1896, was included and a supplementary volume of notes by Pascal Pia added.

This list could be extended, but one of the most important of these posthumous works justifies a few lines to itself. In 1894, Louÿs published *Les Chansons de Bilitis*, prose poems supposed to be translations from the Greek of a poetess contemporary with Sappho (7th century BC), but actually one of the greatest literary hoaxes of the 19th century. Following this, Louÿs took a holiday in Algiers where he composed several more *chansons* which he included in an augmented edition of the book published in 1898 by the *Société du Mercure de France*. After the death of the poet in 1925, two apparently related books appeared: *Les Véritables chansons de Bilitis* and *Les Chansons secrètes de Bilitis*. Of these, the former is certainly a fabrication, having nothing to do with Louÿs save the name 'Bilitis', a view that is strongly emphasized by Pascal Pia in *Les Livres de*

173

LEFT Frontispiece by
Serge Czerefkov to the
first complete edition
of *Aphrodite*. See
illustration page 171

l'Enfer. Interestingly, since he was closely involved with clandestine publishing in France during the 1920s and '30s, Pia is unable – or unwilling – to say very much about this book at all, to the extent of merely noting that it was published '*vers 1930*'. *Les Chansons secrètes de Bilitis* on the other hand is definitely by Louÿs, and was first published in an edition of just 106 copies in 1933, probably by Marcel Lubineau. There is a strong suspicion that Pia was the author of *Les Véritables chansons*, a hoax on a hoax, written in the knowledge of the existence of Louÿs's genuine erotic *chansons* which were to be published three years later. That Pia was capable of such a thing is probable, for he was something of a practical joker in this way, as was shown by his almost certain authorship of 'Guillaume Apollinaire's' *Le Verger des amours* – mentioned above – and also of *A une courtisane* (1925), a poem ascribed to Charles Baudelaire.

RIGHT *Les Véritables chansons de Bilitis* (c. 1930). Erotic poems by an unknown author that were inspired by the *Chansons de Bilitis* (1894) of Pierre Louÿs, whose own, authentic erotic composition ascribed to 'Bilitis' were not published until 1933

The flavour of the authentic *Chansons secrètes de Bilitis* may be judged from the following, entitled *Ordres*:

Priscia, my faithful servant, don't forget especially to place some delicate Burma napkins near the divan, within reach of my hand. You understand they will be to dry myself ... after ... whether it be Mnasidika who pleasures me with his tongue, so moistening the lips of my vagina with a little pungent dew, or whether it be the prick of Lykas shooting deep within me at the right instant its jet of sticky sperm.

By 1925, when Louÿs died, new and younger writers were beginning to emerge. One, Raymond Radiguet, unfortunately did not live long enough to

175

fulfil the early promise of his novels *Le Diable au corps* (1923), which was something of a *succès de scandale*, and *Le Bal du comte d'Orgel* (1924), for he died tragically young in 1923 at the age of 20. These two novels had appeared openly, but in 1926 Radiguet's collected erotic poems were published secretly by René Bonnel as *Vers libres*, an event that did not find favour with Jean Cocteau, the young poet's mentor and intimate.

In 1928, Bonnel published two books that were unlike anything that had appeared before, novels in which for the first time eroticism was approached or examined through the medium of surrealism. These were *Le Con d'Irène* and the terrifying *Histoire de l'œil*. The former has with the persistence of a limpet been ascribed to Louis Aragon (born 1897), one of the founders of the Surrealist movement in literature, and if he is the author his reluctance to admit the fact may not be unconnected with his early abandonment of Surrealism in favour of the Communist Party; Communists are a notoriously conservative crew at the best of times, but doubly so when anything other than a strictly conventional attitude to sexual matters is involved. *Le Con d'Irène* – in all subsequent editions entitled with less directness simply as *Irène* – is a bizarre and poetic account of a paralysed old man's enforced move to a country town to stay with relatives. Here, his infatuation for Irène, a woman who may or may not be real, is fed by voyeuristic visits to the local brothel where he spies on those making love. A paranoid fear of being spied on himself drives him to stop his visits to the brothel and remain at home where he retreats into his own fantasies. Being a surrealist text, it does not always conform to the normal conventions of narrative writing, slipping at times into wonderful cascades of words and images that are clearly influenced in their constructions by Lautréamont and Antonin Artaud.

Influences are less easy to detect in *Histoire de l'œil*, the first book to be published of Georges Bataille (1897–1962). It appeared originally, and in all reprints until the fourth edition of 1967 published by J.-J. Pauvert, under the pseudonym 'Lord Auch', a name which for rather complicated reasons derives from the expression *aux chiottes* – 'to the shithouse'. It was the first of a trio of clandestine books, the others having the added disadvantage of appearing under the Fascist occupation of France, that were entitled *Madame Edwarda* ('1937' [1941]) by 'Pierre Angélique' and *Le Petit* ('1934' [1943]) by 'Louis Trente'. A fourth book, *Le Mort*, is often thought of as being part of the same group, but although as outspoken, it was published from the beginning – in 1964 – under the author's true name.

Bataille, at once a critic, a philosopher and even, in a sense, a theologian or mystic, was never a surrealist in the way that Aragon was, yet he used surrealist techniques in his approach to eroticism. On the surface, *Histoire de l'œil* is a straightforward narrative told in the first person of three youngsters, a boy – the storyteller – and two girls, Simone and Marcelle, who together share an ever more perverse series of sexual experiences. Marcelle eventually hangs herself, and the other two, in order to avoid problems with the police, flee to Spain where they team up with a wealthy Englishman named Sir Edmund, with whom they join in, among other things, a literally murderous orgy with a priest, which

HISTOIRE DE L'ŒIL
PAR LORD AUCH
avec huit lithographies originales

PARIS
1928

Titlepage of the first
edition of Georges Bataille's
Histoire de l'oeil, and one of
its illustrations by André
Masson

results in the death of the latter. The book closes with the three of them escaping to Gibraltar, buying a yacht and continuing their escapades elsewhere in company with a crew of Negroes.

Histoire de l'œil is autobiographical, which is to say that Bataille has created from his past a story not about people but about emotions, psychological disturbances and subconscious terrors that have taken human form. Elements of his childhood, such as the atrocious suffering, eventual madness and death of his father, blind and doubly incontinent from the effects of syphilis, and the subsequent insanity of his mother as well, after a family row that proved too much for her, provided the threads from which the book was woven. The strange and apparently unrelated images that such a disturbing childhood might cause to be retained take on an obsessive relevance as the story progresses: milk, hard-boiled eggs and urine; and then the bullfight in which the matador is killed, the horn of the bull embedded into his brain through the eye and the castration of the animal linking eggs, eyes and testicles. It becomes a quest for the ultimate sexual experience in which orgasm is indistinguishable from death, opposite sides of the same coin, a quest in which nothing is allowed to interfere.

English translations of Bataille seldom if ever work, not because of any lack of ability by the translators but because of the nature of the originals, which apparently are not the easiest texts to read even for the French. They are also not strictly speaking novels, but highly original amalgamations of narrative, essay and prose poem, and often the 'story' is incomplete unless accompanied by an essay in the form of a Preface or Introduction, the two elements being an integral part of the whole. But for those who might care to pursue this strange and unique work, *Histoire de l'œil* has been translated twice, first in Paris in 1953 as *A Tale of*

177

Satisfied Desire under the imprint of the emergent Olympia Press, and more recently as *The Story of the Eye* in 1977, from Urizen Books in the United States.

*   *   *   *   *

As has been mentioned already, censorship of books or the fear that they might be prosecuted began to be seriously challenged in France, at least, shortly after the Second World War. Whereas Bonnel and Duflou and others in the 1920s and later were content to issue their beautiful, limited editions to collectors of means, new publishers with more democratic ideals had been thrown up by the war, and more importantly publishers who had the courage to put their names on the books that they issued. Despite the Allied victory over reaction in Europe and the Far East, reaction of the home-grown variety was still firmly dug in and these new notions of literary freedom were not welcomed with open arms in all quarters, and there were some early skirmishes, with casualties. One of the first publishers to find itself in court was Éditions du Scorpion for a brilliant but outrageously violent and graphically sexual novel entitled *J'irai cracher sur vos tombes* (1946). Heavily influenced by the novels of authors like James M. Cain, it deals with the revenge wreaked on a small Southern town in the United States by a 'white' Negro in reprisal for the brutal murder of his brother, a more normally pigmented black. The author of this was actually the novelist and jazz musician Boris Vian (1920–59), although his name only appears on the book as the translator of the 'American' of 'Vernon Sullivan'. *J'irai cracher sur vos tombes* was successfully prosecuted and found to be an obscene work, remaining a proscribed book until fairly recently.

Although Jean-Jacques Pauvert commenced the open publication of the complete works of Sade in 1947 – and was of course prosecuted as well, but with less success in the long run – clandestine publishing was not completely at an end until about the early 1960s when the first two volumes of the *Emmanuelle* books by Maryat and Louis Rollet-Andrianne were published in editions that while totally anonymous were unmistakably from the Eric Losfeld stable. Most of Jean Genet's books appeared originally in secret editions, one of them, *Pompes funèbres* ('A Bikini', 1947) from Pauvert and Gaston Gallimard.

One of the last clandestine works published by Pauvert was an extraordinary sado-masochist novel entitled *L'Anglais décrit dans le château fermé* (1953) by 'Pierre Morion', actually the writer André Pieyre de Mandiargues. An open, although discreet edition was published by Gallimard in 1979 with the author's real name on it, but an earlier attempt by Régine Deforges to publish it legitimately in 1973 resulted in swift legal action and a swingeing fine. The following extract may explain the attitude of the law:

Poor Edmunde! We were all bent over your arse, none of us wanting to miss the tiniest details of your agonies. Your cries became like the death-rattle of an animal whose throat has been slit and as you gradually slipped into unconsciousness brought on by the terrible burning pain inside, your body took on the soft white consistency of a fresh corpse. We watched as a thin stream of blood and water trickled out from between your buttocks, wetting the cover of the divan. The sight of this little death brought me on to such an extent that I had to remove Viola's hand from my prick so as not to come wastefully into my trousers, and I eyed my neighbours, undecided whether to fill one of their arses, a mouth or a cunt. It was then that I heard a foolish tinkling laugh like a schoolgirl's when teacher breaks her glasses. It was Michelette who had taken advantage of being allowed to eat and drink to the point of over-indulging and now could no longer contain her high spirits.

'Edmunde has got an ice-cube up her arse and she's all white!' she shrilled between fits of laughter.

'That young lady seems to be in a very good mood,' said the German girl. 'She's all one can hear.'

'My dear,' said Montcul to her, 'since you have attended those ante-natal courses which are the custom in your country, you surely know of an effective way to silence noisy children?' The German girl fetched Michelette a stinging blow on the nape of the neck with her foil, behind Montcul, and whispered a few words in our host's ear.

'Hot steaming spunk!' exclaimed the latter. 'What an idea! The little tart will be quite tasty and I shall never make fun of ante-natal education again if that's where you learned these methods.'

He provoked Michelette further by tweaking her nose and threw her, weeping, to the negroes with orders that she should be taken at once to the aquarium room. Montcul with Lina de Warmdreck and I between the mulatress and the negress, all followed the trio, leaving the beautiful Edmunde in her awkward posture to digest her ice-cube in peace. Myself, I hoped that there was some pleasure in store and that I should find a home for my own spunk.

On the ground floor of the adjacent tower there was another round room like the bathroom through which one went up to my bedroom. The circular wall surrounding us was made up of the aquariums which my friend had referred to and which were set into the wall at chest height and separated from us only by a single strip of pebbles. From behind, the background illumination gave a subdued light to the room through its filter of greenish water. Within, the fish and all sorts of sea creatures swam among the mossy little rocks, the shells and the bunches of weed which provided more or less the scene one finds when swimming underwater with goggles. An endless stream of air bubbles climbed to the surface. Just like my bathroom, the centre of the room was taken up with a round pool but here it was covered with a lattice-work grating of brass and only held a few inches of water on a bed of sand and gravel. There were about twenty octopuses beneath, which, excepting two or three, were no bigger than those which one generally finds at low tide in rockpools in Brittany or Normandy, conspicuous by their shield of pebbles. The largest, however, waved tentacles almost as long as a woman's arm. Several of them had climbed from the water and were clinging from where the German girl dislodged them with jabs from her foil.

'Remove the grille,' she said to the negroes. When this had been done she turned to Michelette who had been humiliated by two brutal slaps in the face.

'Listen, you little bitch,' she said, 'You're going into the hole and that should teach you to laugh and be noisy when grown-ups are talking. The octopuses will attack you; you'll feel them biting you and sucking your blood.'

Michelette struggled, screamed with fear between her sobs and shook off the German girl's arm in an attempt to escape but Gracchus and Publicola had grabbed her (I could see that they were both prick-proud and that the tender parts of the little body were being pawed harshly by their big black hands) and threw her into the middle of the pool. Then straightaway they put the cover back on. The octopuses, freshly caught, were quite lively, in fact I should say they were very much alive! To begin with they fled to the sides where Michelette fell in among them but we pushed them back towards the middle. The grille was placed far too low to allow the little girl to stand up or even sit upright and she rolled around underneath like an epileptic tearing to ribbons the delicate cami-knickers which were all she was wearing, and lacerating her face, her hands and the skin all over her body on the metal. Maddened by the activities of this intruder, the octopuses swam in furious fits and starts from one side to the other; they squirted their ink onto the sand and in the water and wrapped their tentacles like whiplashes around the limbs of their little victim. Although these creatures are not as dangerous as some people believe, nevertheless the embrace of those eight arms and the grip of the suckers is quite severe and when the horny parrot's beak of a mouth is placed against the skin of a child it is not exactly a friendly nip that it gives.

To all appearances, Michelette had quite lost her head. She was lying on her back, her hair in the water, her legs spread as wide as they could be and her knees scratching against the grille and bleeding. In this grossly immodest posture she displayed herself to us better (or worse) than simply naked, with odd tatters of crepe and lace still clinging to her wet and bruised body. The five octopuses which had attached themselves to her were motionless, their tentacles closely wrapped around her flanks, her belly and her thighs; another, one of the largest, came and stuck itself to her face forming a ghastly burlesque mask. Such a mingling of childish flesh with that of the cephalopod molluscs in a confused mess of torn silk and lace and all of it swimming in blood, animal ink, sand and salt water, reached such a point of grandiose bestiality in which there was a note of what one rather vaguely calls the sublime that I was quite carried away. I grabbed Viola, tore off her robe and bent her over the grating; but others too had felt the effects of this spectacle and I did not have the time to get my prick up.

'In the name of all the arses in heaven and earth,' cried the master of Gamehuche, 'I think I'm getting hard.'

The women around him at once became attentive and Viola, who had slipped from my arms apprehensively as soon as she heard him, was among the first to help undress him. Stroked by breasts and buttocks, tickled by eyelashes, manipulated, rubbed and sucked, Montcul's yard was soon standing proud. It was a very fine specimen, not hugely long, if, as the learned Viola maintained, it only just reached nine inches, but what was striking was its club-like profile and the enormous crimson knob which topped it (seven inches in circumference!). The most remarkable thing about it, however, was a serrated membrane, rather like the crest of certain reptiles, which was marbled with pink and purple and which hung under this yard from the knob at the top right down to the balls. I have not seen many men with erections, not being a pansy nor much of a lover of orgies, so I cannot say with any certainty whether this magnificent object of which monsieur de Montcul was so proud, is unique. Doctors to whom I have mentioned it later assure me it is and I take their word for it. For the rest, my friend had the body of a hairy Bacchus, in colouring somewhere between chestnut-brown and red, and his face was clean shaven and cold like a clergyman.

'Uncover the pool quickly,' he cried. 'The little slut is perfect just like this in her own special juice. I shall screw her from in front and behind and damn me if this time I don't manage to bring the spunk up.'[7]

Also in France, during the 1950s and early 1960s, there was an enormous amount of really poor quality pornography published which may very roughly be paralleled with the 'Soho typescripts' that were churned out in England at about the same time, semi-literate fantasies, cobbled together on typewriters and duplicating machines, illustrated with smudgy, obscene photographs and sold for a fiver a time in the sex shops in London's Soho. Incredible as it may seem, these things are rare now and although not as desirable as a first folio Shakespeare are not easily found. (Please – no offers!)

But serious resistance to the freedom to publish was gradually eliminated. Side by side with Pauvert, Losfeld and others with their French erotica, Maurice Girodias and his Olympia Press bombarded England and the United States from Paris with the English-language variety; much of it was rather poor it is true, but without *There's a Whip in My Valise* (1961) and similar dubious delights doubt must exist as to whether we should have been able to enjoy books like *The Ginger Man, Lolita, The Naked Lunch,* authors like Beckett, Miller and, in translation, Sade and Bataille.

Today the prosecution of books for eroticism or obscenity is uncommon, and in general publishers are free to put out just about anything, although sensitive areas still exist. This has proved a mixed blessing, for it seems that only at times when the fear of arrest is at its height do really beautiful erotic books appear, and ideas that are interesting, perhaps important, floated. With this paradox in mind, the final word of this all-too brief survey of a very extensive and complex subject must go to Jean-Jacques Pauvert, from the last paragraph of his Preface to the L'Or du Temps/Régine Desforges edition of *Irène* (1968): 'If publishing is a business of which people are growing weary, then it is because new blood is not entering it fast enough, and because the new generations seem to fear any kind of challenge. Nevertheless, we should try single mindedly to use paper and ink to produce the most beautiful and surprising things before libraries have disappeared from our lives, and our children's children have forgotten what books are.'

NOTES TO THE TEXT

CHAPTER ONE

1 It has been suggested, by Ashbee among others, that the *Ragionamenti* was influenced by a Spanish work entitled *La Lozana Andaluza* that was written in Rome in 1524 by Francisco Delicado and printed four years later at Venice. For an extended and enthusiastic notice of an 1871 reprint of Delicado's work, see *Ashbee*, vol. 3, pp. 373–84.

2 Both Sander and Toscanini published articles describing the book. Sander's contribution appeared in *Zeitschrift für Bücherfreunde,* N.F. XXI (1929), while Toscanini's 'Le operette erotiche aretinesche' appeared in *Il Vasari,* anno 19 (1961).

3 Madame Gourdan was one of the most celebrated bawds in France during the latter years of the 18th century. This volume of letters addressed to her is spurious, and is generally believed to have been written by Charles Thévenot de Morande (1748–92), a professional pamphleteer and scandal-monger who may have composed the work while in exile in England where the first edition, entitled *Le Porte-feuille de Madame Gourdan* (À Spa, 1783) is thought to have been printed. The edition of 1784 under the new title is a greatly expanded version. The translation above was done from the edition published at Paris in 1967 by the *Cercle du Livre Précieux,* pp. 51, 2.

4 In itself, the lack of catchwords is not absolute proof that Chorier's book was published in France. Catchwords, for the uninitiated, are the first words of the following page placed in the right-hand lower corner of each page of a book, below the last line of text. Their use seems to have begun in Italy in the 15th century, and from about 1530 they were widely used in English printing until the beginning of the 19th century when they fell into disfavour, except for occasional devotional works which attempted to affect an air of antiquity. Catchwords were uncommon in France in the 16th century, but were in regular use in the 17th. In general, it would be fair to say that

French printing practice was late in adopting the catchword and early in abandoning it, and even while in use it was not universally employed. The purpose of catchwords is subject to argument. The usual reason given for them is to assist the printer in imposing pages; others are not disposed to accept this view, and believe they were intended to aid the reader.

5 Translated as *The Gallant Hermaphrodite* (London, 1688; copy in British Library, but not in the Private Case).

6 *L'Adamiste ou le Jésuite insensible* was first published in 1682, according to *Gay* (vol. 1, p. 25). The British Library has two copies of a reprint done in Holland by the Elzevirs in 1684, one of which is part of the Ashbee bequest.

7 The Grub Street tradition never really survived the 18th century, and the nearest thing that we have to it today is the British satirical magazine *Private Eye,* which combines an entertaining line in sixth form humour with a genuine flair for independent and occasionally devastating investigative journalism that has earned it many enemies but more friends. The celebrated libel case involving *Private Eye* and Sir James Goldsmith, in which readers contributed generously to the *Eye*'s defence costs in the form of the 'Goldenballs Fund', is very approximately paralleled by Curll's spell in the pillory at Charing Cross; he had the foresight to distribute a handbill informing the populace that he was being punished for 'vindicating the memory of Queen Anne'. As a result he escaped the painful, and sometimes lethal, treatment usually meted out to felons in the stocks, and when released was carried shoulder-high to a nearby public house. For an account of Curll's life, and an exhaustive bibliography of his publications, see *The Unspeakable Curll* by Ralph Straus (London: Chapman & Hall, 1927).

8 David Foxon corrected his statement concerning the non-survival of either of the two Curll editions of

Venus in the Cloister in the Introduction to a reprint of his four *Book Collector* articles published in 1965 by University Books of New York.

9 *Amori vera lux*; literally, 'In love there is true light'. I am indebted to Mr Denis Crutch for the suggestion that the anagram here is *Amor e luxuria*, 'Love from excess.'

10 *Venus in the Cloister*, London: 1725; pp. 125–27.

CHAPTER TWO

1 The *Bibliotheca Scatalogica* – 'par trois savants en us' – was first published in 1849 at Paris in *Le Journal de l'Amateur des Livres*. The authors, or compilers, were P. Jannet, J.-P. Payen and Auguste Veinant. In 1850 it was issued separately in an edition of 150 copies with the false imprint 'Scatopolis [i.e. Paris] 5850'. A facsimile reprint of this, done by the Zentralantiquariat der DDR, was published at Leipzig in 1970.

2 Jean-Baptiste Louvet de Couvray (1760–97). The author of a *galante* novel entitled *Les Amours du chevalier de Faublas* (1789–90) that while fairly well thought of in France is still regarded – in the edition of 1966 – as 'frivolous [and] licentious' by *The Oxford Companion to French Literature*.

3 A reference to either the literary critic René Rapin (1621–87) or, more probably, Paul de Rapin de Thoyras (1671–1725), a Huguenot who moved first to Holland and then to England. His *Histoire d'Angleterre* (1724) would have been known to Macaulay.

4 See *Edinburgh Review*, Oct. 1833.

5 Two editions were published in 1748, the other being imprinted 'Au Monomotapa'. An English version appeared the following year: *Les Bijoux indiscrets. Or, the Indiscreet Toys, Translated from the Congese language* ... ('Tobago' [London]: Sold by R. Freeman, 1749). The Germans had to wait twenty-eight years for their edition, which was published as *Die geschwätzigen Muscheln* ('Frankfurt und Leipzig' [Augsburg, Mauracher], 1776); the translation was by Johann Baptist von Knoll.

6 *Les Bijoux Indiscrets. Or, the Indiscreet Toys* (Tobago [London], 1749; 2 vols) vol. 1, p. 8.

7 Op cit., vol. 1, pp. 260–2. It should be pointed out that three chapters found in modern editions of *Les Bijoux indiscrets* were not included in the book prior to the 'Paris' edition of 1833, according to *Gay* (3rd ed. vol. 2, p. 19), or an edition of 1798, according to Yves de Bayser (*Dictionnaire des œuvres érotiques*, Paris: Mercure de France, 1971, p. 64). These chapters are 14, 18 and 19 (cf. *Gay*) and 16, 18 and 19 (cf.

Dictionnaire de œuvres érotiques article). The English edition from which my quotations are taken was published prior to the addition of these three extra chapters, and the numeration of the chapters in it will be at variance with modern editions, especially since the chapters do not run continuously throughout but start again at the beginning of the second volume with 'Chapter I'. Thus, *Rêve de Mangogul* occurs in chapter thirty-two of the Garnier Flammarion French edition of 1968 but in chapter twenty-nine of the English translation of 1749.

8 Op. cit., vol. 1, pp. 20–1.

9 Op. cit., vol. 2, pp. 213–14.

10 *Les Bijoux indiscrets* (Paris: Garnier-Flammarion, 1968), pp. 260–1. The English translation of 1749 renders this passage in French.

11 Even worse, if such a thing is conceivable, is a pornographic film version made in France in the 1970s entitled *Pussy Talk* in the English-language release prints. Since the story is given a modern setting, making satirical observations of 18th-century figures impossible, and displays no discernible artistic criticism, the point of making the film seems, I fear, all too evident.

12 These lines occur in a statement that Cleland made, in the form of a letter, to the Law Clerk in the Secretary of State's Office, a man named Lovel Stanhope. For the full text of the letter see Foxon, *Libertine Literature*, pp. 54–5.

13 The titlepage of the first edition (see illustration), and several reprints and French editions, give the publisher as 'G. Fenton', a transparent alias for Fenton Griffiths. What little is known about this mysterious person is gathered together in Norman Edwin Oakes's *Ralph Griffiths and The Monthly Review* (1961), a Columbia University dissertation.

14 *Le Libertin de qualité* ('À Stamboul' [Paris or Neuchâtel], 1784), p. [1].

15 Op. cit., p. 17.

16 Op. cit., pp. 31–4.

17 Enemies of Mirabeau, the author of the book, had it published shortly after his death as *Vie privée, libertine et scandaleuse de feu H. G. R. ci-devant comte de Mirabeau* (1791).

18 *Lettres originales de Mirabeau écrites du donjon de Vincennes, 1777–1780*, (Paris: J.-B. Garnery, 1792; 4 vols), vol. 4, pp. 166–7.

19 Op. cit., vol 4, p. 189. *Parapilla* is a poem by Charles Borde, written in imitation of the *Novella dell'Angelo Gabriello*, a story that featured in an anthology entitled *Il Libro del perché* (1757). Borde's imitation first appeared in 1776.

20 Op. cit., vol. 4, p. 298.

21 Pascal Pia describes an edition of *L'Anti-Justine* in the *Enfer* (no. 1024) that on typographical evidence he believes to date from the 1840s. I am inclined to think that this is a copy of the poorly printed edition of 1863, especially since it matches exactly such an edition described fully in the *Galitzin* catalogue (no. 112), but without seeing the *Enfer* copy it is impossible to be certain. (See *Les Livres de l'Enfer*, vol. 1, p. 52, col 64.)

22 Restif de la Bretonne, *Pleasures and Follies of a Good-Natured Libertine* (Paris: Olympia Press, 1955), p. [9]. No work by the Marquis de Sade entitled *La Théorie du libertinage* is known to exist, but there is reason to believe that Restif may be referring to *Les 120 Journées de Sodome, ou l'École du libertinage*. This was written by Sade while he was a prisoner in the Bastille, but not published until 1904 for the first time. Restif may have heard of the existence of the manuscript and put down the title as he recalled it.

23 There is in fact a half-length portrait in profile of a young man believed to be Sade done about 1760–2 by Charles-Amédée-Philippe Van Loo (1719–90). It is a charcoal drawing, round in shape. It is reproduced in the journal *Obliques* (no. 12–13, special Sade issue) from the original in the collection of M. Robert Lebel, Paris.

24 A greatly abridged translation of Lély's biography of Sade, by Alec Brown, was published in 1961 at London by Paul Elek.

25 *Les Infortunes de la vertu*, edited by Maurice Heine, was published for the first time at Paris in 1930 by Editions Fourcade. Heine also edited and had published, in 1926, the *Contes et fabliaux* that *Les Infortunes de la vertu* was initially intended to accompany.

26 *Correspondance inédite du marquis de Sade, de ses proches et de ses familiers*, edited by Paul Bourdin (Paris: 1929), p. 290.

27 Sade, *The Story of Juliette* vol. 7. (Paris: Olympia Press, 1965), pp. 199, 200–1. The translation of this volume is credited to John Crombie; the other six volumes were translated by 'Pieralessandro Casavini' (Austryn Wainhouse) or, in the case of vol. 6, by Wainhouse and Crombie jointly.

28 Sade, *The 120 Days of Sodom*, vol. 1 (Paris: Olympia Press, 1954), p. 89. The translation is by 'Pieralessandro Casavini' (Austryn Wainhouse). The edition quoted from here is in two volumes. A one-volume edition, keeping the same pagination and printed on thin India paper, was published simultaneously with a view, presumably, to make smuggling it into England and the United States easier.

29 Op. cit., vol. 1, p. 110.

30 Op. cit. vol. 2, p. 562.

31 Sade, *The Bedroom Philosophers*, trans. by Pieralessandro Casavini (Austryn Wainhouse) (Paris: Olympia Press, 1953), pp. 26, 27.

CHAPTER THREE

1 For my account of the history of *Schwester Monika*, I have drawn on the translator's Notice – signed 'E. L.' [Eric Losfeld?] – of the first French edition, published at Paris as *Sœur Monika récits et aventures* in 1966 by Le Terrain vague.

2 Donald Thomas, *A Long Time Burning*, p. 213, footnote. Cannon also published a French translation of a work that had originally appeared in English: *The Pastimes of a Convent* ('Brussels, 1798' [London: Louis Chappuis & James Ferguson. c. 1830] appeared as *Les Passetemps du Couvent*. (See Ashbee, vol. 3, pp. 154.)

3 *The Inutility of Virtue* ('London: Printed for the Society of Vice', n.d. [Paris? c. 1880]), p. 3. The original edition of 1830 seems not to have survived, nor the reprint of c. 1860 published by William Dugdale.

4 My synopsis of *The Lustful Turk* is drawn from an edition published in 1967 by Holloway House of Los Angeles, California, in a compendium volume entitled *The Harem Omnibus*. Another, similar, work possibly by the same author as *The Lustful Turk* appeared at London in about 1830 entitled *Scenes in the Seraglio*. Ashbee (vol. 3, pp. 136–7) gives a good description of it, but I have been unable to see a copy.

5 *Ashbee*, vol. 3, pp. xlvii, iii.

6 *The Pearl*, no. 17, Nov. 1880, p. 180. I have taken my quotation from the reprint published by Brandon House of North Hollywood, California, in June 1968. I would like to thank Mr Peter Mendes for drawing my attention to this reference to Reddie.

7 Marie Corelli; the nom-de-plume of Mary Mackay (1855–1924), a popular novelist whose books include *The Sorrows of Satan* (1895) and *The Mighty Atom* (1896). If Crowley used her name for any other reason than a convenient rhyme I have been unable to find it.

8 For a very thorough account of the relationships between *L'École des biches* and *Instruction libertine*, see the title essay in G. Legman's *The Horn Book* (N.Y., 1964).

9 The illustrations in the copy of the first edition in Switzerland are coloured as are, of course, those of the reprint taken from it, but it is probable that when *Gamiani* was first published in 1833 they were printed

in monochrome only and it was the purchasers who added colour to them afterwards. Although Devéria and Grévedon are the artists usually cited as providing the illustrations for the book, two others have also been proposed: Horace Vernet and Tony Johannot.

CHAPTER FOUR

1 For the accounts of the activities of Keary and the Ashfords I am indebted to the evidence of Chief-Inspector Edward Drew before the Joint Select Committee on Lotteries and Indecent Advertisements, whose report was published at London in 1908.

2 *Catalogus Librorum Prohibitorum Britannica* ... by Lawrence Forster. Compiled between about 1910 and 1923, this manuscript consists of four loose-leaf albums, one of which – the draft for the whole work apparently – is handwritten, and the other three typewritten. Inserted into one of the volumes are two letters from the Paris erotica publisher Charles Carrington to Forster which indicate that preliminary negotiations were in hand to publish the bibliography, a project that never materialized. The value of the manuscript is limited since it is largely a crib from Ashbee, and in the case of books published after 1885 – the date of Ashbee's last volume of bibliography – most of the information is culled from prospectuses and booksellers' catalogues. I was allowed to examine the manuscript in an office of Dr N. C. Nothmann's bookshop in Covent Garden on 12 November 1973. Its present whereabouts is not known to me.

3 Biographical material on both G. R. Bacchus and Isa Bowman is in part extracted from Morton N. Cohen, *Letters of Lewis Carroll* (1979), vol. 2, p. 710, footnote. I am greatly indebted to Mr Denis Crutch for drawing my attention to this.

4 Quoted in C. R. Dawes, *A Study in Erotic Literature in England*, (1943). Ms. in British Library, p. 326.

5 My discussion concerning late Victorian and Edwardian English erotica, and in particular the area surrounding the Smithers/Nichols/Bacchus trinity, is heavily indebted to conversations over the years with Mr Peter Mendes, based on his research towards his as yet unpublished bibliographical Ph.D., *English Erotic Fiction 1885–1930*. Many of the bibliographical knots that I touch upon will be fully unravelled there.

6 Marcel Adéma mentions a fifth collection of erotic verses comprising poems that Apollinaire excluded from the *Bestiaire ou Cortège d'Orphée* (1911). This was *Le Condor et le Morpion* (Paris: Aux dépens d'un amateur, 1931), illustrated with four woodcuts by Raoul Dufy and limited to twenty-nine copies. I have been unable to see a copy.

7 André Pieyre de Mandiargues, *L'Anglais décrit dans le château fermé*; Paris, 1979, pp. 63–70. I am indebted for the translation of this passage to Mr Merlin Holland.

BIBLIOGRAPHY

To study any class of books historically and as objects in themselves, which is to say bibliographically rather than from the viewpoint of the critic, requires first and foremost that the books themselves are available for examination in a condition that so far as possible is the same as when they were first printed and bound. With erotica this is especially true, for its subject matter has ensured either the total disappearance of many works, or their existence in isolated single copies, later reprints or even, as in the case of the 17th-century play *Sodom*, as imperfect manuscripts. Printed authorities and reference works, then, are not in themselves adequate to pursue studies of this sort, for to use them in isolation requires that the student relies on eyes other than his own, an extremely hazardous practice.

Where then to find these rare or unique volumes? The best place to start is in the national public libraries, or the libraries of the larger universities. It is probable that all national libraries contain *some* erotica because the methods they use to accumulate their holdings, outside the enforcement of copyright laws, resemble a sort of indiscriminate vacuum cleaner that in general accepts everything that is offered, whether through sale (these days rarely though), donation, bequest, gift or even loan. With accession on this scale it would be surprising if erotica of some sort did not sneak through even if not wanted. The problem of course lies in knowing where to look for books of this sort, and by a strange quirk of fate the puritanism of early times has come to the aid of the modern researcher, for until comparatively recently it was thought that the best place for erotic books was a cage all to themselves. This kept them conveniently all in one place in the geographical sense, and as these collections have invariably been saddled with peculiar-sounding names, and pressmarks deriving from these, their contents are fairly conspicuously scattered throughout the volumes or index cards or microfilm of General Catalogues. However, knowing that one's local national library has an erotica collection is only part of the problem for the serious researcher; its extent is another matter

entirely, and to discover that it is an advantage to have access to a specialized catalogue of some description. Unfortunately, while the national libraries have included their erotica in their General Catalogues – an innovation embarked upon by the British Library about 1965 – none of them has seen fit to print a specialized monograph or catalogue of their holdings. In view of the fact that they have published such sectarian guides to other classes of literature, the reasons for the lacuna in the erotica department may be guessed at, but this is no place for gratuitous finger pointing at earlier generations of librarians whose moral sensibilities outweighed their dedication to their profession.

The same situation applies to university libraries, but on a smaller scale; all have erotica collections of some sort, all – so far as I know – are included in their main catalogues, but none is provided with a separate catalogue of their own. Manuscript catalogues or listings may exist it is true, but they are not advertised; and although in my experience access to them is never denied once one is aware of their existence, this is not quite the same as being able simply to pull the volume or volumes or erotica-catalogues off the open shelf in the same way that one is able to with similar volumes devoted to Italian illustrated books of the 16th century or whichever topic it is that takes one's fancy.

There are two major collections of erotica in national libraries, and both have been frequently mentioned in the foregoing chapters. These are the *Enfer* of the Bibliothèque Nationale, Paris, and the Private Case of London's British Library. Between them there are preserved close to four thousand of the world's choicest erotic books, although they are not completely free from rubbish as a quick check through the pages of their independently published catalogues, listed at the conclusion of this note, will show. The old Apollinaire/Fleuret/Perceau catalogue of the *Enfer*, published first in 1913 and re-issued six years later with the addition of a new Preface, has been superseded by Pascal Pia's *Les Livres de L'Enfer* (1978) which gives not only fuller bibliographical detail and corrects a number of mistakes in the earlier book, but brings the whole collection up to date by listing over 800 additions to the collection since 1913 and providing information on other books and editions.

The catalogue of the Private Case, compiled by the present writer and published in 1981, similarly relied on a previously printed source, the *Registrum Librorum Eroticum* of 'Rolf S. Reade' [Alfred Rose], for the bones on which it was built. Whereas Rose attempted a sort of 'world bibliography' of erotica, including the British Library holdings, *The Private Case* is purely a catalogue of the collection of its title.

In the absence of the books themselves, the next most reliable source of information are bibliographies of certain aspects of erotica, the occasional catalogues of private collections that have been printed and, with caution, the catalogues of auctioneers and booksellers. Many of the most important of these will be found below.

PRIMARY SOURCES

ASHBEE 1 *Index Librorum Prohibitorum: being Notes Bio-Biblio-Iconographical and Critical on Curious and Uncommon Books* by Pisanus Fraxi [Henry Spencer Ashbee]. London: privately printed, 1877 (reprinted, New York: Jack Brussel, 1962).

ASHBEE 2 *Centuria Librorum Absconditorum* ... London: privately printed, 1879 (reprinted, New York: Jack Brussel, 1962).

ASHBEE 3 *Catena Librorum Tacendorum* ... London: privately printed, 1885 (reprinted, New York: Jack Brussel, 1962).

ENFER *L'Enfer de la Bibliothèque Nationale. Bibliographie méthodique et critique de tous les ouvrages composant cette célèbre collection avec une préface, un index des titres et une table des auteurs. Nouvelle édition,* (par) Guillaume Apollinaire, Fernand Fleuret & Louis Perceau. Paris: Bibliothèque des Curieux, 1919 (reprinted, Genève: Slatkine, 1970).

GALITZIN *Catalogue du Cabinet Secret du Prince G***: Collection de Livres et Objets Curieux et Rares concernant l'Amour, les Femmes et le Mariage. Avec les Prix de Vente.* Première Partie (Supplément Iconographique). Bruxelles: [Vital-Puissant?], 1887, 1890 (reprinted, London: 1975).

GAY *Bibliographie des Ouvrages Relatifs à l'Amour, aux Femmes, au Mariage, et des Livres Facétieux, Pantagruéliques, Satyriques, etc. contenant les Titres detaillés des ces ouvrages, les noms des Auteurs, un Aperçu de leur sujet, leur valeur et leur prix dans les ventes, etc.* par M. le C. d'I*** 3me Edition, entièrement refondue et considérablement augmentée. Turin: J. Gay et Fils &

Londres: Bernard Quaritch, 1871–3. Six volumes.

HAYN/GOTENDORF *Bibliotheca Germanorum Erotica & Curiosa. Verzeichnis der gesamten deutschen erotischen Literatur mit Einschluss der Übersetzungen, nebst Beifügung der Originale.* Herausgegeben von Hugo Hayn und Alfred N. Gotendorf (und) Paul Englisch. München: Georg Müller, 1912–29. Nine volumes.

KEARNEY *The Private Case. An Annotated Bibliography of the Private Case erotica collection in the British (Museum) Library.* London: Jay Landesman, 1981.

PERCEAU *Bibliographie du roman érotique au XIXe siècle. Donnant une Description Complète de tous les Romans, Nouvelles et autres Ouvrages en Prose publiés sous le Manteau en Français, de 1800 à nos jours, et de toutes leurs réimpressions* (par) Louis Perceau. Paris: Georges Fourdrinier, 1930. Two volumes.

PIA *Les Livres de l'Enfer* (par) Pascal Pia. Coulet et Faure, 1978. Two volumes.

ROSE *Registrum Librorum Eroticorum. Vel (sub hac specie) Dubiorum: Opus Bibliographicum et Præcipue Bibliothecariis Destinatum.* Compiled by Rolf S. Reade [Alfred Rose]. London: privately printed for subscribers, 1936 (reprinted, New York: Jack Brussel, 1965). Two volumes.

SECONDARY SOURCES

ARCANA *Bibliotheca Arcana seu Catalogus Librorum Penetralium, being Brief Notices of Books that have been secretly printed, Prohibited by Law, seized, anathematized, burnt or Bowdlerized,* by Speculator Morum [William Laird Clowes]. London: George Redway, 1885 (reprinted, London: Charles Skilton, 1971).

CHILDS *Restif de la Bretonne: Témoignages et Jugements: Bibliographie.* (Par) J. Rives Childs. Paris: Aux dépens de l'auteur; en vente à la Librairie Briffaut, 1949.

COHEN/DE RICCI *Guide de l'Amateur de Livres à Gravures du XVIIIe siècle.* Sixième édition. Revue, Corrigée et Considérablement Augmentée par Seymour DeRicci. Paris: Librairie A. Rouquette, 1912.

D'ARCH SMITH *Love in Earnest: Some Notes on the Lives and Writings of English 'Uranian' Poets from 1889 to 1930,* by Timothy d'Arch Smith. London: Routledge and Kegan Paul, 1970.

DAWES 'A Study of Erotic Literature in England ...', by Charles Reginald Dawes. Cheltenham: 1943. An unpublished typescript kept in the British Library, Department of Printed Books, at pressmark Cup. 364.d.15. In addition, Dawes's catalogue of his own collection, in two volumes, is kept in the Placer's Room of the British Library. It has no pressmark and is not entered in the General Catalogue of the Library.

DEAKIN *Catalogi Librorum Eroticum. A Critical Bibliography of Erotic Bibliographies and Book-Catalogues.* Compiled by Terence J. Deakin. London: Cecil and Amelia Woolf, 1964.

DICTIONNAIRE *Dictionnaire des OEuvres Érotiques, domaine Française.* Paris: Mercure de France, 1971.

FLEISCHMANN *Marie Antoinette, Libertine. Bibliographie critique et analytique des pamphlets politiques, galants et obscènes contre la Reine ...* (par) Hector Fleischmann. Paris: Bibliothèque des Curieux, 1911.

FOXON *Libertine Literature in England 1660–1745,* by David Foxon. New York: University Books, 1965.

FRYER *Private Case – Public Scandal,* by Peter Fryer. London: Secker & Warburg, 1966.

HOFFMANN *Analytical Survey of Anglo-American Traditional Erotica,* by Frank Hoffmann. Ohio: Bowling Green University Popular Press, 1973.

LEGMAN *The Horn Book: Studies in Erotic Folklore and Bibliography,* by G. Legman. New York: University Books, 1964.

LÉONINA *Bibliothèque 'La Léonina'. III. Curiosa.* Monte Carlo: 1955. Catalogue of the clandestine section of the library of Arpad Plesch; compiled by Jacques Pley.

MASON *Bibliography of Oscar Wilde,* by Stuart Mason [Christopher Millard]. London: Bertram Rota, 1967 (reprinted).

PENZER *An Annotated Bibliography of Sir Richard Francis Burton,* by Norman M. Penzer. London: Dawsons, 1967 (reprinted).

REDDIE 'Bibliographical Notes'. A three-volume manuscript bibliography of erotic literature compiled by James Campbell Reddie, a personal friend of Henry Spencer Ashbee, to whom the manuscript was given after Reddie's death in 1878. It is kept in the Department of Manuscripts of the British Library at pressmarks 38.282, 38.829 and 38.830.

STERN-SZANA *Bibliotheca Curiosa et Erotica* (von) Bernhard Stern-Szana. [Vienna:] Privatdruck für Bernhard Stern-Szana und seine Freunde, [1921].

STRAUS *The Unspeakable Curll: Being some Account of Edmund Curll, Bookseller; to which is added a full List of his Books,* by Ralph Straus. London: Chapman and Hall, 1927 (reprinted, New York: Augustus M. Kelley, 1970).

ILLUSTRATION SOURCES

The publishers would like to acknowledge the following:

Cambridge University Library, by permission of the Syndics of Cambridge University Library: opp. 80 (both)
Bodleian Library, Oxford: 12 (*right*) Phi f. 123, 78 Phi e. 66, opp. 112 Phi e. 100, opp. 113 Phi f. 100, 114 (*left*) Phi f. 100, 114 (*right*) Phi f. 102, 119 Phi e. 112, opp. 128 Phi e. 112, opp. 129 Phi e. 112
British Library, London: frontispiece, 9, 10, 12 (*left*), opp. 17 (*above*), opp. 17 (*below*), 17, 21 (*left*), 21 (*right*), 26 (*both*), 27, 29, 35 (*both*), 36, 37, 38, 39, opp. 40, insert 40–41, opp. 41, 47, 54 (*three*), 55, 57, opp. 64, opp. 65, 66, 67, 77, opp. 81, 85 (*both*), 86, 94, 100, insert 104–105 (*right above* and *below*), 117, 121, 124, 126, 132, 133, 134, 137, 138, 143 (*both*), 144 (*both*), 146 (*both*), 148–149, opp. 160, 164 (*both*), 165 (*both*), 171 (*right*), 173, 174, 175, 178 (*both*)
Mary Evans Picture Library, London: 79
National Portrait Gallery, London: 20
Private Collection: half-title, opp. 16, 25, 67, 68, 82, 90, 91, 92, 102, opp. 104 (*above* and *below*), insert 104–105 (*left above* and *below*), opp. 105, 139, opp. 144, 156, 159, 160, opp. 161, 168–169, 171 (*left*), 172
The Victoria and Albert Museum, London: 70

INDEX